ERIN'S DAUGHTERS IN AMERICA

THE JOHNS HOPKINS UNIVERSITY
STUDIES IN HISTORICAL AND POLITICAL SCIENCE
101ST SERIES (1983)

ERIN'S DAUGHTERS IN AMERICA

Irish Immigrant Women
in the Nineteenth Century

HASIA R. DINER

THE JOHNS HOPKINS UNIVERSITY PRESS
Baltimore and London

Originally published, 1983
Johns Hopkins Paperbacks edition, 1983
18 17 16 15 14 13 12 11 10 9

The Johns Hopkins University Press
2715 North Charles Street
Baltimore, Maryland 21218-4363
www.press.jhu.edu

Library of Congress Cataloging-in-Publication Data

Diner, Hasia R.
    Erin's daughters in America.

(Johns Hopkins University studies in historical and
political science; 101st ser., 2 (1983))
    Includes bibliographical references and index.
    1. Irish American women—History—19th century.
I. Title   II. Series: Johns Hopkins University studies
in historical and political science, 101st ser., 2.
E184.16D56   1983   305.4´889162´073   83-183
ISBN 0-8018-2871-6
ISBN 0-8018-2872-4 (pbk)

A catalog record for this book is available from the British Library.

To the best family on earth: Steve, Shira, and Eli.

Contents

Acknowledgments

This book was written with the generous support of the Eli Lilly Foundation through the Mary I. Bunting Institute of Radcliffe College. I want to express my warmest feelings for the institute, the other scholars there, and to its directors, Marion Kilson and Mary Anderson, who provided a supportive and positive environment, which sustained me in this project. In the most fundamental sense, this book would never have been written if not for the institute.

I would also like to thank the librarians at a vast array of libraries, but particularly the archivists at the Roman Catholic Archdiocese Archives of Boston, at the Schlesinger Library, Radcliffe College, and at the Special Collections of the Catholic University of America.

As in every other project I have been involved with, my greatest thanks go to Steve Diner: expert editor, ruthless critic, and constant source of new ideas.

Introduction

When Hector St. John de Crevecoeur asked rhetorically in 1782, "What, then, is the American, this new man?" he might also have asked if the social realities of America had worked themselves as well upon the "mixture of English, Scotch, Irish, French, Dutch, German" females to produce a "new woman."[1] Yet, most of what we know about the decision to leave one's ancestral home, about the nature of the migratory process, and about the forces of adaptation in the marketplace, church, and club concerns men.

This is particularly true of the literature on the Irish. For a variety of reasons scholars and journalists have sought to understand the quickness and shrewdness with which immigrants from Ireland's four provinces learned to manipulate and master the American political structure. They have also studied the domination by Irish men of the hierarchy of Roman Catholicism in America and the relative slowness of Irish economic mobility in a number of nineteenth-century American communities. These latter studies have relied almost exclusively on census data of male heads of households to show how Irish people made their way from a "pick and shovel" shanty life to the "lace curtains" of the middle class, usually ignoring the data on the women, who composed more than half of the group.

If nineteenth-century Americans thought at all about Irish women, they usually had in mind Bridget, the servant girl, who darted from one American kitchen to another, usually shattering the crockery as she went. Characterized in the Protestant, native-born mind as not very bright or dependable, she was a horrendous cook and fanatically bound to her priests at the local St. Patrick's or St. Mary's. She emerged in American lore in the home of her employer, rather than in her own community or her own home. Although there were some variations to this image, she was generally depicted as a foil to American values and acceptable behavior patterns and not as someone of great con-

Bridget out of the parlor and kitchen and
:ades after the Famine more Irish women
Jnited States; the Irish communities con-
'hat Bridget did with her money and with
:r home, and how she raised her children
'fered from most other immigrant women
he only significant group of foreign-born
they were the only significant group of
marily female cliques. They also accepted
:d down, and their rate of economic and
stanced that of the women of other ethnic
groups.

The relationship of Irish women to the culture of American womanhood
in the last half of the nineteenth century defies easy categorization. Irish
women adhered to a behavioral code that deviated markedly from that celebrated "cult of true womanhood" that commanded American women to lead
lives of sheltered passivity and ennobled domesticity. Irish women viewed
themselves as self-sufficient beings, with economic roles to play in their families
and communities. The ways they migrated clearly established their ability to
make decisions for themselves. In a sense, their work histories and involvement
with trade unions put them beyond the pale of that cult, as did their assertive
family life and frequently boisterous public behavior. On the other hand,
these women subscribed to religious imperatives and conformed to a set of
behavioral patterns enunciated by the Catholic Church and by the traditional
structures of Irish life which had no use for the feminist-women's rights model
of the "new woman." Irish women may have asserted their economic prerogatives in myriad ways and basically ruled their families, frequently leading
them up the ladder into the middle class, but they never rose to challenge the
public hegemony of men. Politics and saloon life, clubs and organizations
belonged to men, but the home and its purse strings as well as its future
belonged to women. The immigrant women knew which sphere was more
important.

The behavior of these women, as immigrants and as wage earners, may
seem to indicate autonomy and independence. It does not. The strong sense
of self that these women had, their ability to decide that Ireland held out
nothing for them and that America was indeed the land of opportunity—for
either work or marriage—did not mean that they thought only of themselves.
Their actions stemmed from family loyalties. They reckoned that they could
support and succor brothers, sisters, and parents better from America than on
the "ould sod." Their actions represented a commitment to Irish Catholic
culture and to its way of life. The move to America did not represent a search
for a new identity, nor did it constitute a break with the past.

The central questions of this book may be as deceptively simple as the
nineteenth-century American view of the Irish woman: What did it mean to

sequence. Yet numbers alone take Bridget out of the parlor and kitchen and into historic center stage. In the decades after the Famine more Irish women than Irish men immigrated to the United States; the Irish communities contained more females than males. What Bridget did with her money and with her leisure time, how she set up her home, and how she raised her children cannot be ignored. Irish women differed from most other immigrant women in terms of numbers. They were the only significant group of foreign-born women who outnumbered men; they were the only significant group of women who chose to migrate in primarily female cliques. They also accepted jobs that most other women turned down, and their rate of economic and social progress seems to have outdistanced that of the women of other ethnic groups.

The relationship of Irish women to the culture of American womanhood in the last half of the nineteenth century defies easy categorization. Irish women adhered to a behavioral code that deviated markedly from that celebrated "cult of true womanhood" that commanded American women to lead lives of sheltered passivity and ennobled domesticity. Irish women viewed themselves as self-sufficient beings, with economic roles to play in their families and communities. The ways they migrated clearly established their ability to make decisions for themselves. In a sense, their work histories and involvement with trade unions put them beyond the pale of that cult, as did their assertive family life and frequently boisterous public behavior. On the other hand, these women subscribed to religious imperatives and conformed to a set of behavioral patterns enunciated by the Catholic Church and by the traditional structures of Irish life which had no use for the feminist-women's rights model of the "new woman." Irish women may have asserted their economic prerogatives in myriad ways and basically ruled their families, frequently leading them up the ladder into the middle class, but they never rose to challenge the public hegemony of men. Politics and saloon life, clubs and organizations belonged to men, but the home and its purse strings as well as its future belonged to women. The immigrant women knew which sphere was more important.

The behavior of these women, as immigrants and as wage earners, may seem to indicate autonomy and independence. It does not. The strong sense of self that these women had, their ability to decide that Ireland held out nothing for them and that America was indeed the land of opportunity—for either work or marriage—did not mean that they thought only of themselves. Their actions stemmed from family loyalties. They reckoned that they could support and succor brothers, sisters, and parents better from America than on the "ould sod." Their actions represented a commitment to Irish Catholic culture and to its way of life. The move to America did not represent a search for a new identity, nor did it constitute a break with the past.

The central questions of this book may be as deceptively simple as the nineteenth-century American view of the Irish woman: What did it mean to

Introduction

When Hector St. John de Crevecoeur asked rhetorically in 1782, "What, then, is the American, this new man?" he might also have asked if the social realities of America had worked themselves as well upon the "mixture of English, Scotch, Irish, French, Dutch, German" females to produce a "new woman."[1] Yet, most of what we know about the decision to leave one's ancestral home, about the nature of the migratory process, and about the forces of adaptation in the marketplace, church, and club concerns men.

This is particularly true of the literature on the Irish. For a variety of reasons scholars and journalists have sought to understand the quickness and shrewdness with which immigrants from Ireland's four provinces learned to manipulate and master the American political structure. They have also studied the domination by Irish men of the hierarchy of Roman Catholicism in America and the relative slowness of Irish economic mobility in a number of nineteenth-century American communities. These latter studies have relied almost exclusively on census data of male heads of households to show how Irish people made their way from a "pick and shovel" shanty life to the "lace curtains" of the middle class, usually ignoring the data on the women, who composed more than half of the group.

If nineteenth-century Americans thought at all about Irish women, they usually had in mind Bridget, the servant girl, who darted from one American kitchen to another, usually shattering the crockery as she went. Characterized in the Protestant, native-born mind as not very bright or dependable, she was a horrendous cook and fanatically bound to her priests at the local St. Patrick's or St. Mary's. She emerged in American lore in the home of her employer, rather than in her own community or her own home. Although there were some variations to this image, she was generally depicted as a foil to American values and acceptable behavior patterns and not as someone of great con-

be a female immigrant from Catholic Ireland in the last half of the nineteenth century? Why would she have immigrated? And how would she make her way from Killarney to Castle Garden? What were the economic and social lures that brought millions of Bridgets and Norahs from Limerick and Tipperary, from County Clare and County Meath to Boston, New York, Chicago, and Philadelphia? How did these women fit into the burgeoning Irish-American communities that were coming to play such an important role in late-nineteenth-century American cities? What institutions served her? What institutions did she create herself? What was her world view and how did the lives of her American-born daughters differ from her own life?

To understand her immigration and adaptation, we must examine the woman's place in Irish culture and in particular in its family life, which had undergone a major restructuring at precisely the time of heavy Irish immigration to the United States. Male-female relations within the Irish social structure mirrored group values and economic realities and helped shape not only the nature of the immigration but the kinds of jobs, voluntary associations, and families that would come to characterize Irish-American life. In other words, Irish men and women behaved in particular ways, and the story of Irish immigration is the story of how this behavior changed and persisted under new conditions.

Despite the strong commitment of Irish women to values and practices of the Old World, they did not remain deaf to the resounding debate on the roles, rights, and responsibilities of women that engulfed American society from the 1840s onward. Irish women responded to this perplexing problem as Irish, as Catholics, as poor and unskilled hands, and as newcomers.

Ethnicity can be a central determinant of human behavior. Immigrant women raised in a particular culture and social milieu—that of the small village of Ireland, the *shtetl* of Jewish Eastern Europe, or the town in Italy's *mezzogiorno*—adapted and acculturated to a new set of values and to new realities in certain discernable ways. They may or may not have responded differently than did their fathers, brothers, and husbands, depending on the level of gender segregation within the group, on the nature of sex role differences as assigned by the culture, and by the different social and economic opportunities offered men and women in the receiving society. There can be no denying that Irish women, Jewish women, and Italian women, for example, experienced migration in different ways. In order to understand those differences, both the nature of the indigenous group culture and the structure of American society *as it affected that particular group of women* have to be balanced and considered in tandem.

Although the primary task of a historian is to document and explain change over time, I have not presented the experience of Irish women in the sixty years following the Famine in a traditional chronological manner. Rather, for two reasons, I have treated the period as a whole. First of all, the story of Irish female immigration in the years after the Famine is one of remarkable, indeed incredible, continuity. The Famine wreaked havoc with the landholding system of Ireland, producing a profound change in every Irish institution, and particularly in the Irish family. For at least sixty years, young unmarried Irish women left for America in huge numbers to avoid the consequences of a new economic and social order that offered them only the most dismal prospects. Although these sixty years witnessed the industrialization of the United States and profound changes in the urban labor market, there remained a striking similarity between the Irish peasant women who immigrated in 1850 and in 1900, not only with regard to their reasons for leaving Ireland but the kind of work they chose here, the family life (or lack thereof) they developed, and their values.

Second, the process of change and adaptation to American conditions occurred generationally and is best understood that way. The movement of Irish women from domestic service to female-dominated professions like schoolteaching has more to do with the length of time they or their forebears had spent in American cities than with changes in the structure of the American economy. Indeed, because of their unique motives for immigration and their distinctive aspirations and attitudes toward family and work, Irish female immigrants sought out certain special kinds of occupations. Unlike Irish male immigrants, male immigrants of other nationalities, and many female immigrant workers of other groups, Irish women did not move initially into unskilled factory work or day labor. Because they were willing to defer or forgo marriage and family, they worked as live-in servants, and later as schoolteachers, who had to remain single. These occupations constituted a restricted and, in a sense, protected labor market for Irish women, and it did not change as rapidly as did the larger market for unskilled industrial labor.

This is not to suggest that Irish women did not change significantly as a result of immigration to America. In the years examined intensively in this study, 1840 to 1900, they changed quite a bit from the immigrant to the American-born generation but without losing their distinctive cultural values. After 1900, when the transformation of Ireland was largely complete and new immigration of Irish women in America was reduced to a trickle, the process of "Americanization" became more visible, and Irish women appeared much less distinctive. Still, there is considerable, fairly recent sociological data suggesting that the distinctive cultural traits of Irish-American women remain strong today, and I suggest in a limited way in this study how the traditional values of Irish-American women survived and changed in the twentieth century. In short, this is essentially a study of cultural persistence over time.

 # Where They Came From: Women's Life in Nineteenth-Century Ireland

N othing thrives in Ireland, but the celibate.
Moritz J. Bonn, *Modern Ireland and Her Agrarian Problem*

Whin Mollie Maloney wor jist sixteen,
No girl in the world wor sweeter than she;
Ivery boy wanted her lover to be—
Dear little Mollie Maloney!
Sure, niver wor eyes as blue as her own, niver wor cheeks as red;
Hair as black as th' night itself, crownin her saucy head;
Carried herself like a thrue Irish queen—
Mollie Maloney, the purty colleen.
Whin Mollie Maloney wor jist twinety-two
The boys wor fightin' to win her;
She drove thim half crazy— 'twas wicked to do—
But she wor a lovable sinner—
Bad little Mollie Maloney!
She'd smile on th' wan that was nearest to her, makin' him think that he
Wor all that she loved—thin turn right around an' give th' same smile to me!
O, such a flirt there nivir wor seen—Mollie Maloney, th' wicked colleen.
Now Mollie Maloney is jist thirty-wan;
Her eyes are as bright, but there's gray in her hair,
An' most av the boys she flouted are done
Wid th' days av their foolish youth, they declar—
(Too bad for Mollie Maloney!)
But Pat, who nivir had blarney enough to get even half a show,
Has won her for life, an' th' joke is on thim—
She chose him so long ago'
Och, Mollie Maloney, I thank ye for that,
For Mollie, me darlint, ye know I am Pat!
The Ballard of Mollie Maloney

Few nations in Europe witnessed as fervent and as drawn out a struggle for national independence as did Catholic Ireland. Few nations in Europe inspired their sons and daughters to fight their bloody battles more fiercely or to praise their native land more strongly than did "the Isle of Saints and Scholars." Yet few nations sent out as many permanent exiles as did that same "Mother Eire." Some of those sons and daughters left in the nineteenth century for other parts of the British Isles, immigrating in droves to London, Liverpool, Manchester, Glasgow, and Edinburgh. Others shifted out to Canada, Australia, and New Zealand, remaining within the empire of the hated Sassenach. The largest stream—more appropriately, a flood—made its way across the Atlantic to the United States, "that happy place . . . thy western home."[1] A centuries-old history of political and economic domination and subjugation by Protestant England and an equally long tradition of grinding agrarian poverty marks Irish history. A passionate commitment to Roman Catholicism, despite the savage repressions of Protestant rulers, and a collective memory of zealous but failed uprisings against an ancient foe seared themselves into the consciousness of the Irish, both those who remained at home and those who chose to live and toil abroad.

If poverty, persecution, and violence seem to have been eternal elements of Irish life, changes in the economic and social structure nonetheless did occur. How those changes came about and what marks they left on Ireland and the Irish provide a convenient starting point for understanding the status and role of women. Historians love watersheds: dramatic incidents that set off one epoch from another; major upheavals that loom as signposts along the historic path. The Great Famine of the late 1840s has generally been considered the event in Irish history which sent shock waves throughout Irish society, whose reverberations could be felt around the world, in Boston, London, Toronto, Sydney, and Melbourne, and whose intensity lasted over a century. Nothing remained the same after the devastation of the Famine. The harrowing memory of the starvation, disease, and destruction that engulfed Ireland after the potato blights of 1845-49 altered all relationships; the footing between landlord and tenant changed, as did that between priest and parishioner. The ruler and the ruled shifted ground as they faced each other. Entire classes of people disappeared. The Famine signaled the demise of the Irish cottier class, that landless mass on the lowest stratum of the social structure.[2]

Sheer numbers also confirm the brutal impact of the Famine. After the four years of continuous blight on the potato crop, the Irish staff of life, at least one million people had vanished. Some were felled by starvation, typhus, and dysentery.[3] In that same year three million were reduced to charity.

Others fled the Emerald Isle. The Famine's shadow seems to have left no one untouched. The memory of the starvation and what was considered the inaction of the British (some saw it as pure malice) would, over the course of the next century, become a major weapon of nationalist propaganda. Irish journalists, poets, novelists, and playwrights would constantly cull the maudlin scenes of those years for pathetic and gripping material. Father Theobald Matthew, who led Ireland's highly popular temperance movement in the 1870s, invoked such wrenching scenes in sermon after sermon:

> There, admist the chilling damp of a dismal hovel see yon famine-stricken fellow-creature; see him extended on his scanty bed of rotten straw; see his once manly frame, that labour had strengthened with vigour, shrunk to a skeleton; see his once ruddy complexion, the gift of temperance, changed by hunger and concomitant disease to a sallow ghastly hue. See him extend his yellow withering arm for assistance; hear how he cries out in agony for food, for since yesterday he has not even moistened his lips!
>
> Who could forget the vision of a strange and fearful sight like what we read of in beleaguered cities; its streets crowded with gaunt wanderers, sauntering to and from with hopeless air and hunger-struck look—a mob of starved, almost naked women around the poor-house clamoring for soup tickets.[4]

People around the world gasped at the horrors of the Famine. Relief poured in. Generous Americans collected money to send food to Ireland's starving millions. American magazine readers were fed a constant diet of grim details about "a widow with two children who for a week had eaten nothing but cabbage. . . . Another woman with two children, and not far from being confined again, stated that during the last week they had existed upon two quarts of meal and two heads of cabbage . . . famine was written in the faces of this woman and her children."[5]

Intimate relationships between men and women, husbands and wives, parents and children, brothers and sisters, were not exempted from this massive restructuring of life. The qualities of personal ties and social bonds were swept away by the Famine's blast. The 1851 Census of Ireland surveyed the ruin of the countryside and lamented that

> the closest ties of kinship were dissolved; the most ancient and long cherished usages of the people were disregarded; the once proverbial gaiety and light-heartedness of the peasant people seemed to have vanished completely, and village merriment or marriage festival was no longer heard or seen throughout the regions desolated by the intensity and extent of the Famine.[6]

If marriage patterns and family life were re-created, so too must have been the status and role of women within those families and that society. To understand, then, how Irish women adjusted to the United States and why they behaved the way they did, one must begin with that Famine in Ireland.

What caused the immigration...

The watershed approach does have its pitfalls. Few of the changes that occurred after the cataclysm were totally unrelated to the nature of the earlier society. The great upheaval merely accentuated trends that had begun earlier and accelerated forces unleashed in more tranquil and stable times. For example, the great upsurge in religiosity that occurred in post-Famine Ireland, the devotional revolution with its tremendous growth in both the number and the power of the clergy, swept a society that was religiously oriented to begin with. Religion had been a powerful political identity for a long time, and the priest, the *soggarth aroon*, had long held a cherished place in the hearts of the masses.[7]

So, too, the trends in Irish demography—a constantly decreasing population with late and infrequent marriage and high rates of celibacy, a social environment of gender segregation and reluctant sexuality, the concomitant ethic of intense gender animosity—had roots that reached far back into Irish folk life and characterized some classes in the pre-Famine structure. Yet after the Famine these elements came to be synonymous with all of Irish culture and these trends became the norm of Irish behavior. Similarly, the Famine did not cause the massive emigrations. For one thing, the Famine of the late 1840s was not the first to ravage Ireland in modern times. In 1800, 1807, 1816, 1822, and 1839 massive crop failures and wide-ranging epidemics had shaken up the rural Irish. Immigration had in fact begun before the Famine and it continued well afterwards. At least seven hundred thousand people abandoned the thirty-two counties of Ireland between 1825 and 1844. As early as 1841 a half million Irish-born men and women had decided to settle permanently in England and Scotland, while in the same year over ten thousand new arrivals to the port of Boston listed Ireland as their birthplace. In the 1831-41 decade a half million Irish emigrated. Long after the Great Famine had become a memory and a closed chapter of Ireland's sorrowful history, twentieth-century Ireland continued to send its young men and women around the world, making people Ireland's chief export.[8]

The legacy of the Famine as it shaped emigration to the United States, and particularly as it stimulated a massive female exodus, involved a demographic transition and an alteration in family relations much more subtle than millions of individuals merely fleeing their native land. Drawing upon older Irish traditions and social trends associated with the more stable classes in pre-Famine society, Ireland became a country that held out fewer and fewer attractions to women. By the last decades of the nineteenth century many young women had no reason to remain in the agricultural towns of Catholic Ireland. They had no realistic chances for marriage or employment. For Irish women to attain either, they had to turn their backs on the land of their birth.

Exodus of Irish women

Ireland became the Western world's most dramatic and stark example of a demographic pattern associated with the shift from traditional to modern societies. Ireland led the world by the 1870s as the nation with the latest age of marriage. Irish men and women decided more frequently than men and women elsewhere to eschew marriage and live out their lives in a single state. Ireland was, in fact, one of the only countries in Europe to enter the twentieth century unconcerned about overpopulation, because decades earlier it had achieved more than "zero population growth." This, however, had not always been the case. Before the Great Famine, more likely than not an Irish peasant or laborer married young. Until the decade of the Famine Irish population figures had risen with alarming rapidity. Ireland's mushrooming—perhaps, more appropriately, exploding—population had, in fact, provided Thomas Malthus with his gloomiest example of the improvidence of the poor and the inexorable cycle whereby population grew far out of proportion to resources.

A large and controversial body of demographic literature has attempted to explain how this happened. The issues in the analysis of Irish population trends are clouded by the difficulty of obtaining accurate statistics on just how many births and deaths occurred in any given year before 1864, when compulsory registration of nationwide vital statistics was enacted. The first official head count of any kind was made in 1821, and that of 1841 is considered the first that approached reliability. Generally, it is accepted by demographers and historians that the 1821 Census counted fewer people than actually existed, whereas the 1831 count overstated the number. Despite the technical problems of portraying Irish demographic movement, scholars and commentators on the Irish scene have sought to come to terms with the ways in which the population changed and why. The impact of the Great Famine is central to this endeavor, and from it we can begin to discern the nature of women's lives in Irish society.[9]

On the eve of the Famine, over eight million people inhabited Ireland. Fifty years later the same island had been home to fewer than three million. This tremendous growth occurred without any industrialization or increase in economic opportunities and without any influx of foreigners. In fact, this staggering proliferation occurred while emigration had already become an established part of life. Over four hundred thousand Irish-born men and women lived in Great Britain in 1841, whereas between 1780 and 1845 more than one million Irish had made their way to the United States and Canada. Thus, despite a continuous stream of Irish leaving Ireland in this same half century, the rate of population increase constituted a major demographic revolution.[10]

One strand of analysis which attempts to explain Irish population dynamics focuses on diet—on the impact of the lowly potato on mortality and fertility trends. The potato culture, which gradually came to characterize all Ireland, triggered a constant and seemingly unending process by which the land was broken into smaller and smaller holdings. Widespread was "the general practice with farmers to divide their land into portions, which were given to their children as they got married. The last married frequently got his father's cabin along with his portion of the ground, and there the parents liked to stop feeling attached to the place where they spent their lives." The fleshy tuber could be grown anywhere, even on the most miniscule of plots, and contained just enough nutrients to sustain the life of the poor.

As the Irish had become potato-eaters by the end of the eighteenth century, they also had become early marriers. The poor, in particular, saw no reason not to marry spontaneously, that is, without protracted negotiations between families, and certainly without the aid of a matchmaker. Young men and women married when they wanted, and since they could always grow potatoes, a family of hungry mouths was not a burden. A priest from Mayo generalized to the Commission of Inquiry on the Irish Poor in 1836 that "small holders are induced to marry by feeling that their condition cannot be made worse, or rather, they know they can lose nothing, and they promise themselves some pleasure in the society of a wife." This testimony typified the statements that were offered by the clerics and laymen alike to this commission, to the Devon Commission, which met in 1841, and to other, similar bodies. One man in County Galway confessed in 1835, "if I had been a blanket to cover her, I would marry the woman I liked; and if I should get potatoes enough to put into my children's mouths, I would be as happy and content as any man." Similarly, very few Irish men and women did not marry. The nature of the economy and the social structure left very little room for the unattached adult. Within marriage, fertility was high. There was no incentive for, or seeming interest in, contraception of any kind as there was in France at the same time. Some scholars even argue that, by providing a cheap and easily cultivated source of nutrition, the potato improved the health of women and gradually led to heightened fertility.[11]

Even before the Famine this pattern of early and improvident marriage characterized the depressed peasants—the cottiers and the poor laborers —much more than any other class. Townspeople, tradesmen, and farmers with more than a potato plot demonstrated greater reticence about marriage. For those with hope of economic stability and with aspirations for a more "middle-class" kind of existence improvident marriage could spell disaster. Marrying too young meant the expense of feeding and clothing a family too soon. Marrying too young was clearly associated with the reckless behavior of the poor, who inched closer and closer to doom as they subdivided and re-subdivided their possessions.

A County Kilkenny observer noted that "those who are a grade above the cottier are more cautious as to marriage, and it is chiefly among small farmers that you will find bachelors." Similarly, in County Limerick one could have found "a greater proportionate number of unmarried men amongst the farmers and tradesmen than amongst the lowest classes of agricultural labourers." This same phenomenon could be plotted geographically. In the wealthier and more fertile East, which supported the cultivation of grains as well as potatoes, people generally married later than in the poverty-stricken West, which was home for the most destitute of laborers and cottiers. Thus, even in the early nineteenth-century, when Irish population grew rapidly, the growth was clustered in the bottom classes.[12]

The late- and nonmarriers of "higher" social status in Irish society provided the link between the pre- and post-Famine eras of Irish history. They undermine the more dramatic interpretation that sees the Famine as the central and defining event in Ireland's development. It is in part because of these more prosperous farmers that the rapid population growth had actually begun to slacken by 1821, and the 1831 Census registered a marked increase in the number of nonmarried adults. What the Famine did accomplish was to dramatically universalize trends that were already in operation. This happened in a number of ways. In the first place, the Famine could claim grim responsibility for the almost total elimination of the cottier class. Second, the memory of the Famine impressed the British lawmakers enough in the succeeding decades to enact legislation that outlawed subdivision and other practices associated with pre-Famine agriculture, thus transforming most Irish men into holders of small, although viable, farms.

The Famine might also be seen as the great convincer. It demonstrated to all the folly of agrarian practices that defined a postage-stamp-size piece of land as enough just because it brought forth potatoes. Irish agriculture was going to have to become much more diversified, and though potatoes could remain a central dish on the Irish family's table, that same farm family would also have to produce a cash crop as well as butter, eggs, and other dairy products for markets. The Famine also demonstrated to Irish parents that no one prospered if they cut up their holdings into equal portions for all their sons. An inheritance came to be the entire holding or nothing. Similarly, the Famine also convinced Irish men and women that early marriage was reckless marriage; that nonmarriage was an option, too. As the Irish changed their marriage patterns, they basically adapted the behavior of the more economically stable elements in the society, convinced that the devastation and destruction of the late 1840s had in part been caused by irrational, carefree marriage and family practices that failed to treat conjugal life as a fundamentally economic enterprise.

Whereas before the Famine commentators on Irish life—Catholic clergymen, economists, and British officials alike—lamented the reckless marriage patterns that seemed to accompany the Irish descent into poverty and destitution, after the Famine concern mounted that the Irish in Ireland were increasingly uninterested in remaining at home, marrying, and reproducing themselves. In 1902 one writer mourned, "In saying all this we are fully alive to the sadness of seeing a grand old race disappear as it were, off the face of the earth." Richard J. Kelly in 1904 shared this pessimism with readers of the *New Ireland Review* and chided the experts, "Economists, so-called, read lessons to us on our over-population and improvident early marriages and, as they said, consequent wretchedness. But they can no longer, with any regard for truth say so now, with a smaller population, lower marriage and a lower birth rate than most countries in Europe."[13] Descriptions of Irish life in the last decades of the century all stressed the gloom of decay, the moribund quiet of a society in decline, although perhaps a decline accompanied by increasing prosperity. A magistrate of County Meath saw his home as

> one of the most melancholy counties I know. This grass grown road, over which seemingly little, if any, traffic passes, is a type of solitude everywhere found. Tillage there is none; but in its stead one vast expanse of pasture land extends. Human habitations are rarer than the bare walls of roofless cottages. Where once a population dwelt, and as consequence, see how lonely and untrodden are these roads.[14]

Census figures painfully recorded the dwindling of Irish numbers. In the fifty years between 1841 and 1891, Ireland lost 3,470,374 residents, plummeting from the pre-Famine population of 8,175,124 in 1841 to 4,704,750 in 1891. Constant migration picked off many of these Irish men and women, but migration could not alone be blamed. The decline in Irish population stemmed most fundamentally from a change in family life and a major demographic shift. There were, to be sure, bad harvests in the last half of the nineteenth century which took their toll, somewhat reminiscent of the Famine, but they lacked the bite of the 1840s devastation.[15]

The bulk of the late-nineteenth-century population decline occurred in the rural areas, siphoning off the residents of farm regions much more rapidly than residents of towns. Ireland was becoming somewhat less overwhelmingly rural in the last half of the century. In 1841 only 17 percent of the population was urban; by 1891 over one-quarter of all the Irish could be found in cities like Dublin and Cork. Even the urban population of the country slumped, however, falling from over a million city dwellers in 1841 to eight hundred thousand in 1891. Only Dublin grew in that same time period, but that growth was hardly dramatic and clearly indicated the stagnation of Irish population and the absence of any industrial development or commercial rejuvenation to draw discontented farm people into the cities. Ireland had basically become a nogrowth nation. It had no urban-industrial attractions to stimulate a massive internal movement. It had in fact become a nation characterized by late and reluctant marriage as well as by a massive voluntary exodus.[16]

In the early 1840s, before the Famine shocked and convinced the Irish out of impoverished, although perhaps comfortable, ways, the rate of marriage was 7.0-8.0 per thousand per year. It bore a close resemblance to the rate of marriage throughout Europe. From 1868, four years after compulsory registration of vital statistics, to 1870 the rate of marriage spiraled down to 5.1 per thousand and then fell to 4.0 in the years 1881-90. Clearly, in any given year or span of years during the second half of the century fewer Irish men and women were setting up families than in years past. Many were merely deferring, that is, they were marrying later than they might have in earlier periods. In 1864, for example, 18.1 percent of all women who married were under twenty-one. In 1911 only 5.3 percent entered marriage by that age. Similarly, in 1864 71.1 percent of all wives in a first marriage were under twenty-five; in 1911 only 51.1 percent were similarly situated. But Ireland also came to be the home of large numbers of men and women who just chose not to marry or who were unable to. In 1861, 11 percent of all men in Ireland sixty-five or over were permanent bachelors; in 1926 that figure had risen to 26 percent.[17] Again using 1841, or the last pre-Famine census, as the point of contrast, the percentage of women age twenty-five to thirty-four who were single in Ireland went from 28 percent to 39 percent in 1851. It did not change in 1891. Although fewer Irish women continued to be unmarried as they approached old age, among women forty-five to fifty-four the number of singles also increased from 12 percent in 1841 to 17 percent in 1891. Figures for men were significantly higher in both age categories, in all years. No longer did Irish society live under the specter of the impetuous young rushing off emotionally to marry and set up homes.[18]

Not surprisingly, this matrimonial trend occurred in tandem with yet another development that characterized post-Famine Irish society. Parents increasingly became reluctant to subdivide their land among heirs, and Ireland as a whole came to have fewer and fewer holdings. In 1841, for example, there were 691,000 holdings in all of Ireland, the largest percentage being the smallest holdings, one to five acres. In 1861, 568,000 estates were primarily of the five- to fifteen-acre size, whereas in 1891 the number of holdings declined to 469,000, most of them over thirty acres. Evictions certainly help account for this trend toward land accretion. The poorest could no longer hold onto their tiny plots, and consolidation in Ireland became the basic trend. The cottiers were gone and increasingly the middling Irish farmer had control of a reasonably viable piece of land, which was to be used for pasture-farming, not for tillage.[19]

These middling Irish farmers either had survived the Famine themselves or their parents had witnessed the harrowing devastation, commonly attributed to the wrath of God, or to the heartlessness of the Saxon ruler, or, importantly, to the impetuous romanticism of the poor. The middling Irish farmers were *not* going to err again. They were not going to find themselves in the same position as had the Irish in the 1840s. To ensure their continuous survival without want and destitution they finally sought to shake off the yoke of

British rule. To ensure their continued survival with a degree of material comfort and security they sought to establish families that enhanced their economic needs. Land and the economic security it brought became obsessions with the Irish. A folk proverb suggested, "Let any man go down to hell and open an Irish man's heart . . . the first thing writ across it was land."

Whereas there is no agreement in sight for the lively and sparring scholarly debate over the cause of the pre-Famine population growth, there is unanimity as to the nature of post-Famine marrage: what it was and why it developed into a more discriminate and rationalized institution. Marriages were based now on economic calculation with parents figuring and weighing the financial benefits and liabilities of their childrens' marital futures. Land would not be divided. An estate would pass intact and undisturbed from one generation to another. Therefore, only one member of the family's younger generation could hope to inherit the land. No systematic or established pattern developed which designated that single heir. Primogeniture was not the rule, nor was the younger son the immediately designated heir. Who inherited the land became the decision of father and mother and they made that decision as late in their lives as possible. Parents held onto control of their fields until well into old age. (Interestingly, Ireland had among Europe's most impressive statistics on longevity.) At the same time they tenaciously held onto control of their children's futures.

Occupation of the land was a prerequisite for marriage. Before the Famine the same had been the case, but then a potato patch sufficed and just about anybody, no matter how impoverished, could aspire to potato farming. In the society created in the wake of the Famine only one son per family could inherit land. Therefore, the male heir was the only son to enter into matrimony in Ireland. The person he married became a matter of some importance, and parents had first and final word here, too. They decided when the time was right to give up authority over land and home. They calculated how much dowry had to be brought in by a prospective daughter-in-law to compensate them for feeding, clothing, and sheltering her. The dowry, its size, its availability, and the haggling that went on in determining it became major themes in the folklore and popular culture of post-Famine Ireland. The *Gael,* a Dublin magazine, printed "The Grand Match" in 1899:

> Dennis was hearty when Dennis was young.
> High was his step in the jig that he sprung.
> He had the looks an' the sootherin' tongue.
> And he wanted a girl wid a-fortune.
>
> Nannie was grey-eyed an' Nannie was tall.
> Fair was the face hid in-undher her shawl.
> Troth! an' he liked her the best o' them all.
> But she's not a traneen to her fortune.

He be to look out for a liklier match.
So he married a girl that was counted a catch.
An' was ugly as need be, the dark little patch.
But that was a thrifle, he told her.

He met pretty Nan when a month had gone by,
An' he thought like a fool to get round her he'd try;
Wid a smile on her lip an' a spark in her eye,
She said, "How is the woman that owns ye?"

Och, never be tellin' the life that he's led!
Sure, many's the night that he'll wish himself dead,
For the sake o' two eyes in a girl's pretty head,
An' the tongue o' the woman that owns him.[20]

Parents surveyed the stock of available "young" women, often through the aid of a third party, to assess who would make the best match with their "boy"—who might by now be well into his thirties or forties. She had to bring with her enough money, or cattle, or land appropriate to the economic status of the family. She had to appear a hard worker, because the life of Irish farm women certainly extracted from them a tremendous amount of labor. She would come in extremely close contact with her mother-in-law, who would continue to live with the new family, so she should be pleasant, traditional in values, and accepting of her role. Certainly, it was assumed that she should have the potential to be a mother of many offspring.[21]

Emotion and that incalculable commodity "love" figured only rarely in these economic arrangements. Even as early as 1852 an observer noted about Irish street ballads, "The romantic or love-in-a-cottage principle, which prevails among the Romeos and Juliets of polite fiction has no parallel here for care is always taken to provide one or other of the amorous couple with 'ample means' and often the exact amount of the dowry is impressively mentioned." Two fathers bickering over a daughter's dowry are reported to have said, "'Not very purty!' 'Faix, I'll maker her purty with cows!'" A dowry could be a very expensive affair. In the 1880s it approximated the amount of ten to twelve years rent for land.

.   The social significance of the dowry extended even further. The money brought in by a woman to her new family basically endowed one of her sisters-in-law. That is, the fortune of one woman became the fortune of another, who in turn allowed yet another woman to marry.

What about the other children in the family, those not chosen as heir? Obviously, a significant number of them increasingly chose to remain unmarried. It is this group that accounts for the growing statistics on permanent celibacy. Many of the unmarried men, called "boys" until the day they died, continued to live on the countryside, sometimes with an aged parent, usually a widowed mother, seeking the company of their peers who had also been passed over for both inheritance and marriage. They could usually work as laborers on farms not blessed with sons or whose sons were too young to lend assistance in the hundreds of tasks that went into Irish farming, which well into the twentieth century was only minimally mechanized. Many got jobs in town, others abandoned the rural areas, and some left Ireland altogether.

Within any family only one daughter could hope to be endowed with her "fortune" and go off to marry into another farm family. Her unmarried sisters had limited options. They could remain single in the countryside, but few employment opportunities existed for them and they could not remain very long with their newly married brothers and their wives and growing families. Unprovided-for "girls" left to work in Dublin shops, the mills of Lancashire and Manchester, the homes of well-to-do Londoners in need of servants and cooks, or they joined millions of other young Irish women crossing the Atlantic to seek fortune or family in the United States.

Marriage was the female equivalent to the male inheritance of his parent's estate. These constituted the greatest rewards that Irish rural society had to offer to its chosen young. Yet, increasingly during the late nineteenth century marriage into an Irish farm family, for a woman, or taking possession of a farm in County Kerry or County Meath, for a man, became less than a glamorous reward. As more and more young people emigrated from Catholic Ireland, sending back their "America letters" from new and exciting places, and as rising literacy brought the outside world to the Irish village, remaining at home seemed dull and unsatisfying. Father Matthew correctly noted that "emigration begets emigration," and when one's aunt or cousin or sister had lived in New York or labored in Chicago or set herself up in San Francisco, rural Ireland indeed appeared even more monotonous and rigid. Certainly, by the beginning of the twentieth century the "boy" who inherited the land or the "girl" whom he married, instead of being the chosen, became the leftovers. A 1914 survey of social conditions in Ireland sweepingly asserted that "no one married until all hope of America faded." The offspring who remained at home might be considered the ones most easily overwhelmed by feelings of guilt about emigration or were the most traditional, conservative members of their peer group. Post-Famine family life in Ireland appeared to many as rigid and authoritarian, limiting and circumscribed. Young Irish men and particularly young women in droves were turning their backs on that kind of family life, the kind of society that was "modern" Ireland.[22]

This independence of grown offspring became a hallmark of Irish family life as it served as a mechanism that allowed, if not unconsciously forced, the immigration of unprovided-for children. Irish families were guided by an inner force propelling members outward by a kind of centrifugal energy that dispersed individuals away from their childhood homes.[23]

The Irish family, however, was not disorganized nor did it lack cohesion. A remarkable degree of family unity persisted as a result of this dispersal.

Family bonds stretched across the ocean. Emigrating members did not forget their parents and siblings and other relatives who remained in Ireland. The emigrants not only sent vast sums of money to kin in Ireland but facilitated other family members joining them in various spots across the globe.[24] According to Conrad Arensberg's widely read study, *The Irish Countryman,*

> one little settlement called Cross, on the Loop Head peninsula which juts out from Clare into the Atlantic at the Shannon's mouth, is locally supported by the Shanghai police force. The first man to go is now Chief of Police in the International Settlement there, and many places in the Force have gone to men of Cross.[25]

Ties of affection between parents and children and among siblings may in fact have been strengthened as a result of immigration. Immigrating family members no longer could be viewed as potential rivals or as drains on the family's budget but in fact turned into thriving assets. The importance of family in Ireland centered significantly on economic production. The family needed the labors of all to survive. Before the Famine cottage industries of various types had dotted the Irish countryside as wives and daughters wove frieze and then fashioned it into garments, gathered turf to warm their homes, and raised chickens. Wives and children in fishing communities fabricated the nets and kept them in good repair.[26] An English observer in 1812 was appalled at the intensity of the work of Irish wives in farms,

> Females in Ireland are treated more like beast of burden than rational beings, and although I never saw anyone yoked to a plough . . . I have seen them degraded in a manner disgraceful to the other sex and shocking to humanity. In the country, they are subjected to all the drudgery generally performed by men; setting potatoes, digging turf and the performance of the most laborious occupations.[27]

Although the culture labeled some jobs as the domain of men and others that of women, some for adults and others a mark of childhood, potato cultivation required that everyone work in the fields at various points in the agricultural year.

The economic functioning of all members of the family regardless of age or gender helped determine how low a family might sink or how high it might rise. One man in County Mayo in the late 1820s related sorrowfully how he had been married to an enterprising woman, who had earned a shilling a day making dresses. The woman died, and he fell almost immediately into destitution and told the Commission of Inquiry on the Irish Poor that "though I am a shabby, poor fellow today, when my wife lived I was decent and fit to appear before a congregation. I had plenty of potatoes, often a bit of meat and was able and willing to help a neighbor."[28]

This dependence on the labor of all did not evaporate with the restructuring of Irish family life into the post-Famine stem pattern. It continued, although it changed form. Fewer cottage industries thrived, since increased industrialization in other parts of the British Isles made weaving and spinning and sewing at home unprofitable. In fact, in the 1890s the Congested Districts Board sent instructors to Inis Beag, a western island community, to teach the women how to knit "ganzie" (a type of sweater worn by children) in order to stimulate a home industry. Also, with the disappearance of the potato culture and the shift in farming from tillage to grazing, wives and daughters would not be found in the fields but instead made their money through a woman's sphere, poultry and dairy work. By the end of the century wives' work had moved away from the actual functioning of the farm. This trend disturbed the *Irish World*, which believed that Ireland needed a "system of agriculture which will employ the energies of each family member within its due bonds," hopefully curtailing emigration. However, the essential shift from pre- to post-Famine agriculture in Ireland involved not the economic importance of women but the focus of their work. Work became much more segregated by gender and to a lesser degree by age, with young children performing their chores with the women.[29]

It is obviously difficult to generalize about how individuals in such a family system felt about it, since the pattern encompassed all rural Ireland. Yet one can say that all parents worked on assumptions of how they would be treated. All children who married knew how they would treat their parents. It was an agreed-upon pattern, so fundamental to the society that it caused little discussion and provoked little debate. Where commentators discussed this relationship and the general subject of parent-child bonds in Ireland they commonly saw it as a harmonious, well-functioning system, based on mutually demonstrated needs and affections. Irish children felt "attachment to parents," and "respect for them, which subsists among the poor Irish. It matters not what may be the weaknesses, the failings of a father and mother, still gratitude and love sway the hearts and conduct of their offspring." At the same time parents "look forward to marrying their eldest son, by the matchmaker's aid, to a girl with a dowry, and then living as lodgers in the same cabin with him and his wife and a new family. The custom is kindly and thriftless."[30] To be sure, conflicts occurred across generational lines. Parents and children might not see eye to eye on the choice of a spouse, for example, or might spar over how best to run the farm or clash over the fate of unmarried brothers and sisters. Generally, however, parents and children respected one another's needs and functioned in peace together, despite the tremendous control parents exerted over the most intimate and personal of human choices—marriage. If Irish children felt frustrated and stifled by parental authority they tended to draw those feelings inward. Instead of lashing out at a domineering father or challenging outright an overbearing mother, they could in fact take solace in drink or opt to leave Ireland altogether. In extreme cases, children withdrew into a delusional world of schizophrenia (since the late nineteenth century Ireland has had one of the world's highest rates of schizophrenic disorder) instead of challenging parental prerogatives and upsetting the intricate web of duties and obligations.[31]

The relationship among siblings in the Irish family provides another important element in social relations particularly as it affected migration. It may have been, in fact, that the relationship among brothers and sisters and particularly among siblings of the same gender constituted the most positive and least problematic human relations in Irish society. Unlike the parents and children, brothers and sisters functioned on a plane of general equality without duty or obligation obscuring feelings. Although a certain degree of competition existed, since only one of them would inherit or be endowed and the others would have to "travel," it was not clear as to who would be the most jealous—those who were chosen or those passed over. After marriage, brothers and sisters basically shouldered no obligation to unmarried siblings who had already begun to disperse themselves. Similarly, brothers had no particular social responsibility to protect their sisters' honor, as did young men in Italy, for example. Brother-sister relationships constituted the only cross-gender relationships sanctioned by the society, and the close bonds among siblings often provided an additional obstacle to marriage—brothers and sisters not wanting to leave their siblings. Much sought after was a match in which a young man's sister married his wife's brother, uniting the family two times and ensuring that brother and sister would not drift apart but continue their positive relationship. Irish autobiographies and memoirs allude repeatedly to these profound feelings of fondness that existed within families. John O'Leary, a major figure in the Fenian movement, never married. He lived with his sister, who waited twenty long years for him while he sat in a British prison. Upon her death, he mourned, that she

> left me behind in a world which is altogether another world to me since. She was everything to me as I was everything to her, and perhaps the sole consolation I have got, or can ever get from her going first, is that I could bear her loss better than she could bear mine. . . . her last years, spent wholly with me, were the happiest of her life.[32]

O'Leary then summarizes his feelings in a ballad so romantic and so amorous as to fool the reader into believing that it was written for a wife or lover.

Sibling solidarity affected migration patterns also. The sister who went to Boston brought over as soon as possible younger sisters or brothers who had not yet made the break with the Irish countryside. The young man in New York saved his money, often deferring marriage so that his brothers could join him and together they could finance the migration of yet some other sibling. These patterns were so common and so widespread as to constitute a chain of sibling migration that linked Ireland to the Irish settlements in the United States, England, and elsewhere. It was as though Irish migrants sought to re-create what they felt were the best and most meaningful elements of their childhood families.[33]

The relationship between husband and wife in the "typical" late-nineteenth-century Irish family present the historian with a difficult and complex picture. The real must be sorted out from the ideal, the substance from the symbol. Clearly, Irish culture gave husbands the upper hand, and wives were admonished by folk adages and by clerics to submit to their husbands' commands. The Irish prided themselves on the devotion of husbands to their wives, on the absence of divorce (obviously a gratuitous pride in a society totally committed to Catholicism), and on a minimum of desertion. The Irish likewise considered themselves to be a patriarchal, male-dominated society, where in the home the husband ruled wife and children alike. It was the husband's parents who usually lived with the new family. It was to the husband's family that the wife carried out her day-to-day obligations; living with them, cooking for them, cleaning after them, perhaps listening to their complaints about her as wife and mother. As late as the 1930s in County Clare anthropologists Conrad Arensberg and Solon Kimball noticed that women walked the obligatory several paces behind their husbands, in an act of clear subservience. Husbands ate their meals first, fresh and hot. Wives had to satisfy themselves with lukewarm remainders. Wives were expected to help their husbands in any task that might come up. Wives' tasks, however, were their own. They could expect no help in their unending series of chores.

Husbands and wives also lived fairly separate existences. Both had their own sphere. Husbands and wives rarely attended church together. If they attended the same social function, they would characteristically arrive sepparately and not interact with one another in public. Importantly, in public —which might even mean in the presence of children and other relatives—husbands and wives never used their Christian names for one another but instead referred to "himself" and "herself."

This is not to say, however, that Irish women as wives accepted subservience or that the subservience amounted to more than symbolic soothing of male egos. In fact, authority was shared by husband and wife, and in some areas of life, the wife ruled. For one thing, Irish women hardly accepted their husbands' behavior passively, particularly when it came to excessive drinking. Wifely assertiveness was often physical, and, according to Arensberg, women's domination was "like that caricature in the cartoon Maggie and Jiggs." Further, he noted, "in the towns where the men have no field and meadow to retire into, and dispute necessitates the men's flouncing out of the house to the screamed recriminations of the wife" they would flee to the sanctuary of the saloon—a male preserve. Folk proverbs underscored the lack of female passivity and lamented that "the three (things) most difficult to teach [are] a mule, a pig, and a woman," whereas the "three things that leave the shortest traces |are| a bird on a branch, a ship on the sea, and a man on a woman."[34] Wives in Ireland had enough sense of self that they could express negative feelings about their husbands' behavior and could make many decisions about their children. Decision making in Ireland tended to be complex and as gender-based as everything else about the society. Men usually played the most significant role in decisions about matrimony and the match: Who should marry the inheriting son? How much should the dowry amount to? Women, on the other hand, usually decided on major expenditures of money and exercised considerable authority over migration.

Women in the post-Famine family had their own economic resources—the proceeds from poultry and dairy. With them they could augment a daughter's dowry or help her raise the fare to go to America. Importantly, Irish culture did not allow mothers-in-law to dominate the new wife, and though the wife might have certain constant obligations to her husband's family, they did not include being controlled by his mother, as was the case in southern Italian families.[35]

Increasingly in the last decades of the nineteenth century there was reasonable chance within an Irish marriage that the wife had lived away from home, as a domestic in Dublin or a shopgirl in Cork or even in London. It was common for young women to leave home before marriage to work in places where they learned about new ways of doing things. The money they earned could very likely augment what their fathers could put together for the dowry and they therefore went into marriage with a sense of having paid their own way. Young women generally were allowed to be more innovative economically than young men, since their labor was less critical to the actual productivity of the farm. Wives came up with new ideas to enhance the family income much more readily than did husbands, who were more thoroughly committed to the older way of life. The wife usually took care of the family's finances. Husbands and children turned over their earnings to the women, who determined what it could be spent on. George Birmingham offered the following description in 1913 in a series of vignettes, *Irishmen All:*

> Small wonder also that she is calm, that no joy has any power to stir her now, nor any sorrow is fierce enough to break her heart. . . . There were nights when she sat anxious in the kitchen, waiting for her husband to return from the fair, knowing that when he did come he would be thick of speech, blear-eyed, staggering in his gait: yet never so drunk but that he has his money safe, the price of the beasts he had sold; never so incapable but that he had sense enough to hand the greasy notes to her. And from then on they were hers; she kept them, spent them, saved them for the rent, or hoarded them for a daughter's portion. James spent what custom ordained that he should spend at the fair, drank luck to a buyer, stood treat to a friend. Afterwards he asked no money of her. She clothed him, fed him: when the time came had the money by her for the rent

and to meet the calls of tax-gatherers. He never doubted that she was the best manager of the money he earned.[36]

Wives were never expected to integrate fully into their husbands' families. Although legally they assumed their husbands' surname upon marriage, they did not go by that name but continued to use their maiden name. John Francis Maguire, surveying the lives of his compatriots in North America in 1869, noted how inconvenient this was, since immigration officials had a hard time tracking down Irish women, known to all by their maiden name yet appearing on official documents by the name of their husbands' family. British officials believed that the Irish in Lancashire fulfilled obligations to aged parents and struggling siblings first; only after those duties were disposed of did they turn to the needs of their spouses. A woman "brought in" to a farming community from the outside might live a lifetime as a "stranger" there, never fully entrusting her loyalty to the kin and community of her husband.[37]

Most Irish women in the post-Famine society could expect to experience widowhood. Irish men typically married women younger than themselves, and despite the worse diet and high rates of childbearing, Irish wives usually outlived their husbands. In 1873, for example, twenty-eight hundred widowers lived in County Wexford, as opposed to sixty-five hundred widows. Although widowhood undoubtedly involved a great deal of emotional strain and often economic suffering, it is striking to see not only the number of widows in Ireland but the range of economic activities they engaged in with an amazing degree of success. Farm widows often kept up production, while bringing in an unmarried son or nephew to help, but they kept control of the farm's operation in their hands. According to Arensberg and Kimball, "Many Irish farm widows with grown sons can successfully manage a farm for many years before they ultimately make it over upon a son's marriage."[38]

The Irish wife played a central role vis-à-vis her children, often overshadowing the husband's. Irish men and women who became writers, politicians, nuns, and labor leaders and who left some record of their childhood lives stressed most frequently the influence of their mother—her strength, her power to control life. In fact, the fathers frequently appeared as the foil of failure against which the mothers' indomitable will and strength contrasted sharply. Irish writers, particularly those concerned with celebrating the national spirit and the virtues of Catholic Ireland, consistently paid homage to the "affectionate mother, such as we have among the peasants of Ireland, where mother love is a passion," and an American priest of Irish extraction traveling in the "ould sod" intoned, "God bless our Irish mothers! we have thank God! thousands and thousands of such angelic women beautifying and blessing the Peasant Homes of our Land!" In the early twentieth century the *Independent* published a series of portraits of "undistinguished Americans as told by themselves." In the reminiscences of an Irish cook readers were told:

I don't know why anybody wants to hear my history. Nothing ever happened to me worth the tellin' except when my mother died. Now she was an extraordinary person. The neighbors all respected her an' the minister. "Go ask Mrs. McNabb," he'd say to the women in the neighborhood. . . . We lived in a peat cabin, but it had a good thatched roof. Mother put on that roof. It isn't a woman's work but she—was able for it. . . . My mother sent Joseph |a brother| to Londonderry to lam the weaver's trade. My father he never was a steddy worker. He took to the drink early in life. My mother an' me an' Tilly we worked in the field for Squire Varney.[39]

Even after migration the McNabbs played out their accustomed roles of "successful" mother and importunate father: "Father died soon after he came. Poor father! He was a good-hearted man, but he wasn't worth a penny when he died. Mother lived to be eighty. She was respected by all Kensington."[40]

Anthropologists who have studied the Irish family forms of post-Famine society have argued that boys were generally more valued by the society. Daughters, considered to be less permanent members of the family, would receive fewer rewards. They would leave upon marrying and go to live with someone else's family or they would grow up to travel far away from their mothers. Sons, on the other hand, could be counted on to remain at home and take care of their aging parents. Sons would also carry on the family name and lands. Boys, therefore, received preferential treatment, particularly from their mothers, being pampered and protected longer than their sisters.

Parental preference for boys exists in many cultures, and maternal dominance characterizes the family structure of a wide range of ethnic groups. Yet, in the United States and in Europe students of the ethnic dimension of psychiatric disorders have linked these family forms with the staggering statistics of Irish male schizophrenia. Many psychocultural studies have asserted that Irish men never could overcome the emotionally debilitating effects of being overwhelmed by their mothers.

Daughters emerged less scathed by these sociocultural patterns because they were deemed less important and, as such, mothers dominated and manipulated them less. Irish women in Ireland have significantly lower rates of mental disorder. We can only guess at the impact this had on Irish immigration and the subsequent adaptation of Irish men and women in the United States. Not only did women leave Ireland more willingly, but leaving involved very little emotional pining. They made the decision to leave with a relatively light heart.[41]

The entire structure of the Irish family and the values upon which it was based had a dispersing, centrifugal effect. In Ireland, though the entire family worked together and functioned as an economic unit of production, it did so in gender-based spheres. Family members, particularly husband and wife, spent very little leisure time together, eschewing each other's company in nonwork hours, with men particularly seeking out the company of other men.

Older sons would join with the men in the local saloon rather than remain at home. Daughters frequently worked away from home, often a first step to the process of leaving permanently. Mothers saved butter and egg money to finance a daughter's trip across the sea. A mid-nineteenth-century Irish magazine writer asserted boldly:

> The Irish peasantry are generally anti-domestic; they miss no opportunity of being in society, and these [opportunities] perpetually occur. . . . The peasantry have generally to build their own houses, and being either possessed of no capital or naturally unwilling to lay out any . . . they build houses to the most wretched description. . . . It is impossible that domestic habits should be formed in these horrid habitations. . . . Being generally illiterate or at best possessing no books, they have no means of amusement at home during the long winter evenings; and as a substitute assemble either at a neighbor's house or a dancing house.[42]

Although this description seems overdrawn it is essentially accurate.

The separation of men and women in the home, the segregation of adults by gender in the family circle, almost universally characterized Irish family life. Irish men and women rarely ate together or sat together in their own homes, with the warmth of the hearth rigidly demarcated. Men's tools were stored in one part of the house, women's in another.[43] A temperance worker in the early twentieth century, trying to point out to a man in Cork that he was wasting too much money on alcohol, instead suggested that he

> put aside every day . . . a nice little sum, and you could go somewhere with your wife and children for a real good holiday. "Go with my wife and children!" echoed the man in disgust, "Sure I never yet walked the length of the street with them!" He spoke in much the same tone of indignation as if he had been asked to go for a walk with a domestic cat.[44]

As might be expected, the world outside the home and away from the hearth mirrored the same marked division of life into the male and female zones. Few institutions in Ireland encompassed both men and women. Obviously, the church ministered to the needs of all; but even here men attended services with other men, women worshipped with sisters, aunts, and other females. One influential analyst of Irish social life, Arland Ussher, has in fact asserted that "Ireland is divided by a boundary even more pernicious than that between North and South—the boundary between the sexes."[45] This rigid gender division had pre-Famine roots, but it blossomed in the decades after the 1840s when marriages had to be delayed in order to ensure the material well-being of those who chose to remain. If marriages had to be postponed and had to be based on the economic considerations of the "match," then romance and courtship must be sacrificed. Although at base the intense gender segregation

[handwritten left margin: husband and wife rarely spent time together]

[handwritten bottom: Men and women were seperated most of the time in Irish society]

functioned to keep "young" unmarried men and women apart, it reflected and exaggerated Irish ideals that stretched back before the Famine. These ideals engendered little or no opposition demonstrated by the absence of any rebellion and the perpetutation of the boundary, although in modified form, even after migration. Not only did Irish men and women, particularly of the marriageable ages, function in separate worlds, but they became enmeshed in an ethos of gender hostility, where each sex had an elaborate rationale of the faults of the other. This became in the end a vicious cycle, as men and women deprecated each other and existed apart from each other.[46]

One measure of the effectiveness of sex segregation among the young in Ireland can be gleaned from the almost universal consensus among contemporary observers and scholars on the low rate of illegitimacy in Ireland and among the Irish in their diaspora. Certainly, after the Famine it became very rare for a young Irish man and woman to be so romantically involved with each other as to indulge in premarital sex. Even before the Famine Irish illegitimacy figures indicated very few instances of pregnancy among unmarried women. English, French, and German travelers observed with awe that "the Irish are remarkable for chastity; natural children are rare, adultery almost unknown." One British visitor commented that the peasants of Ireland were "signally chaste," since "there are no more innocent girls in the world than the Irish." Needless to say, the Irish themselves, and particularly their Roman Catholic clerics, beamed with pride as they declared that in Donegal, for example, "there is scarcely anything known about bastards in the parish," or that a Limerick priest could emphatically point to the "extreme infrequency of a woman being with child at the time of marriage."[47]

If illegitimacy, as an indicator of sexual indiscretion, occurred rarely before the Famine it appeared even less frequently when gender lines became more rigid afterward. One 1890 study found that Ireland had the lowest illegitimacy rate of fifteen countries. Between 1879 and 1889, of one thousand children born in England, forty-six to forty-nine were conceived out of wedlock, as were seventy-nine to eighty-five in Scotland, but only twenty-five to twenty-eight were in Ireland. Interestingly, the highest illegitimacy figures in Ireland registered in predominately Protestant Ulster (four hundred per thousand), whereas Connought, the poorest, most thoroughly Catholic province had the lowest (seven per thousand).

An 1891 ethnographic study of the Aran Islanders commented that "the men do not appear to have strong sexual passions, and any irregularity of conduct is rare; only five cases of illegitimacy having been registered within the past ten years." It is possible that a young woman in Sligo or Killarney who, upon finding herself both single and pregnant, would have chosen to leave home precipitously and go to England, Scotland, or the United States and avoid the shame and dishonor of her condition. Yet areas in the British Isles which were heavily Irish, like Lanarkshire and Renfrewshire, as well as predominantly Irish districts of London had similarly low numbers of children born out of wedlock. The Inspector of Schools in Scotland in 1860 issued a glowing report of Irish sexual morality: "The Catholic mill-girls . . . are remarkable for freedom from the stated corruption which too generally prevails in these establishments." Clearly this kind of tribute from non-Irish sources was greeted with joy by the Irish, who not only sang the praises of "the young women of Ireland who can perhaps carry off the premier prize of the world for maidenly modesty and purity" but also could then feel that the evolving social order in Ireland was working. The low level of sexual activity outside of marriage indicated that young people in particular had come to accept the restraints placed on them, that Irish men and women exhibited almost universal conformity to the system of late marriage, which demanded extremely limited cross-gender contact. No tradition of chaperonage existed, since everyone assumed compliance and expected conformity. No one needed the duenna or the all-protecting brother to guard a girl's chastity. She could guard it herself and it was unlikely that it was in any danger.[48]

The Irish enforced sex segregation through various arrangements. Particularly in the small towns, few places existed where young men and women could mingle. The saloon or pub was a male preserve. No "decent" local young woman would go there to wile away the evening. Schools were segregated by gender. Young men attended church with other males. Young women safely sat through mass with other females. If a man socialized with women, his male friends usually derided him and even ostracized him. Since the camaraderie of the men of the pub or the political club mattered a great deal to any small town young lad, he would avoid assiduously being labeled a deviant by mixing with women. Young women, particularly toward the end of the nineteenth century, commonly spent some years away from home working in domestic service, which further curtailed the possibility of dangerous encounters with men.

The role of the Catholic clergy in enforcing rigid sex segregation and the peculiar pattern of Irish marriage add an important element to an understanding of the social fabric of post-Famine Ireland. Catholic theology nowhere maintained that marriage should be avoided, except by those who embraced a spiritual life under the perpetual vows of the clergy. If anything, the teachings of the church would have encouraged universal young marriage regardless of economic consequences. Beginning in the early nineteenth century, the clergy of Ireland, trained primarily at the seminary at Maynooth, came from the ranks of the peasantry. The clergy increasingly embodied the same attitudes as the bulk of the population. As the Irish masses came to view marriage as something perhaps to be avoided, so too the clergy accepted this position, despite official church dogma. As the majority of Irish farmers believed that marriage basically constituted an economic enterprise, so too the clergy altered the meaning of the sacrament. Memoirs of Irish life as well as Irish literature portrayed over and over again the priest, born of the peasantry, who thundered to his parishioners that "love in the main was devilish, a subtle and odious poison, designed to set young souls in the way of eternal perdition."[49]

The rural priest played a role in keeping any deviant young men and women apart from each other. Irish priests patroled the country roads at night, some armed with cudgels or umbrellas, ready to drive away any amorous couples who had sought some place for romance. Priests in various towns labored to wipe out crossroads dancing and games, theatrical companies, or any other activities where the sexes could mingle. The example of the celibate priest and the eternally chaste nun meshed with the economic dictates of the Irish social order, confirming that nonmarriage was a legitimate option, that male-female socializing not only led to unfortunate and improvident matches but carried with it the stigma of sin.

In the decades after the Famine Ireland had become a society that placed little value on romance and lyrical love. To be sure, ballads were composed and amorous adventures—very tame by French and even British standards—appeared in novels and short stories. The ballads and poetry that presumably dealt with male-female romantic attraction, however, frequently superimposed a nationalistic theme on professions of love, almost as if to make them acceptable. Irish songs might have celebrated the beauty of Irish women, but always in order to contrast them with women of other groups, providing yet another way to celebrate that which was distinctively Irish. A young man in a poem could admire a beautiful woman, but in the largest sense he was admiring Ireland. For example, the following poem appeared in 1871 in the *Irish World:*

> Tis pretty to see the girl of Dunbey
> Stepping the mountain stately
> Though ragged her gown, and naked her feet,
> No lady in Ireland to match her is meet.
>
> Poor is her diet and hardly she lies
> Yet a monarch might kneel from a glance of her eyes;
> The child of a peasant—Yet England's proud Queen
> Has less rank in her heart, and less grace in her mien.[50]

Themes of love thwarted by the wicked landlord or the hard-hearted British appeared much more commonly than those of love for its own sake. More likely, Irish literature, particularly after the Famine, underscored those cultural elements now universally accepted by the farming classes, which approached the relations between men and women cautiously and always with considerations of material well-being. One 1904 story in the *Gael,* "The Whistling Maid," depicted "Shaun Kelly's daughter," a young woman who constantly deviated from the rigid sex division of Knockany. She disrupted the work of the men by her beauty, her "dark eyes that shone," and her eerie whistling. She ended up "in the river, her forehead all black and burnt. The men said it was lightning that killed her. But women knew, 'A whistling woman or a crowing hen was never good for God or men.'"[51]

Not only does the literary testimony of post-Famine Ireland speak to a lack of romance, but personal narratives document a constant chord of male-female conflict. Anthropologists studying Irish folk life noted considerable female resentment over the greater resources available to men and their more extensive freedom in the small towns. Men seemed to feel inadequate when they measured themselves against women's greater economic initiative. Women disliked the time and money their husbands squandered in the saloon, and even politics was frequently deprecated by local women as something of no real value. James Macauly in 1872 related how Barney O'Reagan became inspired at a political meeting against the British, only to come home to his wife who forced him back down to earth, "What's anybody's wrong to us, or all the wrongs of the world, compared with the wrong of not having a cabin to put our heads into?"[52]

Male resentment of females was expressed by James Clarence Mongan, a celebrated Gaelic poet, when he derided "The Woman of the Three Cows," whom he felt had become single-minded in her pursuit of wealth. He warned her with great hostility:

> Now, there you go; you still, of course, keep up your scornful bearing,
> And I'm too poor to hinder you; but by the cloak I'm wearing,
> If I had but four cows myself, even though you were my spouse,
> I'd thwack you well, to cure your pride, my Woman of Three Cows.[53]

From all accounts Irish men clearly realized that the ideal of the patriarchal family bore little resemblance to the actual functioning of their family life and felt very negative about the assertiveness of their wives and the lack of female submissiveness around them.

The only other way that romance and positive light-hearted portrayals of male-female socializing found their way into popular Irish literary and folk idioms was as nostalgic remembrances of earlier times. Thus, the past frequently was depicted as more romantic, merrier, although significantly less prosperous and less thoughtful. James Lyman Molloy, who lived through the Famine, wistfully wrote of those days:

> O the days of the Kerry dancing, O the ring of the piper's tunes
> O for one of those hours of gladness gone alas! like our youth too soon
>
> Was there ever a sweeter colleen in the dance than Eily Moore?
> Or a prouder lad than Thady, as he boldly took the floor?
> "Lads and lasses to your places; up the middle and down again."
> Ah! the merry hearted laughter ringing through the happy glen!
> O to think of it, O to dream of it, fills my Heart with tears.[54]

Significantly, the rigid body dances now so thoroughly considered the proto-
type of the Irish folk dance, which focuses all attention on the feet and not on
the rest of the body, is a post-Famine form. Pre-Famine dancing involved
greater physical contact between partners and the movement of other body
parts, therefore appearing more sexually suggestive.

Leisure time activity also helped keep the sexes apart. The all-male
social group played an extremely important part in rural and urban Irish life.
Although nominally a bachelor group, it also encompassed married men. It
based itself in the pub and surrounded itself with the ritual of drinking and
treating. A man who eschewed the company of the group and who shunned
its ethos of male solidarity clearly deviated from the post-Famine society.
Single men in particular had very few responsibilities to keep them away from
the pub. For married men nighttime freed them from work and there was no
pressure to remain at home in the company of women. Drinking in the pub,
joining in the songs and stories of the men did not just become an expression
of manliness but indicated that one accepted the underlying principles of
society that social life and leisure time ought not be spent with women. The
pub also became a political center where men discussed the issues of
the day.[55]

Even the nationalist movement in Ireland, with its various phases of
action—Ribbonism, Land League, and Fenianism—with its calls for Catholic
Emancipation, Repeal, Republicanism, and Home Rule, constituted an all-
male campaign. With a few exceptions hardly any women participated in the
movement, let alone moved into positions of leadership. Not surprisingly, the
movement had almost nothing to say about the status of women in Ireland. It
was argued that if women suffered it was because they were Irish, living under
the British yoke. The republic that the nationalists dreamed of creating bore a
close resemblance to the one in which they lived, when it came to marriage
and family and the role of women. The paucity of women activists and the
lack of a women's agenda within the movement for Irish independence stands
in stark contrast to almost all the modern revolutions of the nineteenth and
twentieth centuries. In the Russian and the Chinese revolutions women played
a much more extensive role as well as in the Zionist movement and even in
the Italian *Risorgimento*.[56]

Women's social life also confirmed larger cultural patterns. Before the
Famine women involved in cottage industries like weaving might get together
on a regular basis to weave while they "spin, sing and converse during the
whole evening." The disappearance of cottage industries and the centralization
of butter making in dairies resulted in fewer institutions that brought women
together in any kind of systematic way. Yet in some remote, less developed
areas in the west of Ireland, farm women did not even leave their homes to go
to the crossroad shop. Itinerant tinkers periodically appeared hawking goods.
Furthermore, for mothers and daughters on farms, work was unending, and

they began preparations at night for the next day, getting the bread ready and slaking the fire to start work anew in the morning.[57]

Certainly, women had a social life in rural Ireland. It took place before and after services at the church, and when women in the small towns helped each other out, through childbirth, sickness, the marriage of a son or the emigration of a daughter or the death of a husband. Women might spend time in the shop, often run by a widow or a friend, gossiping and sharing news of their children. Women similarly would aid one another in some larger economic project. Importantly, however, their social interaction did not take place in formal institutions as did that of men. The social life of women accepted the cultural dictate that provided greater resources for men in their separate sphere.

The rigid segregation of the sexes operated in a system that allowed women to define themselves in strikingly economic terms, in a system where women measured their worth and aspirations in relation to material standards. The whole family pattern could therefore continue to function without rebellion, without protest. Women articulated their hopes not in the romantic idiom, since that obviously threatened the whole underpinning of the structure of Irish society, but in the economic, since rather than endangering the family order it actually bolstered it. The young women who eschewed marriage to set up a crossroad shop, the female who banished notions of romance and amorous love in favor of accretion of wealth, clearly helped the social order.

Married women could not move around in pursuit of income as readily as could unmarried women. But both single and married females sought to earn money, not only to help support their families, but to assert their own self worth and increase their own power. Contractors paid women cash for knitting, weaving, lacemaking, and sewing for several decades after the Famine. From the 1870s to the 1890s in places like Donegal (which sent a large portion of its residents to the United States) these kinds of activities for women throve. One American visitor noticed that at "land meetings it was common to see in the crowd women intent on the speaker's words while their needles flashed in the sunlight. Often a baby tied in a shawl on its mother's back gazed wonderingly around." A man who grew up at the end of the nineteenth century in the Blasket Islands remembered how "me mother would come in and she in the long black cloak with the hood. She would draw the wheel to her and that was the office for me and my sisters to start carding. She would be singing to the wheel." Married women in the earlier part of the nineteenth century commonly sold jugs, bowls, dishes, and cups at the local fairs, hawked threads, buttons, needles in Dublin, and took up seasonal work in coastal areas involving the salting and barreling of herring. This work provided them with a social life and money. As one woman described it, "There would be twenty women in each shed, laughing and singing, and telling iies—each one better than the last. Oh, we did so love the fishing season."[58]

In towns married and unmarried women ran shops of various kinds, and widows particularly found the proprietorship of a local store an attractive activity. The constant economic activities of women both before and after marriage served as a form of insurance, given the extremely high rate of widowhood in Ireland. Since most married women could expect to be widows, often before their children had come of age, their spinning, sewing, and storekeeping provided an important hedge against the inevitable calamity. Irish women also made money by making whiskey and other alcoholic beverages—legal and illegal. A County Mayo woman brashly told the Commission of Inquiry on the Irish Poor in 1835 as she pointed to a whiskey bottle that it "is my sole dependence. I have no means on earth to keep my children inside the door with me, but to borrow money from one neighbor or another and buy a drop of poteen to sell again." A very popular Irish shoemaker's ballad, heard in the homeland and in Irish settlements in England, jingled:

> When I was at home and I was merry and frisky
> My dad kept a pig and my mother sold whiskey.[50]

Married women had certain prerogatives not available to men when it came to spending money. Husbands first had to use the earnings from the crop for the welfare of the family, whereas women could save or dispose, hoard or spend, as they saw fit. The ways they spent it further strengthened the Irish social system. Women used their money to finance their own migrations or that of other family members. By all accounts—autobiographical and journalistic—parents made little or no effort to block a daughter from earning money to leave home. For many farm families the female-earned income became the factor that tipped the balance between bare survival and a degree of comfort. Even the very poorest women earned money. Begging had always been the domain of the poor female. Despite the shame that begging brought, very poor women, often with their children in tow, would wander through the countryside. Married women in desperation might even go into domestic service, leaving their own homes. Fanny Parnell, one of the few women in the Irish nationalist movement, told of a woman who decided to go into domestic service, despite her husband's objections, in order to avoid the horror of being forced to go into the workhouse.

Interestingly, Irish women had few noneconomic activities. To be sure, the matchmaker usually an elderly widow, played an important part in Ireland, but this too was an economic role. Women did have a central part in the most significant Irish ritual—the wake for the dead. Women in the pre-Famine culture usually prepared the corpse for burial, and even after the 1840s women were intimately associated with the mourning and the ritual of sitting with the corpse. James Macaulay described an 1872 funeral in Ireland, noting that "there were about a dozen elderly women, in two rows, walking in front of the hearse. They had the long cloaks and hooded shawls or kerchiefs of the country. One woman seemed to be the chief keener, leading the dirge, the others joining in the melancholy wail." A number of observers commented on the existence of a class of professional keeners, elderly women who made a living mourning the dead, and fairly recent anthropological studies of Irish rural society reveal that they are still in existence. Yet other than these "semiofficial" positions in the communities of rural Ireland, there were no noneconomic institutions where women met and interacted until the twentieth century.[60]

Even the Catholic orders of nuns and their convent life developed primarily after the Famine. Before the Famine very few Irish women wanted to take the vows. After the Famine, when the number of priests grew dramatically, the growth of orders of nuns eclipsed even those of the male brotherhoods. In 1841 one nun could be found in Ireland to every seven thousand Catholics, whereas a century later there was one nun for every four hundred. Not only did increasing numbers of young Irish women find the life of a nun an attractive option in Ireland but many orders of nuns in the United States regularly came to Ireland to recruit young women.

Irish women started several new orders in the nineteenth century. Mother Catherine McAuley's labors with the poor women of Dublin led in 1831 to the founding of the Sisters of Mercy. Other Irish-based orders, like the Presentation Sisters of the Blessed Virgin Mary, the Loretto Order, the Dominicans, and the Ursulines, gave women a chance to teach, to heal, to organize, and to administer services of all kinds. Importantly, the Catholic female orders rarely were cloistered and contemplative. Irish nuns were activists. They worked very much in the everyday world, confronting the problems of poverty and unemployment, deserted wives and orphaned children, illness and alcoholism. By the closing decades of the nineteenth century the education of girls in Ireland had won public approval, leading to almost universal female education. In part, it became respectable because it was under the auspices of the teaching orders of nuns, who, it was assumed, would not use education to subvert the traditional position of female subservience. The Irish Catholic hierarchy, imbued as thoroughly as the peasants with the traditions of sex segregation, late marriage, and celibacy, welcomed the rise of service-oriented female orders.[61]

The Ireland of the last half of the nineteenth century, birthplace of the hundreds of thousands of women who flooded into the United States, held out very little for women. Few of its resources or honors went to women. It had evolved a family system that of necessity produced surplus sons and daughters, and for those daughters few economic or social benefits could be had if they stayed at home. Such women left Ireland because they could not find a meaningful role for themselves in its social order and because American opportunities for young women beckoned. Different women chose to respond to the pushes and pulls in different ways, but increasingly through the end of the nineteenth century, Ireland became a place that women left.

These young women, the daughters from the thousands of small farms that dotted the countryside, the daughters of the survivors of the great Famine, saw themselves not as passive pawns in life but as active, enterprising creatures who could take their destiny in their own hands. Although possessed of a profound religiosity that belittled what people could do for themselves to alter the course of human events, the Bridgets, Maureens, Norahs, and Marys decided to try just that.

TWO  The Search for Bread:
Patterns of Female
Migration

Amerca: the immigrant from the other lands seeks in it an asylum or
resting place; the Irishman makes it his home.

John H. Campbell, *History of the Friendly Sons of St.*
Patrick and of the Hibernian Society for the Relief of
Emigrants from Ireland, March 7, 1771-March 17, 1892

Farewell to thee, Ireland the land of our birth
The pride and the glory, the gem of the earth
We sail with sad hearts to a land far away
In search of that bread that may fail if we stay
New faces glo bright in the blaze of our fires
And the Saxons abide in the halls of our sires
Farewell, oh farewell to thy beautiful shore;
Tis with tears that we bid thee farewell evermore.

The Immigrant's Farewell

Oh brave, brave Irish girls,
We well might call you brave
Should the least of all your perils
The Stormy ocean waves.

James Connally, *Labour in Ireland*

Beginning in the early nineteenth century, the exodus from Ireland to
the United States amounted to a virtual tidal wave of human beings leaving
one home and seeking another. That more than half of these immigrants were
women, that the migration constituted basically a mass female movement, did
not escape the notice of observers on either side of the Atlantic. No other
major group of immigrants in American history contained so many women.

30

Among the Germans, a group that arrived over the same span of years as the Irish, the women made up 41 percent of the total immigrant population, whereas among the Irish, women accounted for 52.9 percent. The contrast with other immigrants of the late nineteenth and early twentieth century presents an even more striking picture. Southern Italian women, for example, comprised a mere 21 percent of migrants from their homeland; in 1907, 13 percent of all Croatian arrivals were women; and among Greeks only 4 percent of the newcomers were female. The only large foreign-born immigrant population where men and women came in roughly equal numbers were Jews, yet even here men still outnumbered women slightly. Furthermore, a goodly proportion of the new Jewish arrivals were children, indicating that a large number of the immigrants were married and had brought their young with them. The Irish immigrants were primarily still single women and men. Only about 5 percent of all Irish immigrants were children, as compared with 28 percent of all Jewish immigrants.[1]

Why did the Irish male-female ratios differ so fundamentally from those of other groups? What was there about the Irish and their culture to create this particular pattern? Irish female immigration patterns had been distinctive even before the Famine, yet it was only afterward, with the emergence of the modern Irish family structure, that the Irish became so unique, so dramatically female in the migratory habits. As that family form became universalized in Ireland, the intensity of the female exodus became more pronounced. Thus, by the early twentieth century, when the family in Ireland had really hardened into its characteristic form, the number of women leaving swelled to even greater proportions. Women made up about 53.8 percent of all immigrants in 1900, as compared to 35 percent in the 1830s.

Immigration during the Famine differed considerably from the exodus of the Irish before it and contrasted sharply with what would happen afterward. Sheer numbers make the Famine a pivotal event in immigration history, although it was hardly typical. From 1821 to 1850 about one million Irish came to the United States. Of that million 120,000 of them account only for two years, 1845 and 1846. In the eight years between 1847 and 1854, the worst years of the Famine and those following immediately thereafter, over one and a quarter million had made their way to the United States. Another three million immigrated in the half century between 1851 and 1901. Those who migrated during and just after the Famine, more than those before or those afterward, represented the landless and the poor, who just could not remain at home. During the Famine married couples with children immigrated more readily than they had before and certainly than they would later, emphasizing the aberrant nature of the immigration of the Famine years. Thus, during the Famine one sees less clearly the true trends of the Irish movement to the United States and its essentially young, unmarried, female component.[2]

The real impact of the Famine on migration came from the traumatic shock waves it sent through Irish society which accelerated the rearrangement

"Farewell to the Old World": Irish immigrant women aboard ship in the 1870s. (*Courtesy of the Library of Congress*)

of family life and which caused many young Irish men and particularly Irish women to immigrate. Looking at Irish immigration figures in the decade afterward provides a much more profound sense of how the society sought to cope with newly evolving land and family forms. For one thing, age became a more important factor and fewer children emigrated, stressing that single people were leaving. Between 1850 and 1887 over 66 percent of all immigrants fell between the ages of 15 and 35. In the last decades of the nineteenth century, from 1880 to 1897, a mere 7.9 percent clustered below the age of 15,

while a slightly more substantial 9.0 percent exceeded 35 years of age. From 1852 to 1921 the median age for all male immigrants was 22.5, whereas for women it was 21.2, younger than the median age of marriage. In the twenty-three years from 1887 to the century's end, married people constituted only slightly more than 16 percent of all those who arrived in the United States.

This differs sharply with Irish immigration to Britain, where many more children went as well as many more older people, presumably those less able to work. This suggests that when entire families were compelled to leave they could not afford the longer, more expensive trip across the Atlantic. Immigrants to Britain were also committing themselves to a less permanent move, and statistics indicate that the Irish who did not choose America were more likely to return to Ireland.[3]

Other than the very poor, the Irish who immigrated as single men and women did so because of their unfavorable place in the family land arrangements of the Irish countryside. Despite seasonal fluctuations, occasional dips in the number of immigrants, and regional variations, the movement of women out of Ireland continued unabated through the end of the century. Even during the years when prospects dimmed for men in the United States, as during the American depressions of 1873 and 1893, the migration of Irish women continued unchecked. In fact, during these periods the percentage of young women among the arrivals from Ireland mushroomed. Between 1861 and 1870, 21.1 percent of all migrants were women between the ages of fifteen and twenty-four and 23.3 percent were men of those ages. In the years 1871 through 1880 men and women of these ages arrived in exactly equal proportion. From 1881 through 1890, 30.0 percent were women and 27.4 percent men, and from 1891 until the end of the century 35.4 were women and 24.5 percent men. Thus, the percentage and the absolute number of female immigrants from Ireland rose in direct proportion to the hardening of family lines and the circumscribing of opportunities for women in Ireland. Women did not predominate among Irish newcomers to Britain until the 1890s, whereas among those Irish who chose to cast their lot in Australia, men and women came in equal numbers until 1911 and then women took the lead.

The preponderantly female emigration originated primarily from Munster and Connaught, the most rural provinces. The more urban areas like Ulster (home of Belfast) and Leinster (which included Dublin) offered greater employment options to women. In Ulster women still made money through a variety of home-based industries, and therefore they did not have as much reason to leave.

During the last half of the nineteenth century, the immigration became increasingly composed of women as it came to be increasingly centered in the western agricultural areas. Although in 1882 the emigration from all of Ireland had grown two-and-a-half times since 1878, it had grown three times from County Clare and four times from Kerry and Leitrim. In Galway it increased four-and-a-half times, whereas the exodus from Mayo was seven times larger and from Sligo nine times greater than at the end of the 1870s. The female emigration from these western districts originated in environments so scarred by the Famine and now so committed to the single-inheritance system that excess children, particularly daughters for whom no resources could be expended and for whom no alternatives existed, left in droves, de-populating—and defeminizing—rural Ireland.[4]

From the point of view of those who remained in Ireland, the large number of women, "the flower of the population," who left their homes to try their luck in the United States meant that Irish life, particularly in agricultural areas, became increasingly dominated by males. Irish observers during the migration, particularly in the last decades of the century, panicked at the prospect that the migration had reduced "that element of the population which furnishes the natural increase of any people." The censuses of 1861, 1871, 1881, and 1891 confirmed that the population was dwindling, and es-pecially its female portion. For example, 1,542 men and 1,365 women lived in the Aran Islands in 1891; 20 years earlier, men had outnumbered women by 27. Even the nonfarming areas felt the sting of the female exodus. By the 1880s it had become impossible to find young women in places like Donegal who would work in domestic service in Ireland. A London *Times* reporter noted that serving girls were "scarcer everyday" as the lure of America captured them, since they left as soon as they had saved up the needed money.[5]

The women who had immigrated maintained contact with other women, sisters in particular, but also nieces, aunts, female cousins, and friends back home. The steady stream of letters from "exciting" places where women could earn money and where all sorts of activities abounded must surely have whetted the appetites and fired the imaginations of young women who still found themselves in the Irish countryside. The immigration had so charged up the energies of young women that, according to one observer, "indeed the regret belongs rather now to those who stay behind and those who watch the unceasing flow of the hardiest and most vigorous of our race . . . as usual young women, either farmers' daughters or domestic servants, predominate."[6]

Some Irish men, particularly clerics, bemoaned the emigration in general and saw the female exodus as dangerous, risking the "moral murder of countless virtuous Irish maidens."[7] Since traditional communal restraints did not exist in America, Irish girls would face problems in their new homes. Some commentators, who feared for the health of female immigrants, cited "the young girl who left Queenstown with the fresh bloom of health upon her cheeks, with such a complexion as only the genial Irish clime can give," and shortly thereafter, "in America . . . lives the life of a 'slavey' competing in do-mestic service with a Chinaman, or becomes a drudge in a slum, loses her colour and becomes a sickly, dried up sapless creature."[8]

(margin handwritten note, left:) stories of exciting opportunities for women

(handwritten note, bottom:) ⤷ some irish men saw this to be unmoral for women

Opinion in Ireland almost universally agreed that the depopulation of the countryside was undesirable for both those Irish men who remained and those who chose to leave. Importantly, despite this consensus, opponents of the exodus did almost nothing to stymie the outward flow. A few scattered antiemigration societies cropped up but expired quickly. Priests in rural areas and in towns preached against the emigration. The Catholic press joined a chorus of doomsayers who predicted disaster for the Hibernians in America as did nationalist publications. Such admonitions, however, went unheeded. Nothing was done because it would have been impossible to check the tide.[9]

Each emigrant must have had her own story on how she came to the decision to leave Ireland. Yet certain patterns did emerge. Much of the immediate Famine exodus, for example, constituted a flight from hunger, a migration of desperation. *Illustrated London* in 1849 told about Bridget O'Donnel of the seaside town of Kilrush, about to have a baby, whose husband had abandoned her with two children, with no resources of any kind, and on the verge of eviction from her four-and-a-half acres of bog. She left for America, pushed out by overwhelming circumstances.[10]

After the Famine, however, emigrants tended to flee less from actual hunger and disease, although they still intensively yearned to leave. One American who visited Ireland in the early 1850s noted, "There is nothing unnatural in the desire of the unfortunate Irish to abandon their cheerless and damp cottages, to crawl inch by inch, while they have yet a little strength, from the graves which apparently yawn for their bodies."[11]

During the Famine and in its immediate aftermath, several agencies assisted Irish men and women to emigrate. For example, in the 1860s approximately sixty-five hundred (out of nine hundred thousand) immigrants had their passage paid by the Poor Law Guardians. Some landlords, their consciences apparently pricked by the harrowing scenes of starvation and disease, helped their tenants leave. They may also have reasoned that the money for the passage was an excellent investment, since it facilitated the consolidation of holdings needed to shift the land from tillage to grazing. Occasionally the Irish Prison Board, even as late as the 1870s, released well-behaved convicts on the condition that they leave Ireland for either the United Kingdom, for other parts of the British empire, or for the United States.

Some immigration schemes were aimed primarily at women. For example, women, who constituted most of the inmates of the Irish workhouses, were assisted to leave but only in modest numbers. In 1850 2,847 women left the workhouses for America courtesy of the Poor Law Guardians. In the first years of the 1850s Vere Foster, an English philanthropist, organized the Irish Pioneer Immigration Fund and a Women's Protective Immigration Society to finance the migration of thousands of young women to Canada and the United States from the poor counties of the west of Ireland. The emigrants were to be selected on the basis of "their excellence of character and industrious habits." Similarly, in the 1860s a Female Middle Class Immigration Society, organized by Maria Rye, sought to promote the successful immigration of young, educated Irish women, particularly to Australia.[12]

Organized schemes to assist emigrants never accounted for more than a fraction of those who left. Many more came over because relatives already in the United States had sent them the money. Vast numbers of emigrants left through the generosity of their sisters, brothers, and friends, which suggests that the movement was a positive and enthusiastic one. Sometimes the role of family members in bringing one another over contributed to the lightness and almost nonchalance that accompanied the decision to migrate. Maurice O'Sullivan, who grew up in the Blasket Islands in the early twentieth century, described how his sister broached her decision to leave with the family:

> "Well," said Maria one day. . . . The rest of us were sitting around the fire. We turned . . . "What is the 'well'?" asked my brother Shaun. She turned back to the table again, smiling. Then picking up a cup she turned around again "'the well' . . . |is| that I have a great mind to go to America."
>
> "What put that into your head?" said my father. . . .
>
> "Peg is going and I have no need to stay here when all the girls are parting."
>
> "She won't go," said Eileen, her lips trembling, "or if she does, I will go too."
>
> "Well, fly away at once!" cried my father, waving his hands in the air, "away with you over the sea and you will find the gold on the streets!"
>
> That day Maria wrote to her aunt for passage money.[13]

The Irish cook, whose life was immortalized by the *Independent,* noted that after her mother had sent two sons off to Australia and yet another off to Londonderry, the Famine put its "curse on ould green Ireland and we'll get out of it." After working for four years, saving every penny, "we sent Tilly to America. . . . She came to Philadelphia and got a place for general housework. . . . She had no expenses and laid by money enough to bring me out before the year was gone. Me and Tilly worked till we brought Joseph and Phil over . . . and they saved and we all brought out my mother and father." These kinds of descriptions were typical of almost all portrayals of post-Famine leave-takings. Immigrants showed little remorse and decided to leave on a positive, cheerful note.[14]

Such stories also illustrate the relationship of migration to the Irish family structure. Most migrations moved in long lines of kinship and, to a lesser extent, bonds of friendship. Almost all observers of Irish life on both sides of the Atlantic confirmed the overwhelming tendency of the Irish to journey "one member of a family at a time" and of the Irish here to provide for the migration of yet one more family member. Relatives came to the United States and tended to live near each other.[15] Importantly, much of the migration occurred along female lines. Women brought over other women: sisters bringing sisters, aunts bringing their nieces, cousins assisting one another. In many cases migrating married couples set themselves up in the United States under the auspices of the wife's kin already here and settled near them. For example, the parents of Charles Francis Donnelly, a major political figure in late nineteenth-century Irish Boston, began their lives in America in Nova Scotia "where Mrs. Donnelly's two uncles were men of property and position."[16]

Occasional Irish arrivals followed the pattern more common to other immigrants of the father coming first to the United States and earning enough for passage and support of his wife and children back home, like the father of labor leader Mary Harris Jones, better known as "Mother Jones." More typically, either the entire family arrived together, or single family members, sons, and daughters made the move. Sisters played strikingly important roles in bringing over other sisters, as did other female kin and, to a lesser extent, brothers. Ellen O'Grady, the first female Deputy Police Commissioner in the United States, was brought over in the 1870s by two of her sisters, as was Alice Lawlar a century earlier, the founder of the Order of the Visitation Nuns. The mother of James Michael Curley, the controversial mayor of Boston, journeyed here an orphan with her two sisters, and Ellen O'Keefe, Mother Mary Zita originator of the Sisters of Reparation of the Congregation of Mary, immigrated by herself to Lynn, Massachusetts, in 1864 and four years later paid for the fares of her sister and brother-in-law. Catherine Mehegan, Mother Xavier of the Sisters of Charity, arrived first with a sister in 1825 and few years later financed their brother's migration. The mother of Elizabeth Gurley Flynn immigrated alone to the United States in 1877, joining a sister who had come earlier and who had first arranged for the migration of a brother. Kate Kennedy, a pioneer organizer of public schoolteachers in San Francisco, journeyed to New York with one brother and one sister. Two years later enough money paved the way for their mother and four older sisters. Mary Mountain, a domestic servant in Gardner, Massachusetts, unknown for any great achievements—at least publicly—did, however, earn enough money in domestic service to bring over several sisters and brothers, who together became the nucleus for the Irish community in that town.

Aunts, too, were agents of migration for Irish women like Mary O'Toole, first woman judge in the Municipal Court of the District of Columbia, and Margaret McShiftery, Mother M. Annunciata of the Sisters of the Holy Cross.

Numerous biographical sketches of Irish widows likewise demonstrate the centrality of women in the migration process. Hannah Corcoran, a young servant girl in Boston; Patrick Collins, the mayor of that city; Margaret Sanger, crusader for birth control; and Irish nationalist Joseph Clarke represented just a few Irish-Americans whose mothers or grandmothers emigrated with young children after experiencing widowhood in Ireland.[17]

Women actively promoted migration and traveled along what might be seen as female chains. They made the trips together, they helped finance one another, and they met and greeted one another. Although they certainly assisted male kin as well, particularly brothers, the primary emphasis focused on their sisters and other female relatives. Journeying to the United States to a sister, an aunt, or a friend became the typical pattern for Irish migrant women.[18] In 1897 the St. Vincent de Paul Society in Boston surveyed Irish female arrivals and found that out of 2,945 that year only 76 were not met by "friends."[19] In 1907 a survey of foreign arrivals in Boston uncovered that of the Irish women, 106 came to join relatives, 7 came with relatives, 1 came with a friend, and yet another had a friend to meet her. A grand total of 2 came to marry. In terms of passage money, 2 had their passages paid by husbands and 46 were aided by older relatives. Seventy of the women had raised the money themselves, and 120 had been financed by "relatives of the same generation," most likely brothers or sisters, and none by fiancées.[20] These kinds of statistics and others collected by a variety of institutions reveal the basic pattern and underscore the ways in which Irish women migrated.

Journalistic accounts and life histories confirm the accuracy of the quantitative data and put the numbers into a more personal perspective. A reporter for the New York *Sun*, for example, in 1880 reported that

> one day last week a young Irish girl, who had come over alone, was sighted in the passageway between the rotunda and the Information Bureau—which is an out building—by four women relatives who had gone down to meet her. Her back was toward them, and she was unaware of the proximity, until with a wild 'whillillilew' they precipitated themselves on her.[21]

Charles Dickens, in one of his forays to America, observed about the Irish in 1869 that "some go in response to the urgent entreaty of relatives who have already tried the experiment. This old man is going to join his daughter Biddy, a prosperous maid-of-all-work in New York."[22] In a few extreme cases, married Irish women left their husbands and children in Ireland and came to America to work as domestics, eventually sending over the money to reestablish the family. These cases, however, proved exceptional, and the most typical situation involved those who had not yet married and in which sisters and brothers as well as other relatives helped and pooled resources to bring over their loved ones.

The migrations did not always occur without problems or disruptions and occasionally the colleen arrived with no one to greet her. All of the Irish-American newspapers, like those in most immigrant communities, ran columns for people attempting to locate missing friends and relatives. The *Irish World*, a New York-based paper, in the 1870s reported a roughly equal number of men and women as "missing" (a striking contrast to the Yiddish newspaper during the zenith of Eastern European immigration in the twentieth century which aptly titled its service "A Gallery of Missing Men"). Usually sisters or brothers sought one another out, with sisters looking for sisters most often and then brothers looking for sisters. Similar grim listings of the lost and the lonely appeared in the Boston *Pilot* as well as the other Irish newspapers and again demonstrated the female bonds and ties between siblings.[23]

Immigrants frequently failed to find one another because they constantly changed residences, expecially if they were poor, and because Irish women continued using their maiden names after marriage. Sometimes misconceptions about America hampered immigrants. A settlement worker in 1890, representing Rutland Corner House in Boston, reported that "a young girl from Ireland was met at the steamer by an Agent of the Traveler's Aid, and brought to the Home. She said she had come to join an aunt who lived 'somewhere near Boston.' When asked how she expected to find her, she said she was going to the 'chemist's' to inquire."[24] Mary Mitchell, newly arrived from Ireland in 1875, "went to Brooklyn on the 22nd of April in search of her brother who she had heard lived in Bolivar Street, and was a policeman. In Maddon's Liquor Store in Myrtle Avenue she was told that one Mitchell lived at 15 in that street. Four who eyed her in the saloon followed her into Bolivar Street. There they brutally assaulted her."

The Women's Educational and Industrial Union of Boston frequently came in contact with immigrant women from Ireland who had met some confusion. It reported such typical cases as the one in 1908 where "an Irish girl crossed with a chum by an earlier boat than her aunt expected. The chum's sister met them and acted as a guide for both." In another case the "chum paid her passage over from Ireland, and had a place waiting for her, but she did not get to the wharf in time. A steamer acquaintance, a woman, took the girl to the House of the Good Shepherd for the night."[25]

Whether they had migrated alone or with a sister, whether they left Ireland in the company of parents or children, or friends, the overwhelming majority of the Irish consciously eschewed rural life in the United States and became urban dwellers. For one thing, it took money to venture far beyond the port of arrival, and to leave New York, Boston, or Philadelphia to farm required more capital than most Irish had with them. Also, Irish newcomers harbored very negative sentiments about the agricultural life. Since they had left Ireland precisely because of the limited—or, more accurately, shrinking—opportunities of farm life, they showed no eagerness for it in the United States. That the migration was so heavily female and single also helps explain the apathy of the Irish for rural living here. Most importantly, farming involved a family effort—an effort in which husband, wife, and children labored together—an undertaking totally inappropriate for the single women who comprised so large a portion of the immigrants.

On the other hand, the cities and industrial towns of the North and the urban Middle West offered economic opportunities for women and men. For unskilled hands, factory and millwork, domestic service, and the physical labor of public work projects were the prizes to be had in the cities. In 1860 the Irish had already so engulfed urban America as to be the single largest immigrant group in Boston, New York, and Philadelphia and the second largest in Baltimore and Cincinnati. In 1869 they also predominated in Providence, New Haven, Albany, and Pittsburgh and occupied the rank of second most numerous in Buffalo, Milwaukee, Chicago, and St. Louis. Substantial Irish communities exploded in size across the last half of the nineteenth century in San Francisco, Omaha, Memphis, New Orleans, Cleveland, Detroit, and Denver. The Irish showed up in large numbers wherever workers were needed. In milltowns like Lawrence, Lowell, and Pawtucket, Irish women appeared, too, making many of these Gaelic communities predominantly female as well as providing Americans with the largest ethnic group of domestic servants.[26]

Throughout the nineteenth century a debate raged in the Irish communities and in the Catholic Church over the propriety of urban life and the reasonableness of the Irish clustering in the cities. Some church officials, like Archbishop Hughes in New York, believed that an Irish scattering to the frontier would spell their spiritual and political doom in the United States. Some, like Thomas D'Arcy McGee, an active proponent of settling the Irish in the West and taking them out of the industrial cities, prophesied in 1852: "Whatever we can do for ourselves, as a people, in North America, must be done before the close of this century, or the epitaph of our race will be written in the West 'too late.'"[27] Irish urban concentration was seen as the cause of their continuing poverty, their unflattering crime statistics, their high rates of marital desertion, and their continued problems with alcohol.

Even critics of the group did, however, recognize an essential reason why the Irish preferred the cities over the rural areas. In the cities the Irish could create communities where links of kinship and bonds of friendship could be reconstituted to ease the shock of migration and cultural change. In massive Irish neighborhoods of New York and Chicago, "the Irish man can dance as lively and attend a wake or a wedding with as light a heart and as free from hinderance as if he had never left his own green isle."[28] One young Irish man who had listened to the rhetoric of the frontier and went out to Missouri in the 1820s mournfully wrote home, reminiscing first, "I could then go to a fair, or a wake, or a dance . . . I could spend the winter's nights in a neighbor's house cracking jokes by the turf fire. . . . But here everyone can get so much land . . . that they call them neighbors that live two or three miles off."[29] Yet in the cities, proximity and a high degree of residential segregation meant that they could create the kinds of networks and institutions they chose. Americans were frequently struck by the extensive social ties of the

Irish. Edward Everett Hale commented in the early 1850s to readers of the Boston *Daily Advertiser* that

the clannish spirit of the Irish, which has ruined them in one country, and does a great deal to ruin them in another, attracts them at once to persons who may have the slightest tie of community or neighborhood. For instance, it is within my own observation, that in the winter of 1850 to 1851, fourteen persons, fresh from Ireland, came in on the cabin-hospitality of a woman in Worcester, because she was the cousin of one of the party—all of whom had sailed together.[30]

Irish hospitality not only was legendary in Ireland but transferred itself to the United States, providing informal institutions to assist and orient new immigrants, since "Paddy is never known to show a cold shoulder to a former friend, or to disown a compatriot, however poor and destitute." Even in smaller mill towns the same tendencies and social life, coupled with the economic opportunities of industrial rather than agrarian pursuits, helped to shape the settlement pattern of Irish immigrants.[31]

Because of the nature of the migration and its high proportion of women, it should not be surprising that the Irish communities of the United States were likewise predominantly female. With the exception of the Irish settlements in the Far West, like San Francisco, Los Angeles, and Denver of the middle and late nineteenth century, most of the cities of the East and Middle West housed more Irish women than men. This held for New York, Boston, Baltimore, Philadelphia, Providence, Newburyport, Worcester, Buffalo, and elsewhere.[32]

A young priest, just arrived in St. Louis from Ireland in 1854, was stunned by the extent to which young women in his parish outnumbered men as they did in other Catholic churches in the city. He discovered that

young Catholic Irishmen not obtaining occupation in the city had been obliged to seek employment of the railroads and move about as the work progressed. These types of employment and the separation of Catholic young men and women on account of lack of fixed abode for the former seems to preclude the probability of otherwise suitable Catholic marriages.[33]

Even Dubuque, Iowa, in 1860 had 183 single Irish men, as opposed to 317 single women, as well as 18 Irish-born widowers and 98 widows.[34] The continuous stream of migrant women helped to create this pattern as did the tendency of Irish men in the face of high rates of unemployment to take jobs as construction workers on canal and railroad crews, which took them away from settled city life. Furthermore, Irish men in the United States had an extremely high rate of industrial accidents, having been forced by circumstance to take the most dangerous job, and as such further compounded the tendency toward female-dominated communities.

Because women outnumbered men as migrants and as new Americans they played a strikingly significant role in the economic life of Irish America as well as in the creation of informal networks that linked Irish America to the homeland. Edward Everett Hale should not have been quite so surprised that it was an Irish *woman* in Worcester who acted so improvidently as to give lodging and shelter to new Hibernian arrivals or that in neighboring Danvers, Massachusetts, "there was not an immigrant that came . . . from Ireland that Johannah O'Neill didn't take in . . . a good, big, hearty woman. She took them in for a week or until they got a job, most always without hope of reward."[35]

What effect did the preponderance of women as migrants have on the economic, social, and cultural patterns of Irish America? The kinds of family the Irish carved out in America as well as the work patterns, educational achievements, and sense of self of Irish women all need to be examined in light of the female-dominated migration.

Just because women surpassed men in number does not necessarily imply that women achieved greater power and authority in the formalized institutions of their communities. Just because more Irish women than men had chosen to migrate to the United States does not necessarily mean that equal or even greater resources and services in the communities went to them. Just because the "typical" immigrant was a young, single woman does not mean that women's actions were fully autonomous. In fact, it may have been that the older Irish traditions of gender antagonism and segmentation plus the numerical insecurity of Irish males in the United States caused them to cling to power in formal institutions even longer and more tenaciously than if they had not been so outnumbered.

More importantly, Irish women immigrated in huge numbers to the United States because of the greater opportunities that awaited them. Irish women migrated not as depressed survivors of Famine, but in the main they made the journey with optimism, in a forward-looking assessment that in America they could achieve a status that they never could have at home.

THREE  Undefeated, Unafraid:
Women in Irish-
American Families

I
n all the vicissitudes of fortune an Irish man clings to his wife and the wife
clings to her husband, and is the joy of his life and the light of his day. If he turns
out bad and comes home drunk, she says "I've made a bad bargain and must
make the best of it."
Irish World

It is not the fashion among them to speak in praise of "marriage life" as the Irish
women say. "If I had it to do over I'd never marry" was almost the universal
remark.
Karen Anthony, *Mothers Who Must Earn*

If it were possible to peek through the cracks of a quickly improvised
shack of a mid-nineteenth-century Irish shanty town in a dilapidated section
of New York or Boston or Philadelphia, huddled on the dirt floor would likely
be a mother and her children, poor and desperate. The male "breadwinner"
probably has died, a victim of an accident, or perhaps he has deserted his
family, ashamed of his inability to find a job and incensed at his lack of
authority within the domestic circle. Three or four decades later, the father
still might not have returned as a constant family member, and the household
might include a boarder or two, as the family eagerly seeks any extra sources
of income to ensure upward movement for at least one of its large brood.
Living close by that same family might also reside an unmarried aunt, a
bachelor uncle, or a widowed grandmother, contributing to the survival
of all.
Drawing aside the freshly washed fabric of the "lace curtain" that sym-
bolized the arrival of the Irish into the realm of the middle class, one would

Irish squatters in New York's Central Park in the 1880s. Note that only one man appears in the picture. (*By permission of the J. Clarence Davies Collection, Museum of the City of New York*)

note changes. In this two-parent household, the father holds down a white-collar job; a number of daughters in the family attend high school or normal school; the mother, who would not have dreamed of being employed after marriage, sets the tone of refined, civilized living which would announce to all the world—or at least the relevant part of it, the surrounding parish community—that this family had permanently liberated itself from shanty, tenement existence. A stable family was viewed as an important piece of evidence in that announcement.

Yet, no matter the relative economic class, certain features of the Irish family as it had evolved in post-Famine Ireland and was carried over as cultural baggage by the millions of young women and men persisted. In a survey of the nature of Irish family structure and the position of women within those families over the course of two generations, that is, the immigrating generation and the first crop of American-born Irish men and women, a pattern of remarkable stability appears. The propensity of the post-Famine Irish to view marriage as an economic arrangement that ought not be rushed into too young and too precipitiously linked the Irish on both sides of the Atlantic. The striking number of Irish who somehow never married bore further testimony to the retention of cultural patterns despite a radical change in the nature of economic arrangements.

links between siblings

The importance of sibling relationships in adulthood also survived the transoceanic journey. As brothers and sisters provided the links of movement from Ireland to America, so too after settlement they succored one another and provided support in the cycle of crises of poverty and illness, desertion and widowhood, in the tortuously slow climb of the Irish from shanty to tenement to lace curtains. Furthermore, despite official dictates of the culture and teachings of the religion, women within their families continued to play roles far from subservient and passive in the United States, underscoring the strength and centrality of female family members. The economic assertiveness of women before marriage and the continued gender segmentation that defined the home as woman's turf and kingdom placed immigrant Irish women and their daughters in positions of strength and dominance within.

Certain major aspects of life, however, changed dramatically. The United States was not Ireland—the economy of New York represented the polar opposite of Connomara, Boston bore little resemblance to County Cavan, and Chicago and Sligo, Pittsburgh and Kerry shared few social or economic characteristics. The Irish family bent and stretched to accommodate itself, within the imperatives of the traditional value system, to confront new situations. A whole range of problems unknown in the Old World beset the Irish arrivals and forced family members to rethink certain roles and patterns. Widowhood became an even more common life experience for Irish women in the United States than it had been in Ireland and, coupled with male deser-

(margin handwritten notes: Irish female head of household)

tion in America, made the Irish female-headed household a strikingly common element of the social tableau.

Irish men generally experienced a decline in status and power within their families as a result of migration, pushing women—wives and mothers —into authoritative roles far greater than they had experienced in the country-side. The daughter in the Irish family no longer occupied the lowest rung of importance and respect, and the comparatively open range of economic options for young Irish women—in domestic work, in white-collar employment, and in the professions of nursing and school teaching—made her someone of note in her family and, by extension, in her community. These changes—the general augmentation of female family authority—importantly occurred without any active rejection by women or men of the dictates of traditional Irish cultural values which split the world in two—into a male and female sphere. These changes in real power within the household did not herald a rebellion in attitude or a revolution in ideals, but silently and thoroughly changed the way Irish women—and men—lived.

Studies of the Irish in New York, Boston, Milwaukee, Buffalo, Pittsburgh, Detroit, and elsewhere all documented the continuing tendency of the Irish to marry reluctantly. The rate of marriage among the Irish in the United States did outpace that in Ireland, since people no longer were bound to the single-inheritance system. The Irish in the United States, however, married less frequently than any other immigrant group, Catholic and non-Catholic alike. Nineteenth-century Irish-Americans hesitated to marry. In 1850, one Irish person in fifty in Boston married, as opposed to one German in twenty-seven. In New York in 1873, more than two decades after the Famine, only ten of every thousand Irish-Americans chose to marry, as opposed to forty-two per thousand of the German residents. In the 1880s and 1890s, Irish men and women throughout the Commonwealth of Massachusetts married in numbers more typical of native-born Protestants than of other Catholic immigrants or even immigrants from Protestant countries. Early-twentieth-century comparative studies confirmed these nineteenth-century traits. A Boston social service agency in 1907 attempted to track down five hundred single immigrant women who had landed at the port a number of months before. Twenty-three percent of all the Italian women had married, as had six percent of the "Hebrew" women and 4 percent of the Scandinavian women. Of the Irish women, the largest group of arrivals, a scant 1 percent had since married. In short, the low rate of marriage, born of the economic necessities of rural Irish life, remained a common practice among the Irish people who had chosen to leave Ireland and who confronted an economy of a very different sort.[1]

The continuity of peculiarly Irish family patterns can be seen not only in statistics on marriage rates but in data on ages of marriage. In most cultures, marriage for a young person heralded the emergence from youth to adulthood. Among the Irish the transition from childhood had occurred long before, and individuals married when they were well established as grown-up members of their community. Although the Irish in America married younger than did their brothers and sisters who remained at home, they married later than German, French-Canadian, or Italian immigrants or their children. One study of Providence, Rhode Island, highlighted three couples marrying on the same day in 1879. The two American-born couples comprised a man of 21 and a woman of 22, and a 26-year-old fellow and his 21-year-old fiancée. The Irish-born bride was 27; her groom, also a native of Ireland, 29.

The persistence of these Irish forms can be measured by looking at Irish-born men. Irish male family heads in Holyoke, Massachusetts, in 1880 averaged 45.7 years of age, while American-born and Canadian-born male heads of household averaged 42 and 41, respectively. In the same year, among Irish-born men in Cohoes, New York, age 20 to 29, only 24 percent had married, as compared to 32.3 percent of the French-Canadians, 39.3 percent of the English-born, and 52.5 percent of the American natives. The marriage age for Irish men in Lowell, Massachusetts, actually rose during the last half of the nineteenth century, with 1.8 percent of them marrying before age 20 in 1845, yet none marrying before that age in 1880. In Lawrence in 1910, 71 percent of the Irish male mill hands 20 to 29 had not yet found a spouse, whereas 68 percent of the native-born whites, 63 percent of the Canadians, and 65 percent of the British found themselves similarly unattached. In the next age category, 30 to 44, 36 percent of the Irish men still had no wife, whereas the same held for only 14.8 percent of those born in the United States (not of Irish-born parents), 7.1 percent of the Canadians, and 28.7 percent of the English. Twenty-four percent of the sons of Ireland after age 45 still were single, as compared to only 3.8 percent of the American-born and none of the Canadians or British.

Furthermore, nonstatistical sources confirmed this trend. For example, a volume celebrating the Irish of Troy, New York, and its *Representative Young Irish-Americans* found that the majority were unmarried men or men whose marriages took place well after they had turned thirty. Three sons of Erin who were worthy enough to have their pictures included in an 1880 history of Lawrence—Michael Rinn, 33, single; Daniel F. Dolan, also 33 and single; and Timothy Dacy, 43, single—all bear testimony to the retention of the Irish ideal.[2]

Like their brothers, immigrant women from Ireland opted to marry much later than other American women—native-born and immigrant alike—and this pattern changed little during the final decades of the nineteenth century. In Buffalo, New York, Irish women who married Irish men between 1877 and 1882 averaged 31 years of age while their "young" men averaged 35 when they entered into the married state. In places like Cohoes, New York, a cotton textile town with a large number of mill jobs for women, Irish women vastly outnumbered Irish men. Only 8 percent of the Irish women age 20 to 29 found themselves married, and among those age 30 to 39, only 44.2 percent had found a life's partner. By contrast, 13 percent of English operatives in their twenties and 83.3 percent in their thirties were married. Just as marriage ages rose for male Irish residents of Lowell over the course of the last half of the nineteenth century, so too for Irish women. Similar figures could be marshaled for almost every Irish community. Even where Irish women did not outnumber their fellow Irish men, as in San Francisco, Irish women still demonstrated a reluctance to marry.

Irish women passed on this tradition to their American-born daughters, testifying to the retention of the Irish ideals, and among second-generation Irish-American women the tendency to marry late persisted in force. Once again, Lawrence textile employees serve as good examples. In 1910, 97.7 percent of native-born women with Irish fathers were not married in their twenties, and 66.7 percent of those between the ages of 30 and 44 were still single. The female mill hands undoubtedly provide a skewed sample because most Irish women refused to work for wages after marriage. A study of comparative marriage patterns in Rhode Island in 1970, however, showed women of Irish ancestry with the latest age of marriage. Among Rhode Island women of all ages, 35.3 percent of the Irish women were classified as marrying old (age 45 and up), as opposed to 23.1 percent of all other Catholics (with Italians marrying old in only 20.2 percent and Portuguese in 22 percent of the cases). Among older women 49.5 percent of all Irish women had entered into marriage late, whereas 28.4 percent of the Italians and 32.4 percent of the Portuguese fell into that category.[3]

Again, literary and biographical evidence reinforces the trends suggested by the statistics. Elizabeth Gurley Flynn, the "rebel girl" of the American Communist Party, noted that her mother, a coat maker, an emigrant from Ireland, worked for thirteen years at her trade and "because of family responsibilities, my mother did not marry until she was thirty years old, an 'old maid' in those days." Mother Jones, after teaching school, decided to marry at thirty-one. One of Kate Kennedy's sisters married at twenty-three but the others, almost all schoolteachers like herself, married at thirty-one, twenty-eight, twenty-six, and thirty-two years of age. Eleanor O'Donnell McCormack, an active club and culture promoter in Memphis, had migrated as a child with her parents; after a career in teaching and several years in service as the first woman to be elected a county superintendent of schools in Tennessee, she married—at 33. Although all these women were "famous" and lived lives and achieved rank far above the "typical" Irish immigrant they were not statistically aberrant and behaved strikingly like Mrs. Lyonns, who died in 1873 in New York at the age of 112 and had married at 35, not too old to bear nine children.[4]

Yet another index of the retention of Irish family forms emerges from the data on nonmarriage, that is, from those Irish men and women who chose never to marry. Once again, local statistics from Massachusetts, New York, Rhode Island, Pennsylvania, and New Jersey demonstrate that the Irish in the United States were behaving in the late nineteenth and early twentieth centuries somewhat like their kin who had not made the transoceanic journey. Among the young men and women who chose to leave Inis Beag, an Irish island community, 37.4 percent of the first generation never married. In Pittsburgh the Irish had the highest rate of nonmarried women of any white group in the female population. Among the Irish, twenty-three per thousand eschewed marriage as did only thirteen per thousand among the German and eleven per thousand among native-born in the two-and-a-half decades from 1865 until 1890.[5]

Furthermore, the life histories of Irish-Americans, those who grew up to be famous and infamous as well as those whose lives remained obscure, rescued for a brief moment from anonymity by a historian or journalist or parish chronicler, abound with unmarried relatives and friends. The vast majority of prominent Irish women—labor leaders, schoolteachers, religious leaders, and actresses—never married. Moreover, the presence of unmarried sisters, brothers, aunts, uncles, and cousins made the Irish-American social fabric unique. Unmarried women and men dotted the Irish-American landscape, clearly and unabashedly. Community studies and parish histories, biographical sketches and autobiographical memoirs, church bulletins and charity reports yield over and over again the profusion of the unmarried in Irish life in the American cities. Few Irish-Americans did not have unmarried aunts or uncles, brothers or sisters, friends and neighbors. Of the forty-nine women who served as aids at the twenty-fifth anniversary to commemorate the founding of St. Mary's Parochial School in Cambridgeport, Massachusetts, in 1900, only four were married. Of the former pupils of that school who got together in 1895 for a reunion, only one woman out of sixty had added "Mrs." to her name. Settlement workers Robert Woods and Albert Kennedy, surveying social life in South Boston in 1907, were quite amazed to find that many Irish families housed sons between the ages of twenty and forty-five still living at home and still unmarried.[6]

Why did the Irish in industrial America continue to marry—or not to marry—in the fashion of the rural countryside of Ireland? This family pattern had grown out of the harrowing experience of the Famine, which convinced the agricultural Irish to mend their ways and eschew early marriage and land division with a vengeance. Why then should the Irish immigrants to industrial Buffalo, to urban New York, to metropolitan Pittsburgh, to cities like Chicago carry over this particular rural behavior? The commitment of the Irish to this form is particularly striking when one considers that it had become universal in Ireland only recently. Unlike the Irish commitment to Catholicism or the zeal of the Irish to shake off British rule, it did not have a centuries-old history rooted in the soil of Ireland's antiquity. For the young single migrants this

marriage pattern was fairly new and sprang from the very immediate experiences of their own or their parents' lifetime. There certainly must have
been something extremely appealing and meaningful to them in the family
forms of post-Famine Ireland, that they depended so nearly on them to
survive the migration, and that they flourished so well in the new urban, industrial clime. The appeal and the meaning must have struck a very responsive
chord in the way Irish women viewed themselves and in the kinds of options
they defined as important for their lives.

That the Irish in America chose to marry reluctantly and comparatively
late in their lives indicates sharply the stability and continuity of cultural
patterns among the migrants. It indicates that the economic motives for
migration remained paramount. Irish women did not migrate primarily to find
the husbands they could not find at home. Whereas their chances for meeting
an eligible man and falling in love were certainly better in the United States
than in Ireland, the opportunities for marriage to an Irish man were not
favorable in the United States either.

Irish women across the last half of the nineteenth century continued to
flock to Boston, Lowell, Chicago, New York, Lawrence, Buffalo, Providence,
and Philadelphia, and in all of these cities Irish women continued to outnumber
Irish men. These cities and mill towns did not offer large numbers of eligible
bachelors. Instead they proferred jobs: factory jobs and millwork, domestic
service and, later in the century, clerical and shop work. Probably the most
rational thing for a young Irish woman to do if matrimony were indeed her
primary goal would have been to immigrate temporarily to the United States,
work here, probably as a domestic in order to incur the least expenses, and,
after squirreling away her "fortune," return to Ireland and find herself an
unmarried boy who could not quite afford a local girl with dowry. This certainly happened occasionally. The literature of late-nineteenth- and early-
twentieth-century small town Ireland alluded intermittently to the returned
"Yank" woman who brought back her money, her stove—to the wonderment
of the residents of the town—her newly acquired twang, and her memories of
life in America.[7]

Of the millions of young Irish women who made the move to the United
States a statistically insignificant number returned to find a husband back
home. For those who stayed in the female-dominated Irish enclaves of the
New World, one way to find a spouse and settle down in matrimonial bliss
would be to marry a non-Irish man, since there were just not enough sons of
Erin to go around. The comparatively low rates of outgroup marriage once
again underscore that marriage was not the single overriding object of Irish
migrant women. To be sure, Irish-born women married non-Irish men more
frequently than Irish-born men married non-Irish women.[8] In Lowell, for
example, in the first generation, 2.7 percent of the Irish-born men married out
of the group, as did 6.8 percent of the women. In the second generation these

figures climbed to 37.8 percent among the men and 28.1 percent for the women. In New York during the four years between 1908 and 1912, 9.6 percent of the first generation Irish men and 18.6 percent of the females chose a non-Irish-born spouse. The greater willingness of Irish women to choose non-Irish mates certainly made sense in light of the statistics: If an Irish woman were to marry at all, she had to consider the possibility of marrying someone from outside the group. Perhaps, also, with the traditions of gender segmentation within Irish life and the culture of gender hostility, Irish women might have found a Catholic of British or German descent, for example, a more appealing life's partner. One study of intermarriage in Woonsocket, Rhode Island, in the 1930s suggests another explanation: "In Woonsocket, as elsewhere, Irish women are most assertive of their marital freedom to marry out of the group. Seven and eight-tenths percent more Irish women intermarry than men. This difference is even greater for the first generation, where 9.6 percent more women than men marry out."[9] Irish-born women in this polyglot mill town preferred British men over any others—a group that commanded greater status and certainly greater income than any other, including the Irish men. Generally, however, the rates of Irish outgroup matrimony tended to be small, with women engaging in it more frequently than their brothers. In Cohoes, in Lawrence, in New Haven, in Boston, even in Denver and San Francisco, where Irish men outnumbered women, Irish women usually married Irish men, if they married at all. Even studies that extended far into the twentieth century indicated a high rate of Irish endogamy, particularly when compared to German or French-Canadian Catholics.

Irish women could have chosen from the large number of German Catholics, and, later in the nineteenth century, Italian, Polish, and French-Canadian Catholics. In these groups, men migrated in greater number than women, so they offered a constantly increasing pool of Catholic bachelors. Despite this, a significant number of Irish women continued to eschew marriage or to put it off until well into their thirties. Certainly, the hesitance of Irish women to marry in the United States cannot be explained primarily by their lack of opportunity to do so.

Although Irish women brought over from Ireland a tradition, admittedly a relatively new one, of late marriage or nonmarriage, the tradition remained strong in America because it continued to make economic sense. What did it mean for an Irish woman to get married? What did she give up? What did she gain? Upon marrying an Irish woman ended her life as a worker, as an earner of income. Although married Irish women worked for wage under situations of duress—when their husbands were incapacitated or when they deserted —Irish wives generally had among the lowest rates of employment. In Fall River at the turn of the century 30 percent of all French-Canadian wives held down factory jobs, as did 28 percent of the Portuguese, whereas only 12 percent of Irish wives found themselves on the assembly line. In the paper mills of Berkshire County, Massachusetts, Irish females were "more likely than American-born girls to work before marriage but less likely to work after marriage," and in Poughkeepsie, New York, 6 percent of married Irish women in 1860 were employed, and 2 percent were in 1880. A study of Irish women in Holyoke, Massachusetts, once again revealed that unlike women in other groups, "hers was the role of homemaker, and husband and children alike bent every effort to maintain her in it. In consequence the Irish family had a unity and dignity which neither poverty nor prosperity could destroy."[10]

Furthermore, Irish families were unique in their aversion to homework. Eastern European Jews on New York's Lower East Side engaged in sweatshop labor at home, making garments, and Italians made buttons and artificial flowers in their apartments. Social workers, government investigators, and settlement house observers who studied the sweatshop syndrome almost never reported any such enterprise among Irish wives. Occasional literary and journalistic references noted married Irish women taking laundry into their homes. Irish widows were another story, and they often opted for homework as a way to care for their children and earn an income. These were the exceptions, however. Generally an Irish woman's earnings ended with marriage.

For Irish women, therefore, the large sums of money that they collected to send home as remittance to those family members holding down the farm in Ireland dried up upon marriage. When they were single Irish servant girls and mill workers they made a staggering contribution to the Irish economy in the form of these remittances, but all nineteenth-century observers agreed that when a girl changed her state to that of a married woman she no longer continued to underwrite the expense of her family back home. Given the tremendous loyalty of Irish children for parents and love for their siblings, this certainly constituted a sacrifice in order to marry.[11]

Yet married Irish women abandoned their jobs with the same zeal and ardor with which they had rushed into them as single women. Traditional Irish culture stressed the centrality of the woman in her home with her husband and children as did the cultures of most other European immigrants. Yet Italian and French-Canadian women, who worked in fewer numbers than did the Irish before marriage, remained in the labor market more frequently afterward. The Catholic church frowned gravely upon such behavior and insistently thundered that a married woman belonged in the home and the only work of importance that she ought to engage in was motherhood. Irish women seem to have agreed with this position, in that they rarely sought work after they married and did not consciously limit the number of children they bore and raised. To the Irish the Church represented the single most important institution in their lives and probably the only source of real authority— authority to be adhered to with devotion. Not so for the Italians who, in the United States as well as in the *mezzogiorno,* had a much more ambivalent and less intimate relation with the Catholic church and its clergy.[12]

Irish marriage quickly brought with it the burden of a growing and hungry family. This may have deterred Irish women and men from taking the plunge into matrimony. Marriage was synonymous with economic hardship and duress for unskilled workers. Importantly, many of the successful Irish political and business figures, young men who dedicated their lives to rising into the middle and upper classes, consciously chose money and power over marriage and family.

Marriage involved a profound change in one's economic status. Irish women by all possible measures made that change with deliberation and assessed the advantages and disadvantages of the polar states of singleness and matrimony. Lelia Hardin Bugg, a novelist of American-Irish life in the late nineteenth century, noted quite clearly the weighing and the calculations involved when she moralized in her sketches of *The People of Our Parish*, "the sensible woman realizes that any sort of work is a thousand times better than an unhappy marriage, and the unselfish one often chooses to earn a living rather than to be a burden on an overtaxed father or brother."[13]

In a series of lessons for working Catholic girls, appearing first in 1868 and reissued in 1892, George Deshon spent a great deal of time painting the ideal Catholic marriage for his young female readers, and he advised that although "marriage is a state of life instituted by God Himself," young people should "not be too hasty in making a decision" as to their life's partner. The wrong choice, a poor decision, could have disastrous results. He asked:

> Who is that bloated, coarse-looking woman who has not apparently combed her hair for a week, with a lot of ragged children bawling and fighting and cursing around her in her miserable, dirty hovel? That was, a few years ago, a pretty, modest girl, who was innocent and light-hearted, earning an easy living in a quiet pleasant family, and attending to her duties regularly and with great delight in her soul.[14]

Deshon, therefore, cautioned that women wait patiently for a partner, although he believed that the typical girl wanted "to settle herself in life by marriage. She may be happy enough, and well enough off, at the present, but she has to consider the future; her life in middle age and when she is old."[15]

Equally romantic views of marriage abounded in late-nineteenth-century Irish-American literature penned by women as well as men and in the sermons and religious tracts of the Catholic church. Many of the Irish women who consciously chose the single state might have agreed with Elizabeth Gurley Flynn about this (but probably about nothing else) when she remembered her mother's hours of drudgery and labor, her parcel of children, and her inability to act on her own. As she recalled, "A domestic life and possibly a large family had no attraction for me. My mother's aversion to both had undoubtedly affected me profoundly. She was strong for her girls 'being somebody' and "having a life of their own.'"[16] The hesitancy of the Irish to marry grew out of the economic needs of the Famine. The economic needs of American life allowed Irish women and men to keep that tradition alive.

If Irish women upon marriage gave up their careers as servants, mill hands, shopgirls, and factory operatives, they did gain large numbers of children. The actual fertility of Irish married women varied from place to place and altered slightly from the middle to the end of the nineteenth century, but what emerges most strikingly from a huge array of statistics and a plethora of data sources on comparative immigrant childbearing patterns, measuring both crude and refined birth rates, is the high number of Irish births when considered against the low rates of Irish marriage. Fewer Irish women from a given cohort actually married and became mothers than did French-Canadian or Italian immigrants. Therefore, a smaller number of women were responsible for a larger number of children per woman.

Women of Irish extraction also married later than German women, for example, therefore commencing their childbearing years later, but for the Irish those years extended far longer than for others. Among married women in the shoemaking center of Lynn, Massachusetts, in 1880 Irish women bore more children in every age category than French-Canadian and native-born women, except in the twenty- to twenty-four-year-old group, when the Irish gave birth to no children. Among the forty-five to forty-nine year olds, French-Canadian mothers had 85 children, whereas 188 children were born to Irish women. Studies of Irish family patterns elsewhere in Massachusetts, in Milwaukee, in Pittsburgh, in a number of Rhode Island towns, in New York City, in Buffalo, and in other areas all yielded very similar pictures. Importantly, Irish women were more likely to become widowed or deserted than Italian or German women. Irish husbands more likely would take a job on a railroad construction crew or a canal-building gang, which took them away from home, often for years at a stretch, limiting the opportunities for conception. The nonmarrying and late-marrying Irish women and widows therefore brought down the total of Irish births.[17]

The kinds of families they formed bore a very close resemblance to the arrangements of social life in Ireland. Although changes occurred and the Irish-American birth rate dipped in the twentieth century in the United States, this occurred quite gradually, and second- or even third- generation Irish families did not differ radically from those of the immigrants, particularly in terms of family size.[18]

While much of Irish-American family life preserved the functional element of the Old World, new realities added strains and tensions to the lives of women within their families. The family life among these immigrants and their children was ravaged by a whole range of problems—a high rate of domestic violence and discord, the frequent desertion of the male breadwinner, and a high rate of industrial accidents that created many a widow and orphan. Taken together, these forces produced a striking number of female-headed households. An Irish immigrant woman who chose in the 1860s or 1870s to marry a construction worker in Boston or Providence or a factory hand living in New York or Worcester ran a very high risk of having some day to be sole support for a house full of children, existing indeed on starvation's edge.

This certainly does not imply that *all* Irish families rocked and reeled under the strain of disorganization; that all Irish families as they settled in and sought to adjust to American life were the scenes of disarray and chaos. Clearly, families existed in which husband and wife, children, and other kin lived and worked together, earning enough money to propel the next generation into a somewhat more comfortable station. But since they did not add to the cases on the police docket or the charity files nor did their harmony and stability make material for newspaper vignettes, they have escaped into anonymity. The jottings of some of the more sensitive social settlement workers, on the other hand, attempted to canvass a broad spectrum of life styles among urban dwellers, noting the organized as well as the disorganized, the tranquil and the explosive, the harmony and the discontent. Similarly, priests and nuns serving in the urban parishes made a point of celebrating the lives of their parishioners who did not end up deserted or abandoned, drunk or defeated; in fact, the clergy had a stake in down-playing deviance. Using therefore a wide variety of sources, considering those observers who looked for the bad as well as those chroniclers who sought to reveal the good, one can make some headway in trying to characterize the trends in Irish-American family life and how they left their mark on women's lives and consciousness. Robert Woods and Albert Kennedy, who made an exhaustive study of social life in Boston's South end in what they called the city's "zone of emergence," may have best summarized the extremes in Irish family life, the polar patterns in the Irish homes. On the one hand, they confronted the "empty larders, the unshod feet of little children, brutal fathers and husbands, ill-natured loud scolding mothers and wives. . . . But likewise there will be found the lives crowned not by the sordid care of the struggle against the empty larder but by loyalty and devotion."[19] Yet by all accounts, from the group's detractors and apologists, from the opponents and the supporters of the Irish in America, one can see that the incidence of domestic violence and heated fighting in the home, usually in the form of wife-beating, occurred not infrequently and that the Irish home of the middle to late nineteenth century hardly provided a haven from the tumult of the industrial world.

The literature on the Irish in nineteenth-century America abounds in descriptions of brutality toward wives. A female prison matron interviewed the various women—almost all Hibernian—under her charge in the 1860s and having, for example, asked McMullins about her marriage before incarceration, got this answer: "'I don't care so much for the old man, he used to beat me sometimes.'" Benjamin O. Flowers peopled his admittedly biased *Civiliza-tion's Inferno* with many an Irish man like Pat, who, having woken up from a drunken stupor, "demanded, 'Give me some money!' But there was no whiskey and no money. He overturned the table, cursed and blasphemed until, with demoniacal rage, he drew a knife and caught his wife by the throat." Helen Campbell, author of many social reform descriptions of the miserable lives of the poor in the late nineteenth century in New York, depicted Mrs. Maloney a comforter of her desperate Irish neighbors: "Women beaten and turned out into the night fled to her for comfort." Workers at the North Bennett Street Settlement House in Boston's North End reported a case of an Irish man, "in a fit of drunken frenzy, one day, as he dragged his wife up the dark staircase by the hair of her head, with the little puny five weeks' old baby in her arms, and flung them into the street." Even in far away New Orleans one Jemmy O'Brien had been charged with the attempted murder of his wife and pathetically told the police, "Bedad sir, I wouldn't hurt a hair of her head only the dhrop was in me." Similarly, police accounts contained many Irish men in prison for wife-beating, and most of the commentators on Irish-American life might have agreed with Katherine B. Anthony, an early-twentieth-century social settlement worker on New York's West Side, that "the German poor man tends to cruelty, and the Irishman to brutality. In German homes were tragedies unrelieved by humor, and in Irish homes, brutalities enhanced by an easy-going acceptance."[20]

Anthony erred, however, in seeing acceptance in wives. From all types of source it is clear that Irish women, when they could, struck back and rarely took the blows passively or submissively. Irish women, like Annie O'Brien, whose temper "was like a lucifer match," held her own and frequently dealt out the first fist when, for example, she was confronted with a drunken husband, who had squandered the family's meager resources on an evening at the saloon. "'I'll tache yees, ye ould hound, to coom home like a baste to yer supper,'" shouted old Kathleen in an 1863 description of Irish life in New England, as she "shook him up and down as if he were scarcely a feather's weight in her hands." Over and over again in the literature Irish couples "on a drunken bout discarded all Queensbury rules," as the "bottles flew about the dwelling, smashing windows and knocking heads, and frequently rendering the doctor's attendance necessary" to patch the wounds of domestic life.[21] A French traveler to America in 1895, Charles John Paul Bourget, has left us with perhaps the most graphic description of the Irish-American household as an armed camp, fighting within itself:

> Those terrible Irishmen, so astonishing with their poetry and their cruelty, their patriotic flume and vindictive rage, their eloquence and drunkenness, their spirit of enterprise and disorder, it is noteworthy that the caricaturists only show the drunkenness and disorder . . . it is an Irishman coming home intoxicated, whose

state the sketcher represents by multiplying the head of his wife seven times, as she looks at her husband and out of her seven mouths says: "If you saw yourself as I see you, you would be disgusted." "And if you saw yourself as I see you," replies the drunkard, "you would be astonished." Sometimes it is a domestic quarrel in which everything gives way, the man assaulting his wife with a chair, and she retorting with a flatiron.[22]

Importantly, the Irish themselves, writers, clergy, publicists, and journalists, recognized the high incidence of violence in the Irish home. One of the most extensive activities of the Irish-founded Sisters of Mercy in American cities was to provide a place of refuge for battered Irish wives, who had no other place to escape the wrath of their husbands. Irish newspapers and those Irish leaders who defined the curse of the Irish man as drink and city life frequently pointed out the grisly details of wife-beating and even murder. Typically, the *Irish World* told of a countryman in 1874 in New York whose fiancée had consistently urged him to give up drinking and, when he could stand it no longer, he came to her place of work and shot her. Although the typical journalistic-moralistic view stressed the violence of Irish husbands toward their wives, one sterling commentator of Irish-America, Mr. Dooley, placed the shoe on the other foot, and his narratives of life on Archey Road depicted Irish wives who rendered effective assault. Poor Malachi Duggan, for example, "won day he had a fallin' out with his wife, f'r the championship iv th Duggan family," wrote the sardonic Finley Peter Dunne, creator of this immensely popular genre of Irish-American narrative,

> an' Malachai was winnin' when Mrs. Duggan she r-run him into a clothes closet and shtood ga-ard at th' dure like a sinthry. "Come out," says she,' "an' fight" she says, "ye Limerick buthermilk" she says. She come fr'm Waterford an' her father was th' best man with a stick in Ireland till he passed away to his repose iv pnoomony iv th' lungs.[23]

The Irish homes of Chicago, as portrayed by Dunne and described by Dooley, indeed provided an arena for physical violence with women in a position of strength. However accurate this assessment of female physical prowess may or may not have been, observers of all kinds stressed the extremely high level of tension in the Irish homes of urban America which sparked into domestic discord and ignited into violence with striking frequency.

Domestic violence was not unheard of in Ireland. It grew in part out of the Irish traditions of sex segregation and gender animosity. It underscored the basic tension in the culture between men and women, between husbands and wives. This tension surfaced in America as a major domestic problem in the Irish enclaves. Other families might have coped with marital tension through the divorce court, but as devout Catholics the Irish could not consider divorce. A marriage made in heaven was forever. Official records of charity organizations, Catholic and non-Catholic, as well as social settlements indicate that the tone of male-female relations within the Irish families was indeed characterized by intense animosity. Settlement workers, usually women of native-born Protestant origin, did in fact often get a chance to observe the day-to-day workings of Irish domestic relations, and the notations of the representatives of the North Bennett Street Industrial School, for example, etched a portrait of deep hostility across gender lines within the family. Irish women confided to the settlement workers that they would not live with their husbands one more day and pleaded with the settlement workers to provide them with some shelter or assistance to free them of dependence on their husbands. Irish women appeared repeatedly as either deserted or deserting and their feeble attempts at reconciliation proved fruitless. While such reports weighed the evidence toward the deviant and problematic, emphasizing the intensity of conflict, stressing the most extreme cases of discord among the poor, the Irish themselves confirmed their essential accuracy. The generalized lack of interest that Irish men displayed toward women, the rigidly segregated world in which they functioned, and the disdain they demonstrated for interacting with women made the deviant patterns not so aberrant at all. Martin Lomasney, the leader of Boston Irish politics in the late nineteenth century, prided himself that he "never married, never had a romance, never attended a wedding"—a bit extreme perhaps in the degree of the sentiment, yet not out of line with the general tone of expression in the self-descriptions of Irish-American life. Although James Michael Curley did marry, at age thirty-two, he informed readers of his autobiography that "I had no time for girl friends," and when he and the new Mrs. Curley went on their honeymoon he "visited every town office or city hall possible, picking up pointers from officials." His descriptions of the honeymoon mentioned his new bride only in passing, as he used the occasion to meet Irish-American political luminaries along the way. Boxer James J. Corbett, who also married in his thirties, devoted a grand total of one paragraph to describe courtship, wedding, and marriage. Clearly, these events figured only in a minor way in his view of what merited attention. When John Morrissey, a heavyweight champion of the 1870s, was seen dressed up in "swallowtail coat, patent leather boots, white kid gloves," a friend asked, "'John, what's up now? Going to a wedding?'" "'No,'" answered Morrissey, "'not so bad as that.'"[24]

Irish-American culture de-emphasized romance. Social realities created a pattern whereby marriage and the interaction between husband and wife was at best one of irritability and separate spheres and at worst one of tension and domestic violence. This grew out of the combined influence of old-world patterns, in which sex segregation and hostility measured even greater, and the influences of American economic conditions, whereby individuals married as adults, with women particularly having experienced any number of years as independent wage earners. Women in such marriages rarely submitted pas-

sively to the domination of their husbands, and the high level of female assertiveness within the home offered a direct challenge to their spouses' view
that authority belonged to men. Interestingly, even mid-twentieth-century
studies of family life had noted an extremely high degree of tension in the
Irish Catholic family, a tension produced by the confluence of female assertiveness within the framework of a culture that supposes male dominance, a high
level of mutual disdain across gender lines, and a lack of a social basis for
male-female interaction.

One way men responded to such patterns of domestic discord and
eroded authority was to desert, to simply pick up and leave their wives and
children to fend for themselves temporarily or permanently. How much of the
desertion actually involved Irish men going off in search of work—on railroad
gangs, on construction crews—is unclear, since official records were always
spotty. Yet if women admitted to being deserted, they most likely were. There
is no reason to assume they were hiding something or prevaricating and, in
fact, many of the Irish women who listed themselves as "widows" may really
have been abandoned wives too proud to admit it, finding it somewhat more
respectable and sympathetic to be in the role of the bereaved. Where Irish
men engaged in the backbreaking tasks of pick and shovel labor, like in
Worcester, Massachusetts, before the 1840s, they lived alone in the camps
without wives or sisters or mothers near them for over a year. Yet in other
cases, as among the Irish male workers on the Baltimore & Ohio Railroad in
1831, female relatives and children accompanied them and they all lived
together in the shabby facilities provided by the B & O.[25] Certainly, the quest
for work took many Irishmen away from home and family. Yet even allowing
for the excuses of employment, the Irish families of the United States from the
middle to the last decades of the nineteenth century found themselves wracked
by high levels of male desertion. Irish desertion of wives reached far beyond
the teeming Irish communities of Boston and New York; it also extended past
the earliest years of settlement after the Famine exodus to America. The
Associated Charities of Washington, D.C., reported that among the Irish
denizens of the capital city were large numbers of deserted women and their
children, and the Sisters of Mercy aided abandoned Irish women in Omaha,
New York, San Francisco, and Providence. One 1898-99 study of Boston
claimed that "the largest number of deserted wives becoming known to us . . .
was Irish." Data on 574 cases of desertion from around the country found that
no group of men figured so prominently among the deserters as did the sons
of Erin.[26]

Once again the life histories of Irish-Americans confirm the tendencies
pointed out by the statistics. Not untypical was the case of actor James
O'Neill, the father of dramatist Eugene O'Neill. The son never forgot the
tragedy of how his father, a Famine emigrant, refused to adjust to life in

America and abandoned his wife and eight children to return to Ireland. His mother spent the rest of her years "slaving as a charwoman, the family always was ill-fed and poorly clad."[27]

An Irish immigrant woman almost any place in the United States might well have contemplated the possibility that if she married an Irish man she ran a good chance of someday being abandoned. She would have known the deserted wives in her neighborhood her friends and kin. She would have seen how they lived and what it meant to be a woman left alone with children in urban America. She also would have been familiar with dozens of widows who also provided the sole support for their families of young ones. Typically, Irish women on both sides of the Atlantic married men quite a bit older than themselves. From an economic point of view this pattern involved choosing a mate who had been in the work force long enough to have saved a bit of money, but it increased the probability of widowhood. Furthermore, Irish men as a result of job discrimination fell victim to industrial accident at a staggering rate. Between 1884 and 1890 in New York, Irish men led all the groups in the number of victims of on-the-job mishaps. Irish men took jobs no one else would take, as in the cutlery industry of the Connecticut Valley, where one axe manufacturer noted, "There have been so many deaths among the grinders that no Yankee would grind, and the Irish were so awkward and stupid that we did not get the quantity needed even by having extra men working at night." Needless to say, the extra workers were also Irish. They too risked injury in the job, and their deaths contributed to the legions of Irish widows who appeared in force in song and story, in biographical material, in parish histories, and in descriptions of Irish America. Irish laborers died so frequently and so young that Boston's Theodore Parker labeled them a "perishing class," alluding also to the spiraling rates of tuberculosis and other diseases associated with the poverty, overcrowding, and unsanitary living conditions of the Irish poor. Irish husbands and fathers rarely provided any hedge against this eventuality, and despite the plethora of benefit organizations and clubs that the sociable Irish joined in droves, few provided meaningful death benefits for widows and orphans. Most likely, an Irish-American family struggling to keep afloat did not have the resources to spare for life insurance, although the *Irish World* believed that life insurance, an "absolute duty—of throwing around their families' . . . protection," went against the Irishman's "natural" instincts. In encouraging Irish men to think about their wives and children the newspaper asserted, "We cannot conceal the fact that our country-men are less provident in this respect than other nationalities. Not because they are less solicitous for the welfare of their families, but because many entertain erroneous ideas of, and senseless prejudices against life insurance; many saying they 'would rather trust to Providence.'"[28]

An Irish widow with children became a prime candidate for charity, and the most pathetic descriptions, the most harrowing scenes of Irish-American poverty, involved the indigent widow, surrounded by hungry children, with no visible means of support. The ranks of the almshouse women swelled with Irish widows as did the workhouses, the prisons, and the charitable homes set up by religious orders, such as the Sisters of Mercy and the Sisters of the Good Shepherd. Widows took what work they could, attempting to maintain the integrity of their now fragmented family, and engaged in domestic day labor by running boarding houses, hawking goods in outdoor markets, and going into the mills and factories while setting up makeshift arrangements for those children too young to work themselves.[29] The mother of the future governor of New York and 1928 presidential candidate Al Smith returned to her trade as a hoop-skirt maker the day after her husband, the victim of an accident, was buried. Shortly thereafter she took over the management of a neighborhood grocery store. After Mother Jones had lost her husband to an epidemic that ravished Memphis, she took up her needle once again and with another woman opened a dressmaking business. Elizabeth Gurley Flynn lived for a number of years at the turn of the century with an aunt in the Bronx, a widowed tailoress whose sewing supported five children, and Catherine Donnelly, the mother of populist leader Ignatius Donnelly and his five sisters (four of whom became schoolteachers and one a poet), went back to teaching to feed and shelter her large brood. In fact, the first woman public school principal in Brooklyn, Mrs. McCloskey, entered the classroom through the sheer necessity of widowhood. The impact of widowhood on Irish-American life loomed clearly as a social phenomenon. Hardly anyone was untouched by its pervasiveness; hardly any biographical sketch fails to turn up a widow or two.[30]

With so many widows, with so many deserted wives, it was only natural that the Irish-American world contained a large number of female-headed households, families supported and controlled by women. By all accounts, statistical and literary, quantitative and qualitative, the female-directed family appeared often in Irish-America. Among the Irish in Philadelphia in 1870, for example, female-headed households appeared more often than among any other white group, although the black rate exceeded that of the Irish. Of the Irish families, 16.9 percent were headed by a woman, as opposed to 5.9 percent of the Germans and 14.3 percent of the native white Americans (a significant portion of whom were of Irish stock). In Buffalo in 1855, 18 percent of the Irish homes had a woman at their head. Ten years later the number had dropped to 14 percent, and then in 1875 it jumped back to 16 percent. Among the ten Irish households that constituted the entire Hibernian community of Danvers, Massachusetts, in 1837, two had no male as chief breadwinner. Boston's South End not only housed the city's largest Irish enclave but it also registered the highest percentage of female-headed households of any neighborhood of the Hub City.[31]

Once again, charity and settlement notations and observations of priests and nuns provided first-hand testimony to the frequency with which women were called upon to assume the responsibilities of both father and mother.

Dozens upon dozens of reminiscences and autobiographies underscored the hardships endured by Irish women as they struggled to take care of their families without male support. The dismal statistics on Irish female arrest records and the astounding figures on alcoholism among these women confirm the graphic descriptions of their grim lives. American observers repeatedly stressed the disorganized family life of the Irish and the particularly harmful effects it had on women. American journalists, social reformers, charity workers, and others generally believed that the Irish man in particular bore responsibility for the discord and suffering.

According to American observers, the double burden of families that were too large and the Irish curse of drinking caused the pathological condition of Irish family life. Many native-born Americans, infused with an anti-Irish ideology laced with anti-Catholicism, believed that Irish women and men were breeding prolifically; that not only would their incessant childbearing ensure an Irish political takeover of American cities but Catholicism would become the reigning faith of the hitherto Protestant nation. Social settlement workers, conscience-pricked journalists, evangelical do-gooders all saw the large number of Irish children, new ones who appeared with almost yearly regularity in the poverty-stricken tenements, as the source of the Irish man's misfortune, second only perhaps to his bottle of whiskey.[32] Esther Barrows, a Boston settlement worker in the South End, in 1905 recalled her lively neighbor Mrs. Murphy, who had just borne a set of twins:

> The smiling mother introduced the little pug-nosed mites by saying "More insurance for me old age, you see!" "And how many have you now, Mrs. Murphy?" On busy fingers she counted them, boys and girls, and Bridgy is twelve and the twins make thirteen. No one on earth has ever been able to persuade Mrs. Murphy that the twins "Is" more than one, and she always speaks of little Sonny, who came eighteen months later, as "me fourteenth and last kid."[33]

Barrows and other settlement workers in Boston, New York, Chicago, and elsewhere claimed also that no one on earth could persuade Mrs. Murphy and her sisters to think about having fewer children. That native-born Americans viewed Irish women as reckless breeders, to their own detriment, might help explain why one daughter of Irish immigrant parents, Margaret Sanger, who rejected her religion, her home, and her family, emerged as the most vociferous and effective champion of birth control. Yet most of these analysts erred in viewing the Irish as reckless in their childbearing patterns, since the low rate and late age of marriage in fact served as an effective way of reducing conception without having Irish women and men engage in behavior that they viewed as sinful, threatening their eternal souls.

Needless to say, the sentiments of the organized Irish Catholic world did not conform to those of Margaret Sanger or Esther Barrows, nor did it concur with those Americans who believed that the Irish were reproducing themselves into both poverty and power. The Irish, so shrewdly political, clearly recognized the connection between numbers and influence and believed that the two operated in tandem in a democratic country. Speculating on the ethnic make-up of Brooklyn in 1871, the *Irish World* took a long look forward and prophesied, "Whichever Race has the most children commands the future of Brooklyn." Most Irish commentators, on both sides of the Atlantic, in fact gloomily predicted that the sons of Erin would lose that race because of the perpetuation of the Irish syndrome of reluctant and late marriage which had the effect of cutting the number of potential voters for the Democratic ticket. Irish-American newspapers, to provide models for the young, loved to retell the life histories of obscure Irish women who gave birth to bountiful families, and obituaries appeared regularly which celebrated individuals like Mary Cleary, eighty years old, born in Tipperary, who "lived many years in this city, where she has left many descendants, a credit to her as she was to them." Irish spokesmen in Ireland in fact viewed a sluggish Hibernian birth rate in the New World as one of the major problems of immigration, and they lamented that "in America large families—the pride and glory of a virtuous people—are a rarity, every year becoming more and more rare." A moroseness pervaded the American church where Catholic prelates, mostly Irish-born or of Irish extraction, noted unhappily that Italian, French-Canadian, and Portuguese Catholics increased their number with greater speed and relish than the Irish since they *all* married and married young.[34] The Irish concern with their relatively low birth rate continued unabated into the twentieth century, culminating in the 1920s with a series of mournful articles in the Catholic *America* bearing such Cassandra-like titles as "Are Irish Catholics Dying Out in This Country?," "The Disappearing Irish in America," and "The Suicide of the Irish Race." Different statistics, a range of quotes, and a variety of anecdotes distinguished one article from another, but they all harked backed to the common theme:

> Everybody seems to presume that the Irish are a prolific race and are beyond all doubt not only reproducing themselves but besides that distinctly adding to the population of the country . . . |that| the national bird of the Irish is still the stork, and our race is following quite literally the Biblical injunction, "increase and multiply." . . . The Irish Catholic families are failing to reproduce.[35]

The authors, James J. Walsh and M. V. Kelly, and the numerous Catholic priests interviewed for these articles not only blamed the actual childbearing patterns of the Irish-Americans, but pointed an accusing finger at the selfish "old maids and bachelors who are to be found in Irish families in this country." That the Irish had merely continued a pattern brought over from

Ireland escaped the analysis of these commentators. Similarly, most of the participants in the discussion about Irish family life seemed not to have noticed that Irish women and men frequently chose not to marry and bear children precisely because they had other kinds of goals—primarily economic ones—and that given what lay in store for them, Irish women frequently either abjured or just put off the decision to marry until later in their lives.[36]

Given the sensitivity of an issue like family and the degree to which native-born Americans judged Irish domestic lives, it is hardly surprising that the official organs of Irish America, the community press and the Church, for example, did not draw sharper attention to the problems, the "pathologies" of Irish home life. If anything, the general tone of description in periodicals like the Boston *Pilot* and the *Irish World* and in the very popular literature of writers like Maurice Egan and Mary Sadlier focused on the bliss and tranquility that pervaded the Irish existence. These writers and periodicals painted the picture of the Irish in America, infused with a "love of home and kindred which is one of the most beautiful as it is one of the strongest traits in the Irish character." Catholic convert Orestes Brownson, who used his *Quarterly Review* as a vehicle for defending Catholics in the United States, admonished those who believed Irish family life was discordant and volatile to "visit their families and you feel that you are in a pure and healthy atmosphere, and your hearts are melted by a love of parents to children and of children to parents, of brothers and sisters for each other that you have never found in the families of Puritan origin." (Interestingly, Brownson did not include in his list of loving relations that between husband and wife.)[37]

Writers for the Irish secular and religious press did not consciously ignore problems nor did they craftily gloss over issues like desertion and domestic violence. They saw the problems. They recognized the plight of the immigrants. Nonetheless, they universally asserted that the major impediment to a pleasant and tranquil family life stemmed from excessive Irish drinking. The basic thrust of sermons and speeches, poems and prose, asserted that the essential structure of Irish family life appeared sound and healthy, but that drinking, caused by external forces like poverty, could insidiously and stealthily undermine the most solid of foundations. To the leadership of the various constituencies of Irish America, the patterns of family life, as transferred from Ireland and molded to fit the needs of American realities, seemed perfectly appropriate. The nature of male-female relationships, so similar to that which had characterized the hamlets of the Emerald Isle, seemed just fine. Excessive drinking, without the controls of the village, unfortunately undermined that basic stability.[38]

The formation of Catholic Total Abstinence societies on the parish level and the consolidation of these local temperance groups into a national Irish organization emerged as one of the solutions to the problems of the Irish immigrants. Aided by the charismatic Father Theobold Mathew, who inspired huge numbers of Irish men in Ireland to the cause of total abstinence, the movement spread to the United States, and the appearance of the Capuchin monk in the Irish enclaves of North America gave further impetus to those who believed that the tragedies of Irish families all began with the Irish man's fixation on his bottle of *poteen.*

Other voices in the Irish forums believed that the root of Irish family discord and domestic disarray grew out of the alien, unnatural atmosphere of urban life. Bernard O'Reilly, a priest, concluded in 1878 that "a family transplanted from a quiet country district in Ireland finds itself utterly lost in a large city in the New World, all ties, affections and holy influences of the ancient home and neighborhood are gone forever." According to a writer for the *Catholic Review* in 1879, among the Irish in the cities "some of them toil their lives through as common labourers, without a hope of ever putting their own roof above their heads and with the mortification of seeing their children grow up in hunger and dirt, the girls to become hard workers like themselves, the boys to go to the devil as rapidly as possible." The intimate connection between city life and family breakdown, between urban concentration and domestic disorganization, appeared over and over again in the Irish musing over their lot in their new homes. Since the Irish had been an overwhelmingly rural people and, at least as they remembered it, families had functioned harmoniously back home, then the solution to the disruptions should be sought in the promotion of the westward movement. Places like Iowa, Nebraska, Oregon, Wisconsin, and Kansas had readily available tracts of cheap land, which would solve their manifold problems. A whole range of experiments was started, launching Irish agricultural colonies in western states. Guided by churchmen like Bishop John Lancaster Spalding, who orated that the "religious mission of the Irish people" lay precisely in the rural areas where they would not be beset by the plethora of social ills, Irish men marched off to the Sweetman Colony in Minnesota, for example, and to O'Connor, Nebraska, to try their hand at breaking sod. Few of these attempts worked; few of the colonies made any headway in attracting the Irish from the slums of New York and Boston. Importantly, it appears to have been hardest to lure Irish women off to these bucolic or frontier settings, and despite editorials in the Irish press which told them straight out that if they made the move, they could "take their pick out of the many thrifty, young farmers that are out here," they did not budge. Clearly, economic opportunity beckoned in the cities and despite the problems of urban life, the Irish were not tempted by the rhetoric that if they moved out West they could marry and live peacefully in happy, thriving families.[39]

Despite all sorts of problems, Irish women had a fierce determination to sustain their families and to ensure some degree of upward movement. In fact, Irish women exerted tremendous influence within their families. Families with fathers present could also have been described as mother-centered. The impact of these matricentered families on Irish-American social development shaped the American-born children of the immigrants strongly. The tradition of strong, assertive Irish women which had its roots in Ireland's rural economy became even more pronounced in America and its urban environment.

The status of father in the Irish family eroded after migration since the father no longer exerted the same degree of authority connected with the whole process of the transfer of land. Since sons in urban industrial America were not expected to take over their father's job on a construction crew or a factory assembly line, fathers generally lost the power that accompanied the role of passing on the skills and expertise that they had held in agricultural Ireland. As the male role weakened, the female one accumulated greater prestige and authority. From scattered autobiographies, from the fragmentary evidence of letter collections of Irish immigrants, one can see that Irish men endured a harder process of adjustment to life in America and demonstrated less emotional flexibility in learning to cope with their new home than did Irish women. Perhaps the tremendous advantages that Irish society accorded to men and the preferential treatment they received from their families made them yearn more for their home communities than did the young women, who in Ireland clearly occupied the lowest rank in the scale of prestige.

The Hibernian Society of Cincinnati, for example, founded in 1850, began its existence in order to help a young Irish man who had recently arrived and "was seized with sickness, accustomed to have a mother's care in his slightest ailment he had to learn the chilling power of neglect." A young Irish woman no doubt would have learned it long before and would have been forced early in her life to learn how to cope. Many of the biographical details of Irish-Americans depicted the father who never came to terms with America, who had migrated reluctantly and never adapted. Winifred O'Reilly, the mother of labor activist Leonora O'Reilly, had come to the United States as a small child. The move had been her mother's idea. The father had always balked at going, but the persistent Mrs. Rooney of County Sligo won out. Her recalcitrant husband died on ship. Anne Sullivan's father never learned to make adjustments to life in America, nor did Margaret Sanger's nor Eugene O'Neill's.[40]

Generally, American society placed greater emphasis on carrying out domestic responsibilities—cooking, keeping a clean house, raising well-disciplined children—than had rural Irish society. Similarly, American popular culture and public opinion held up a strikingly more negative view of the Irish man than of the Irish woman. Although the "Bridget" of comic strip and theater stage fame acted foolishly and impetuously, she clearly behaved more acceptably as an American than did "Pat"—always drunk, eternally fighting, lazy, and shiftless. In fact, when American commentators compared Irish women to men, particularly in terms of how responsibly they carried out their family duties, women clearly received higher marks, constantly being portrayed as self-sacrificing, noble mothers who did what they could for their children without the assistance of their either inebriated or absent mates. Jacob Riis's descriptions of the lives of the urban poor depicted many a strong mother set against the foil of a weak, ineffectual father, both pitted against the overwhelming odds of poverty and slum life. On the popular stage similar characterizations gave Irish women respectability and sympathy.[41]

Significantly, many of the organs of public opinion in the Irish communities themselves confirmed this belief, with Catholic clergymen in particular celebrating the heroic efforts of the Irish woman as compared to her feckless—although affable—husband. The Irish man was seen by his own priests as wild and reckless, improvident and pugnacious. The ruin of any Irish woman—by drink—always began with the man first, and he was to blame for the destruction of his family, the erosion of parental influence, and the misfortunes of Irish-American life. Irish commentators, clerical and laymen, as they analyzed the foibles and frailties of the group, stressed the image of the man as the source of family disorganization, the woman, the pillar of strength. Women, it was asserted, not only held the family together, providing the only anchor of comfort in a hostile world, but they propelled the family out of poverty and into the respectability of the middle class.

In much of the Irish popular literature, the women were "civilizers," constantly attempting to stop men from drinking, and fought with their husbands over the number of hours they spent in the all-male drinking group. In this activity wives operated in league with the priests, who also made a valiant effort to discourage excessive Irish male drinking. Irish women in play and poem, in story and satire, bore the burden for the economic well-being of the family, hoarding the money their husbands would otherwise squander. They decided where and when to spend and, particularly in the fertile imagination of Mr. Dooley, women used the money for items that would enhance the family's image and status in the community. Molly Donahue, for example, insisted that the family's income allowed them to buy a piano, which "in Archey Road . . . is the one sure and visible symbol of the achievement of social ambition. It served as the landmark of progress towards wealth and culture." She also made her husband Malachi wear a stiff collar so that he, too, could bespeak the family's respectability. That collar

> was the shadow on his hearth; it was the skeleton in his closet, it was the fly in his ointment, it was in short, anything Irish you wish to call it. And it was the weapon of domestic discipline that converted a proud assistant foreman, sure of his decision of great problems, like the dumping of slag and the switching of freight cars, into an irresolute, apologetic serf.[42]

This darker side of the uplifting Irish female image was played out also in Harrigan and Hart's popular vaudeville act of the 1880s, "The Mulligans," in which Cordelia went from being a hard-working, frugal woman to an ambitious social climber.

When Irish people wrote about their group they portrayed the women as strong, exerting a great deal of influence on their families and articulating clear aspirations for middle-class status. Non-Irish observers, both those who sympathized with the plight of the immigrants and those who clearly harbored anti-Irish feelings, shared these views.[43]

According to sociologist Andrew Greeley, the forceful Irish matriarch "exists in America," and was a phenomenon that "is obvious to anyone with any experience of Irish-American life or novels." Greeley, also a priest, generalized from his experiences that "many if not most of the alcoholic Irishmen I know come from families where the mother rules the roost and have married women who are very much like their mothers." The pathological implications of the female-dominated family, of the rule of "herself," have also been explored in extensive literature on the high rates of male Irish mental illness, particularly schizophrenia. Psychiatrists such as Marvin K. Opler and Jerome Singer have linked the mother-dominated culture of Irish America with the mental disorders of delusion, guilt-ridden alcoholism, and "anxiety, tinged with fear and hate." According to Opler, the Irish male schizophrenics all came from homes "dominated by the mother; the father is often a weak and shadowy figure, the mother, assuming most of the major responsibilities, may treat her sons as forever boys and burdens."[44]

It is obviously difficult to draw an accurate portrayal of decision-making patterns within Irish-American families. Autobiographies, memoirs, and journalistic accounts generally point to greater female authority in major life decisions among the Irish than among most other immigrants, with more clearly defined patriarchal traditions. Terrence Powderly, the driving force behind the mid-nineteenth century Knights of Labor, wrote in his autobiography that "before their marriage my father and mother were Terrence Powderly and Madge Walsh; after marriage they were one, and I always held to the belief that my mother was the one. She was to me anyway." William Cardinal O'Connell, archibishop of Boston, son of a Lowell widow who managed to support and raise eleven children, described his pilgrimage to her birthplace in Enagh, County Cavan: "The place where my mother was born is a sacred place to me. The little village Church where she worshiped as a child, and was married, the little school she attended, — all these things, lovely in themselves, have now become to me *loca sacra;* consecrated to her memory and all that she has been to me." Big hefty James J. Corbett, a champion in the pugilistic ring, prided himself that "for six years I was a bank clerk, I gave my monthly salary to my mother each day." Corbett lived for many years in what he called "my mother's house." A young man of Irish parents, born in 1867 in Chicago, christened Peter Dunne, decided to take on his mother's name "Finley" at the moment of his first journalistic success. James T. Farrell, creator of Studs Lonigan, remembered his Irish-born grandmother: "She dominated the household, she was a spirit, she had the fear of God but I doubt she had any other fear in her. She and her older sister had 'come out' from the Irish midlands. . . . The world never defeated them."[45]

Importantly, a striking number of Irish-American writers, actors, labor organizers, churchmen, nuns, politicians, schoolteachers, boxers, and lawyers had grown up in female-headed households. Few knew their fathers. When they did, somehow their fathers merited only a passing reference, a sketchy paragraph at best. These autobiographical details do indeed confirm the patterns obvious also to contemporary observers, group members and outsiders, who stressed emphatically the centrality of Irish women to their families and the strength they demonstrated as they coped with hardship and stress or as they helped guide the family's journey from Ireland to America, from poverty to comfort, from shanty to lace curtain.

Since married life held out so many pitfalls, since being the wife of an Irish man in America during the mid-nineteenth to the early twentieth century held out so many possible tragedies, many Irish women reluctantly entered into blessed matrimony. Because they had immigrated to the United States in order to better their lot, to guide their own destinies, Irish women exchanged their roles as wage earner and income producer to that of wife and mother with a degree of circumspection. Given a long Irish tradition that called upon women to assert themselves, particularly in the home, and given the grim realities of life for the poor in urban America, Irish women, as wives and mothers, found themselves thrust into positions of power and authority. Significantly, the late age of marriage and the extended number of years spent in the labor force may have cushioned the shock and blunted the pain for the Irish wife who found herself pushed into central responsibility for her family, with few sources of support or solace.

FOUR  Broom, Loom, and
Schoolroom: Work
and Wages in the Lives
of Irish Women

Tell Mary McKinerly that if she were here she would make 100 dollars a
month knitting.
Quarterly Review

We all put every cent we earned into building associations. So Tilly owned a
house when she died and I own this one now. Our ladies told us how to put the
money so as to breed more and we never spent a cent we could save.
"The Life Story of an Irish Cook"

The millions of young single Irish women who chose to immigrate to
America emphatically opted for a life of remunerated work. The very culture
that caused these women to leave in the first place, that caused them, like
their sisters across the Atlantic, to develop a uniquely Irish family structure
highlighted by late age of marriage, nonmarriage, high fertility, and gender
segmentation, provided the means by which Irish women actively saw themselves in economic terms. Many of these women, in fact, experienced real
success in terms of their own definitions of mobility. Because they adhered to
a tradition whereby women functioned apart from men, they could take
advantage of the expanding American urban economy, which offered a wide
range of opportunities for unskilled, unmarried women in the work force.
Here, too, continuity over time emerged more dramatically than did change.
Although Irish women found themselves in a variety of occupations, the
nature of their migration and the structure of their families allowed the
majority to opt for domestic service more readily than any other group
of women.

Women left Ireland because it held out nothing for them. America offered them a chance to earn money and the respect that money brought. Theirs was an economic migration. Therefore, it is hardly surprising that the friends and relatives already here who had paid for their passage often arranged jobs for the newcomers even before they set foot on American soil. Immigrant letters sent home to Ireland depicted abundant jobs women could get and the high wages that they could command. Young Irish servant girls enthusiastically corresponded with friends and relatives back home, endorsing the migration because "there is already a demand for them [domestic servants] as few native girls care to go out as house servants," or "Good Girls to do housework in respectable families can readily get from one and a half to two dollars per week and good board and food."[1] A young woman, who worked as a seamstress in Connecticut, similarly glowed. "I am getting along splendid and likes my work . . . it seems like a new life. I will soon have a trade and be more independent . . . you know it was always what I wanted so I have reached my highest ambition."[2] The money that American women of Irish birth sent back to their parents and kin bore further testimony to the possibility of earning a good living in America, all the more so since the money that poured into Ireland in the millions came primarily from single women. (Married women generally stopped sending remittances as they had to devote their attentions to their own budding families.)[3]

The immigrant woman who came for a trip to the homeland or the occasional one who drifted back from America in order to find a husband among the local boys arrived with clothes and appliances and possessions that clearly bespoke economic success by Irish standards. The structure of the American job market as it translated into opportunities for the unskilled and uneducated tended initially to favor the Irish immigrant woman over the man. This pattern continued into the century's end as young Irish women moved into teaching, nursing, stenography, and clerical and sales work—all white-collar, semiprofessional positions—with greater ease than young men showed in their abandonment of unskilled, blue-collar occupations. One study conducted in Buffalo as late as 1920 demonstrated that Irish men made a less successful showing when compared to other immigrant men in terms of longevity on the job, education, and level of skill than did Irish women, as compared with other groups of immigrant women.[4] Generally, Irish women as a whole suffered less overt job discrimination than did Irish men, and while employers might have tried to find a servant other than an Irish girl or a school district might have looked for teachers other than Irish women, the pool of available candidates was relatively small and Irish women faced little competition. Furthermore, the generalized image of the Irish woman, the stereotype of Bridget or Norah, carried with it fewer negative implications than did that of Paddy. Although the stage caricature and the cartoon strip portrayal depicted Irish women and men as lacking in intelligence, manners,

differences of stereotypes in Paddy vs Bridget

and common sense, Bridget was generally lovable despite these failings. The Irish man, however, bore the stigma of the violent, drunken, rabble-rouser whose apelike physiognamy was witness to his degraded social and cultural development. Irish men faced greater social prejudices, and they had more difficulty moving out of the ranks of unskilled and semiskilled work. Furthermore, Irish men and women migrated with different expectations and attitudes. For Irish men the abandonment of home involved a greater break with the past; for them the move meant leaving a society that accorded men the greatest honors and where their superior social position was acknowledged by all. For Irish women the move almost universally constituted a positive upgrading of their status by bringing them to a society that offered greater respect and paid greater homage to women and women's activities. If Irish men left Ireland because of the constricting of possibilities in the place of origin, women left because of the prospect of the opening up of opportunities in the place of destination.

This is certainly not intended to imply that Irish women encountered no hardships, that they worked in pleasant environments, reaping high wages to sustain a luxurious life style. Indeed, they entered the labor force at the very bottom of the female job hierarchy, occupying a place perhaps equal to that of black women—a group with whom they shared many employment experiences. They worked for paltry wages in mills, factories, and in the thousands of private homes of the United States. They labored long hours and endured all of the dangers and discomforts associated with the lowest rank of the work force. But when one considers the material and economic standards of life they had had in Ireland and understands the dearth of options for them there, the work histories of these millions of laboring women constituted a rise in both actual conditions and in expectation.

Winifred O'Reilly, for example, and her life history may provide a case in point of the laboring patterns of Irish women. She was born in Ireland in the 1840s just before the Famine, and her family, particularly her mother, Mrs. Rooney, opted for immigration to America rather than remain in Ireland. With her recalcitrant husband and three little girls Mrs. Rooney left. Her husband had never wanted to come to the United States and got his wish, dying on board ship. Earning money to support the family became everyone's responsibility and seven-year-old Winifred became a nursemaid, and at eleven took a job as an errand girl for a dressmaker—providing her a start in the industry that would dominate the rest of her life. From errand girl she began to learn the rudiments of needlework and she took tremendous pride in the skills she learned. Years later she remembered, "It was all hand sewing in those days. I well remember how, while I was there, I learned to make sleeves. I could make a whole pair of sleeves ready to sew in and I was very proud of the accomplishment." She shifted over to making men's clothing, and noted, "The best pay I got was for men's heavy duck suits. But they were not always to be had, and then it was shorts or drawers or overalls." By age twenty-seven Winifred Rooney had become Winifred O'Reilly, marrying a man who owned a grocery store. Together they operated the store, but she never gave up her needlework, doing the two simultaneously; when the grocery store failed she could still bring in money to the family. More tragically, when her husband died she had total responsibility for an infant daughter. Once again she picked up her needle—actually by this time she operated a sewing machine—and went back to the factory, supplementing her wages by bringing work home to do at night and also taking in two lodgers to help defray the rent. Her daughter, Leonora, entered the ranks of laboring women at age eleven, as a worker in a collar factory. Both mother and then daughter came to realize that the roots of their struggle against poverty grew out of the nature of economic arrangements and both became ardent members of the Knights of Labor. Both, however, also retained a strong and abiding pride in their craft and in their skills as needle women. While in terms of income neither rose above the ranks of the working class, the daughter became one of the most significant and charismatic figures in the American trade union movement, moving in reform and intellectual circles with poise and self-confidence.[5]

The work history of Kate Kennedy may also provide a glimpse at how Irish immigrant women viewed their work and defined their importance through economic activities. Born into a wealthier family than Winifred O'Reilly in Ireland, the Kennedys of County Meath lost most of their money during the Famine and decided to emigrate. Kate Kennedy and a brother and sister went first, taking work in New York as embroiderers of cloaks and vests, saving money to bring over their mother and four other sisters. In the two years it took to accomplish this the three Kennedys in New York also earned enough money so that Kate could go to school and prepare herself for a career as a schoolteacher. By 1857, less than a decade after migrating, the entire family not only was reunited but had moved across the continent to San Francisco, where Kate was in fact able to teach and rapidly moved up to a principalship. All of Kate Kennedy's sisters were schoolteachers at one time or another and she went on to lead one of the earliest trade unions of public schoolteachers, focusing particularly on the issue of salary discrimination against women and demanding equal pay for equal work.[6]

Dozens of other biographical sketches and profiles could be summoned to demonstrate how important Irish immigrant women viewed work and the process of earning money. Community histories of the Irish in a variety of locations as well as Catholic charity and parish records indicate that a significant number of Irish women—almost all single—were successful, or at least parsimonious, enough to save up impressive sums of money, which they used to buy land or send back to Ireland or endow their parish church with bells or stained glass windows or underwrite some charitable endeavor. Similarly, the vast array of statistics accumulated particularly by state labor departments indicated that work and labor force participation was an experience that just about all Irish women had at one time or another. The woman who had never worked rarely figured in the Irish-American social portrait. Typically, Irish female immigrants and daughters of immigrants worked from the earliest possible age and remained in the labor force until marriage. Few married Irish women worked outside the home, fewer than women of other immigrant groups and fewer than native-born women. Among the Irish women in the Lowell mills in 1860, for example, only 8.9 percent had been married, and of these the vast majority had already become widows. With widowhood, such a common experience for the Irish woman in her late twenties or thirties who married a man older than herself, a woman re-entered the labor force, working until such point that her children could support her. Widows with small children had different needs and as such different options than they had had when single. Young women who migrated alone or with female friends or relatives experienced different pressures than did those women who migrated and lived with their parents. These differences in situation came to shape employment options.[7]

Domestic work was the Irish female immigrant's preferred job. By dint of circumstances, however, some could not take service positions and had to look to the factories and mills for income. These Irish women worked in almost every industrial endeavor where females found employment over the course of the last half of the nineteenth century.[8] The intense activism of Irish females in the industrial labor force occurred every place the Irish settled. Irish women comprised the single largest group of foreign-born female workers in Massachusetts, accounting for 17.19 percent of all women in industry as late as 1889 (French-Canadian women were the next largest at a mere 4.11 percent), in keeping with the intense clustering of the poorest Irish in the Bay State. Yet just one year earlier in Minnesota, where the Irish did not represent a sizable group and where those Irish who had migrated that far west were most likely among the more prosperous, more Irish women worked in industry than did any other foreign-born group.[9] Similar figures could be marshaled for places as diverse as Connecticut, Rhode Island, California, and Colorado, and all indicate that most industries in which female labor was used found Irish women among their ranks. In many instances more Irish women tended the machinery and performed the various operations to produce goods than any other females born outside the United States.[10]

Industry had not been their first choice. Particularly in the first generation it was less desirable than domestic service. Some women, however, found themselves forced into factory employment, particularly married women and widows. Millwork in the mid-nineteenth century brought whole families—that is, fathers and single offspring, both sons and daughters—into the same factories. The more family members, the better. Therefore, due to family pressure and loyalty, Irish daughters labored in textile or paper mills, even though they might have preferred other kinds of jobs. Widows, furthermore, could not accept domestic work because they usually had responsibility for children, and domestic work required them to live with their employers. So these women went into factory work as their only reasonable alternative.

Some industries, however, were more important than others, and two in particular employed so many Irish women that working in the cotton textile mills and in the various needle trades became standard life experiences for millions. Furthermore, since these were the two largest industrial employers of the daughters of Erin, the nature of work there helps one understand why they preferred domestic service. When Archbishop John Lancaster Spalding lamented that "the work of the factories is especially fatal to women," he particularly bemoaned that "there are few sadder sights than the poor women of the cotton mills of New England, so many of whom are Irish girls, whose cheeks once bloomed with health as fresh and fair as the purity of their hearts." Whatever the actual assessment of the impact of millwork on either morals or health, Spalding in fact accurately measured the Irish female preeminence in the textile mills that clustered in New England—in Lowell, Lawrence, Holyoke, Chicopee, and Fall River, Massachusetts, as well as in Rhode Island, Connecticut, and Cohoes, New York. Young Irish women entered the mills as the daughters of laboring families and remained there until marriage, returning with alarming rapidity as they swelled the ranks of the widowed and the deserted. The 1870s represented the zenith of Irish female employment in Lowell, the City of Spindles, and in that year females of Irish birth constituted 57.7 percent of all cotton textile employees.[11]

The cotton textile industry in Lawrence essentially began simultaneously with the great migration from Ireland, and at no point from 1847 on did the giant mills operate without Irish female labor. Like Lowell's Irish females these single women, most of whom lived in some kind of family grouping, and the widows worked for long years amidst the noise and the dust in order to sustain themselves. Not only did they endure unpleasant working conditions but poor safety features made the mills hazardous. Certainly, the owners of the Pemberton Mill had taken few precautions to protect their nine hundred workers, mostly Irish women, and on January 10, 1860, the massive structure just collapsed without warning and then broke out in fire. Trapped in the rubble were hundreds of female operatives, and when the final count was made, 88 women had been killed, and 116 had sustained severe injury. The grisly list of victims yielded forth many Irish names, a testimony to the large numbers of daughters of Ireland who had immigrated to America and found that they had to work in the factories of New England. Similarly, a fire in a mill in Fall River in 1874 claimed the lives of 14 women, all of them Irish spoolers, spooler tenders, drawing-in girls, warper tenders, or slasher-helpers. Most were widows.[12]

The Irish-American press followed the scores of industrial accidents in the textile mills that felled many young colleens in the decades after the 1850s and noted the consequent growing number of orphans. Not only did the Irish press and the sermons issued by the Catholic clergy note the high rate of Irish female victimization in disasters like the Pemberton Mill, but they also discussed the evil impact of factory labor on the health of these women. Yet despite the gloomy statistics and the maudlin portrayals of factory work in communities like Lawrence or Lowell or Warren, Rhode Island—yet another grimy center of the American cotton textile industry—where jobs as operatives in the mills existed for women, Hibernian females had no choice but to work there.

Most of these women came to the textile towns with brothers and sisters and even parents. Millwork encouraged all family members to work together within the mills, and owners of the mills offered bonuses and other advantages to employees who brought in kin to add to the ranks of the operatives. Therefore, economic pressures militated against the movement of the Irish women into other kinds of jobs, the kinds of jobs they would have held had they lived in New York, Boston, Baltimore, or Philadelphia. Furthermore, towns based on textile production generally housed that one industry only and supported a very small middle- and upper-middle-class, decreasing the number of opportunities for young Irish women to go into domestic work, as they surely would have had they lived elsewhere. Male employment in the mill communities ran a steadier course than male employment in the large cities, and for Irish men Lowell or Lawrence provided greater chances for uninterrupted work than did Boston or New York. Staying in these towns offered greater lures for Irish males than it did for Irish females, yet the desire for parents and children to remain together, rather than sundering the family unit, operated to keep Irish women in the mills, despite the hazards and dangers accompanying such work.

Employment in the textile mills for Irish women amounted to an act either of desperation, for the legions of widows supporting young children, or of family loyalty, for the daughters of mill hands, who put family solidarity above their personal concerns. Also judging from the very high rates of female-headed households in Lowell, Lawrence, and Cohoes as well as the plethora of millworking widows, the motivation for millwork among Irish women frequently grew out of the empty larder and the hunger of dependent children. Irish women did not go into millwork because they defined it as an appropriate occupation but because they had to and because it suited the needs of the state of widowhood in which so many found themselves.[13]

The variety of jobs conveniently lumped together as the needle trades also provided Irish daughters and widows with an income. In one of New York City's most thickly clustered Irish neighborhoods, the Sixth Ward, 40 percent of all Irish women age fifteen to nineteen sewed and stitched for a living as did 30 percent of those between the ages of twenty and twenty-nine. In men's clothing and in women's clothing, in millinery work and in the various miscellaneous branches of the industry, most women who emigrated from Ireland had the basic skill necessary to secure employment in the American cities of the post-Famine decades, as the garment industry grew tremendously. The occupation also proved to be particularly appropriate for widows with small children since in the nineteenth century so much of the work was done on a contract basis and women could labor at home, casting a watchful eye on their children who might also be enlisted to help work on collars or buttons, sleeves or seams. Sewing of various kinds basically provided the most frequently chosen form of employment except for domestic service. Yet the difference between the two trades was great. In 1855, for example, in Kingston, New York, 254 Irish women appeared in the census as wage earners. Of them, 240 were servants and 14 seamstresses. At the same time that 40 percent of the Irish female residents of the "bloody old" Sixth Ward sewed for a living, over 50 percent cooked and cleaned in the homes of New York's middle class.[14]

Changes certainly occurred over the course of the last half of the nineteenth century and by the end, although more Irish-born women still found themselves employed as servants than as needle-trade workers, the gap had narrowed considerably. By 1900 women of Irish birth made up 33.8 percent of all seamstresses and dressmakers in the United States and 41.2 percent of all white servants. For Irish women immigrating to the United States in the immediate aftermath of the Famine and in the next few decades, needlework represented not an active employment choice but something they did when they had no alternative. Like those women who worked in the mill with their children, Irish widows found sewing a way to combine watching their children with the imperatives of making a living, since they could not go out into domestic service. Young girls, not mature enough to cook and clean and tend to the duties of an American home and who still lived with parents—more likely than not a widowed mother—similarly could make garments while remaining part of their struggling families. Later in the nineteenth century and into the first decades of the twentieth century, however, garment-making and the various other branches of the needle trade employed a greater percentage of Irish women than they had ten or twenty or even thirty years earlier.

The shift in employment choice, from a preference hierarchy that in the mid-nineteenth century rated domestic work above needlework for Irish women and by the century's conclusion found the two jobs about equal, can be explained by a number of factors. Throughout much of the nineteenth century few occupations existed for women, particularly for the masses of women of the poor and working classes, regardless of race, national origin, or religion. Of all the options that existed for them, needlework represented one of the worst in terms of pay, working conditions, and opportunity to advance oneself. In the large cities, however, it also drew in the largest number of females, desperate for some way to earn money. In New York, Pittsburgh, Baltimore, Philadelphia, Cincinnati, and elsewhere more women than the market could bear sought work sewing, driving wages constantly downward. Matthew Carey, an Irish-born economist and writer residing in Philadelphia, witnessed the plight of the poor needle women in the 1830s, documenting their paltry wages, which could hardly sustain life, and the damp, dark garrets where they worked making clothing. He took to task the economic system that had reduced to starvation the needle women, who earned approximately seven cents a day, which had to be spent on food, fuel and clothing; they could spend only half of that on such necessities if they had to support children.[15] Studies and surveys of sweatshoplike conditions where women and children sewed in their homes in a dozen cities of the mid-nineteenth century abound in the details of poverty, dirt, poor wages, and instability. Even the factories, which gradually came to encompass more and more of the garment labor force after the Civil War, operated under unhealthy, unsafe conditions, paying women workers pitiable wages. Throughout much of the nineteenth century seamstresses appeared more frequently on the rolls as charity recipients than did servants: live-in cooks and other forms of "help" showed up less often in the annals and yearly reports of either general or Catholic charity societies than did dressmakers. In 1875, for example, the largest group to be "relieved" by the New York Association for Improving the Conditions of the Poor was Irish women, among which 44 percent were "sewing women" while an equal number worked in their own homes as washerwomen. No domestic servants that year appealed for alms. As late as the 1880s grim conditions and miserable earnings characterized the trade. One young Irish woman mournfully described her plight to the Colorado Labor Bureau in 1886:

> My parents live in Ireland and are entirely dependent on myself and sisters for support. I served an apprenticeship of three months, seven years since. I have worked at the trade ever since. I am a good seamstress and work hard. I try but I can not make over $1 per day. I pay rent for machine, $2.50 per month. Am not able to afford to ride on street cars, therefore I have to walk, and if I happen to be one minute late, I have to walk up long flights of stairs and am not allowed to go on the elevator.[16]

By the end of the nineteenth century and certainly into the twentieth century's first decades, however, the garment industry had gradually advanced in terms of wages and working conditions, and with the earliest successes of trade unions in the various branches of the industry a marked improvement occurred. For Irish women, in particular, work in garment-making at the end of the century became somewhat more bearable as the lowest ranks of the industry, the most oppressive conditions, the worst-paid positions came to be occupied by newer groups of immigrant women, especially Italians and Eastern

"Scene in Sitting-room": New York City New Labor Employment Bureau. Jobs in domestic service were always plentiful for single women, and Irish immigrant women took advantage of the opportunity. (*Courtesy of the Library of Congress*)

European Jews. Irish women in essence were pushed up by the appearance of these more recent arrivals, less schooled in the industrial marketplace. Young Irish women who entered garment-making in 1890 or 1900 more likely possessed a greater level of skill than did Italian women entering at the same time, and the woman of Irish origin would more likely be entering a factory where other Irish women and men now held supervisory positions than she would have earlier. Thus, Irish women came to consider garment-making a more appropriate occupation when it became a better paying, less oppressive way to earn money. One study of female earnings in the women's clothing industry in 1915 found Irish women earning the second highest wage per hour of any group of women similarly employed, including German, French-Canadian, Italian, Polish, and Portuguese women and exceeded only by women born in England. Irish females also earned more than most other women in the men's clothing field. In the years when the needle trades in urban America commanded only starvation wages and forced women into unsafe working environments, Irish women chose domestic work when they could. For thousands of Irish women, however, sewing was the only choice they had, domestic service being an unattainable goal.[17]

If Irish women viewed domestic work as the best chance they had to fulfill the economic goals of migration, why did other groups of women—native-born Protestant women and, later in the nineteenth century, Italian, Jewish, and French-Canadian women—view it as the worst possible form of employment? What was there about both the nature of domestic service and the cultural dictates of Irish life that allowed these millions of young women to take what others would not, to enthusiastically embrace what others eschewed? Since Irish women did, in fact, take jobs as domestic servants with relish, diminished only as the floods of Irish immigration dried up, there must have been something in the nature of the job that appealed to them as women, shaped by a specific culture, with definite goals, ambitions, likes, and dislikes. By examining the nature of domestic service and the ways in which Irish women functioned in it one can indeed see some of the fundamental patterns of Irish female life as migrants and as new Americans. Certainly, the nature of Irish family structure and the contours of Irish male-female relations played a very important part in setting the conditions that brought these women to the point where they eagerly accepted the jobs that others refused.

The shortage of domestic servants is a theme that consistently runs through the history of work in America. The difficulty American housewives had in finding suitable "help" can be traced back to the earliest years of European settlement in the New World, as "Americans" experimented with indentured servants, redemptioneers, and slaves to cook and clean and mend

Employment office, 1866. (*Courtesy of the Library of Congress*)

and engage in the dozens of tasks of running an affluent home. Young American women basically refused to do this kind of work. Native-born Protestant girls in the nineteenth century found the notion of domestic work so odious, so demeaning, so beneath their sense of self that they in fact often took lower paid jobs in mills and in factories and even willingly accepted less as seamstresses and needle women rather than humiliate themselves in someone else's home. Louisa May Alcott once found herself as a servant and considered the experience so wrenching that her mother noted, "Every sentiment of her being revolts at it—and I am not sure how long she will remain." Less than two months provided the author of *Little Women* with just enough degradation to quit as well as enough material to write "How I Went out to Service," in which she stressed the constant sexual innudendos made by the man of the house and the lack of autonomy. Catharine Beecher, in her *True Remedy for the Wrongs of Women: With a History of Enterprise Having That for Its Object,* confirmed this and asserted that the reluctance to engage in domestic work stems from pride, and that "caste has the strongest hold of any other on the human mind; and so long as servitude places a woman in the lowest and most despised rank, no consideration of health and no pecuniary offers will draw American women into it, if they can escape it." Importantly, as more and more Irish women did consider health and money and entered—flooded —the ranks of domestic servants, American girls became even more adamant in refusing it, because now it was not just demeaning, it was not just degrading, but it bore the Irish label and as such was something no American girl would touch if she could avoid it. A London *Times* correspondent in New York during the Civil War was struck by the desperate straits of needle women, the vast majority of whom were American women who chose slow starvation as they plied their needle rather than humiliate themselves and do domestic work and thereby risk equating themselves with Irish women. One American girl who served, albeit reluctantly, confessed to Helen Campbell, as she collected material for her study of women toilers, that among her main objections to domestic work was that "the cook and the waitress here [are] just common, uneducated Irish, and I had to room with one and stand the personal habits of both, and the way they did at table took all my appetite. I couldn't eat, and began to run down."[18]

So pervasive, in fact, was the antidomestic service prejudice among American women that the American-born daughters of Irish immigrants, acculturated in part to the values and beliefs of the world around them, also snubbed their noses at domestic work. One such young woman, the daughter of an immigrant Irish cook, confessed to the readers of *Good Housekeeping* in 1890 (many of whom at that very moment either were looking for a new "girl" or were unhappy with the one they had) that she and her five sisters all had chosen millwork over the domestic work their mother had done: "I hate the word service. . . . We came to this country to better ourselves, and it's not bettering to have anybody ordering you around! . . . If there was such a thing as fixed hours and some time certain to yourself, it might be different, but now I tell every girl I know, 'Whatever you do, don't go into service.'" Significantly, as was the case with the Protestant American women who refused service, the reasons given by these women were not economic but psychological.[19]

If American and Americanized women considered domestic work beneath their dignity, particularly as it came to be synonymous with Irish female labor, women of other immigrant groups, with a few exceptions, also chose lower-paid jobs rather than serve a strange family in a strange home. Recognizing the ethnic inclination for or against domestic service, a Y.W.C.A. employment survey remarked in the early years of the twentieth century that no other group even came close to equaling the Irish in their preference for service since

> the Irish are about the only race which can be said to prefer housework. In general they desire positions of this sort, but the influx of Irish immigrants is past and now it is a very small stream which comes when compared with the hordes which came before the Italian invasion. Italians do not take kindly to housework; they drift into the North End or into mills. Jews never do housework in any but their own homes, and most Jewish women marry young.[20]

Italian women never took jobs that threatened the traditional structure of family life; the prospect of living away from the protection and watchful eye of father and brother seemed anathema to them. Since Italian women in the United States married universally and young and had immigrated to the United States less frequently than did their brothers, the Italian communities had no excess of unmarried, unattached females to be domestics. Eastern European Jewish women also preferred either sweatshop work, where all family members sewed together, or the garment factory over domestic employment. One 1905 study traced three hundred young Jewish immigrant women who had been placed in private homes on their initial arrival in New York, and within less than a year, two-thirds had either married or rushed off into factories and stores. Certainly, migration patterns need to be considered because, like Italians, few Jewish women migrated alone but tended to make the move within family units, and though more Jewish women migrated proportionately than had Italian women, even among Jews there was no excess of females as had been the case among the Irish. Whereas in the Middle West Scandinavian immigrant women did choose domestic work, in the East the Irish were basically the only group of white women who did not consider the job odious and degrading. The Domestic Reform League of Boston in 1909 was in fact quite struck by the ethnic proclivity for or against this kind of employment and noted,

> Habits of life, social ideals, standards inherent in race and past environment, ability to speak the language—these with many other factors enter into the immigrant's choice of an occupation and affect her attitude toward housework. In one year, to July 1, 1906, there entered the port of Boston or vicinity 2482 immigrant women between the ages of 11 and 30, unmarried or childless. An invesigation of 398 cases, divided approximately among the nationalities represented in the 2482, showed that . . . 172 . . . somewhat over two-fifths—entered domestic service. These were almost entirely Irish. The women who did not go into domestic service—Hebrews, Italians and other southern Europeans—were . . . living with their families.[21]

Daughters of New England farmers and of Italian *contadini* as well as newcomers from the *shtetlach* of Eastern Europe rejected domestic service as a result of the dictates of their own cultures and opted for other kinds of jobs that they defined as more harmonious with their values. As was the case with Irish women, they did not make this employment choice on economic grounds. The reasons offered ran the gamut, including lack of autonomy, lack of free time, not wanting to live away from their families, the unpredictability of hours, and the like. Yet wages rarely appeared as a motive for this choice. Working women who were interviewed in 1898 by the Women's Educational and Industrial Union of Boston, in fact, admitted that "housework was more healthful and paid more. Yet while they were situated as at present their health was good enough and a little larger pay was no great inducement." Lucy Maynard Salmon, probably the most exhaustive late-nineteenth-century researcher of the whole field of domestic work, asserted that "one of the striking conditions of the service, especially in view of the unwillingness of many persons to enter it, is the fact that the wages received are relatively and sometimes absolutely higher than the average wages received in other wage-earning occupations open to women." If others then refused it for non-economic reasons and in fact turned down better wages for higher social status, it was all the more striking that Irish women almost universally rushed to "household industry."[22]

One reason why Irish women flocked to domestic labor stemmed from the almost unabated demand for household workers. That other women—native-born and immigrant—refused it and that daughters of middle- and lower-class American families experienced greater educational opportunities from the mid-nineteenth century onward, thereby being less available to "help" in the routines of home tasks, all helped to create a labor vacuum that Irish women filled. Irish women from the pre-Famine decades well into the early twentieth century recognized the workings of the law of supply and demand and supplied to American homes their services and labor, which were in such demand.

Since Americans hungered so for servants, Irish women generally had an easier time getting work than did their brothers. Employment agencies that served both men and women found Irish females easier to place than males. The *Irish World* in 1870, for example, noted that a Free Labor Bureau in New York provided jobs to 81 Irish men and 628 females. John Francis Maguire in the late 1860s had a chance to examine the register book at the Intelligence Office and Labour Exchange at Castle Garden, noting, "The chances of employment are generally more in favor of females than of males and that they are terribly against the latter, if they come out at a wrong season—which is towards the Autumn, and all through the Winter." Irish women could also hold onto their jobs longer than could Irish men, because in periods of economic disorder and decline job security for domestic servants did not seem to suffer as severely as did the jobs Irish men normally held in public works, construction, and factories. Not atypically, during a period of severe unemployment in Albany, New York, in 1855, the wives, daughters, and sisters of Irish men endured little job dislocation and continued to work in their places. In 1887, 19.4 percent of all Irish-born men in Massachusetts found themselves unemployed, while only 13.3 percent of Irish-born women also were out of work. Among French-Canadian- and English-born workers, however, an equal number of men and women suffered from lack of work, according to the Massachusetts Bureau of Statistics and Labor.[23] Even in periods of economic decline, which saw the reduction in factory and mill jobs, the need for houseworkers seemed almost untouched. One Irish writer seeking to discourage the outward flow from the Emerald Isle noted that golden economic opportunities did not await the Hibernian newcomers in North America. "Pauperism is already upon us. The market for all the lighter calling is overstocked, and I doubt whether . . . there is much demand for mechanics, though there is still a demand for farm labourers and domestic servants." Year after year, in prosperity and panic the New York Association for Improving the Condition of the Poor reported to charitable-minded New Yorkers that domestic servants rarely appeared among the ranks of the needy, and in 1866 after chronicling the miserable wages of launderesses and needle women the commission's annual report asserted, "Of females in domestic service, chiefly foreign born, it need here only be said that they occupy the places for which they are best fitted, and having abundant employment and very liberal wages they cherish no higher aspirations."[24]

Statements about "suitability" of ethnic groups for particular work and about the paucity of aspirations aside, nineteenth-century New Yorkers and Bostonians and Philadelphians did in fact hunger for the labors and services that basically only Irish women would provide. Josephine Goldmark, a twentieth-century progressive activist, noted in her autobiography, as she retold the stories of her midwestern childhood, that the shortage of servants was perceived so sharply there that "the advent of an Irish newcomer on the streets of the little town was almost immediately spotted. Any prospective employer made haste at once to accost and engage the stranger, and for the sum of $4.50 per week her not unwilling but usually quite unskilled services were obtainable."[25]

Partly because of the ample opportunities to find work few domestic servants showed up in the various studies of prostitution, and one 1867 survey of women's work, *The College, the Market, and the Court; or Woman's Relation to Education, Labor, and Law* noted that among prostitutes, "almost none of these women are drawn from domestic servants." So acutely did American women feel the need for servants that they overcame the intense American prejudice against the Irish and the deep-seated distrust of Catholicism and brought Irish women into their homes.[26]

Employers kept hiring "green" Irish girls to cook and clean and sew as well as care for the children and the household despite the pervasive judgments offered—almost universally—against the colleens who, it was said, could not cook, whose standards of cleanliness fell below that considered appropriate for middle-class Americans, and who might in fact be disguised agents of the Pope bent on converting the Protestant children in their charge. Despite these prejudices against Irish servants, despite the constant litany against Irish habits and lack of skills, employers seemed to have lived in constant dread of the moment when Bridget or Norah might decide to quit. Knowing this, Irish servant girls seem to have moved from job to job with ease, recognizing that their services were needed and that they therefore operated out of a position of strength. They could, in fact, set some of the terms of their employment and in essence could "shop around" for an ideal situation. So secure were these servants in the knowledge that they could always find work that one Boston domestic from Ireland responded forthrightly to Frances Kellor's query as to why she did not want to receive training in cooking and other household craft, "Shure, now, why should I be l'arnin' when I kin shove my ear in anywhere and get a good job?"[27]

Irish women entered American homes despite the almost universally stigmatized image that domestic service carried in American society. Irish women had migrated precisely because domestic work abounded, and they seemed almost impervious to the demeaning, if not scathing, things being said about them on the stage and in the popular press, in employers' letters and diaries, in fictional and in what purported to be factual accounts of nineteenth-century American life. Travelers to the United States in the nineteenth century repeatedly remarked on the plethora of Irish servant girls and noted how dependent Americans were on the new arrivals. British visitors, with their own anti-Irish heritage, found the phenomenon somewhat amusing, noting that now Americans who had expressed support for Irish home rule demands were getting a real glimpse of what the Irish were really like.[28]

Autobiographies and reminiscences of upper-middle-class life in nineteenth-century America similarly abound with memories of Irish servants, some warm and tender recollections, others humorous mockeries of the foibles and failings of the "help."[29] Even advertisements for household products emphasized that it was the Irish servant who would use them; the *Ladies' Home Journal* sang the praises of Kirkman's Soap, as it was heartily endorsed by "Mrs. McCarthy."

Dozens upon dozens of statements, evaluations, judgments, and comments were offered during the last half of the nineteenth century about the merits—and mostly the demerits—of the Irish servant girl. The greatest attribute of the Irish female domestic worker rendered during her heyday was her availability. Most commentators, when searching for other words of praise, emphasized that she was chaste and that her employers rarely had to contend with sexual deviance and with the problems of having to fire her, unmarried and pregnant. Despite these grudging compliments, the bulk of the material describing and detailing the "Doings and Goings of Hired Girls" lamented that Irish servants were: terrible cooks, poor house cleaners (having been born and bred in the mire of the bogs), temperamental if not violent, and clumsy and awkward in handling the family's precious china and crockery. Whereas some employers thought that Irish girls worked slowly, out of a combination of laziness and impudence, others were convinced that the Irish servant sped through her work at an amazing speed, so as to get through her tasks no matter how sloppily.[30]

Typical of the voluminous testimony offered against the Irish domestic was the following, which appeared in 1889 in *Our Day*:

> Introduce into a home thoroughly fitted up with them [improvements] a green daughter of green Erin, whose sole training for domestic service has been in her native cabin, and to whom furnaces, gas, and water pipes are unknown quantities; keep in mind the antagonism which seems to exist between ignorance and labor saving machinery, as indicated frequently by Nora's refusal to use even a wringer, and you have a reason other than incompetency of the mistress for things not running smoothly. . . . Nora has faults which we can hardly put up with in any position, faults plenty and glaring; she is often untruthful, dishonest, slovenly, impudent, and generally provoking.[31]

A group of household servants in the early twentieth century. Service was the single largest category of Irish female employment in the United States at that time. (*By permission of the State Historical Society of Wisconsin*)

Elspeth MacDonald shared with the readers of *Success* in 1907 the trials and tribulations she endured with the "Hired Girls I Have Met," and described one Mary McGuire, the only person available who had an "infinitesimal share of common sense . . . her mistakes seemed almost diabolical." Edwin Lawrence Godkin, editor of the *Nation,* went so far as to say that the behavior of the Irish Bridgets in American kitchens had been a major factor in turning American public opinion against the Irish cause in Ireland. Whether intended as serious analysis or as satire, the massive outpouring of the American employer class drew an unflattering portrait indeed of Bridget and Norah and their ability to perform their jobs in the homes of middle-class Americans.[32]

No matter how much American employers disliked Irish servants and despite complaints about Irish failings, middle-class Americans in fact depended heavily on this single source of help. As a result of the twin forces of dependence and dislike yet another common theme emerges in the contemporary literature on the "servant problem," that of the employers living in fear of their social inferiors. Throughout the material that sought to dissect the nature of servant-employer relations runs the constant leitmotif that since servants were scarce, employers could not ask too much of them. Since servants could find work just about any place, it was the servant who set the terms of the job.

In an article titled "Which Is Mistress?" the *Ladies' Home Journal* described the "poor little mistress [who] yields tremblingly, because 'it would be too dreadful if Bridget were to leave.'" This 1886 piece noted that servants held the trump card and used it. Typically, Bridget or Maggie would announce, "'In all the iligant first-class families I've lived in (an' ontil I cam to yez I've lived in none but quality houses) I niver was axed to send up soup on Sunday afore.'" Margaret Polson Murray, an active proponent of the women's club movement, believed that the middle-class American woman was trapped. "In her household from January to December, from start to finish, she lived under the nineteenth-century dictatorship of homesick young women from foreign countries, spinsters and widows who must 'support' themselves." Bridget, it was said, "knows that no 'character' is needed to find a new place; so if her tea is not strong, or her mattress not of good hair, if breakfast is ordered too early, or dinner kept waiting, she packs up her traps, demands her wages, and off she goes." A British traveler in the 1870s went so far as to attribute the growing tendency of Americans to live in hotels and therefore not being required to cook (that is, not requiring an Irish girl to do the cooking) to the "terror of the Irish servant." Particularly hard hit were employers in smaller towns, since they had the most difficulty in replacing discontented Irish servants, as few were willing to live outside the teeming cities. One such American woman in the 1860s, Harriet Jane Hanson Robinson of Malden, Massachusetts, became so obsessed with her annoyance and fear of her servants that she devoted extensive passages in her diaries to various servants.

After firing one she determined to "wash . . . my hands of the Tribe called Paddy and mentally painted on my door posts . . . 'No Irish Need Apply!'" Unable, in fact, to liberate herself from Irish help, Robinson found a new Irish servant named Julia. On March 29, 1864, the employer confided to her diary that Julia "told me that my work was too hard unless I would pay her two dollars a week," and two days later, she poured out her heart with trepidation, "I am preparing for another *domestic revolution.*" Annie Adams Fields, a wealthy Bostonian and a dabbler in charity, recalled how in 1875 she had helped place an elderly Irish woman in a domestic job. The woman quit and, according to Fields, "went to see my Irish washerwoman who told me she would not work for her because she locked up everything and called her by her Christian name when she was an aged woman."[33]

Clearly, domestic service carried a stigma for the Irish just as it did for women of other origins. Yet Irish women closed their eyes to the grotesque cartoons, shut their ears to the mawkish portrayals of "Biddy the Kitchen Canary," and continued to cook and clean and scrub and tend. It was almost as though Irish women remained impervious to the mockery and scorn that accompanied the job. Despite the mockery, domestic service constituted an almost universal experience for women of Irish origin in the United States. As late as 1900 60.5 percent of all Irish-born women who labored in the United States worked in domestic capacities. In Buffalo in the 1850s 90 percent of all daughters of Irish families had left home by age eighteen, most apparently taking jobs as live-in servants. In the 1850s Irish women cornered the domestic market in Milwaukee, Janesville, and Madison, Wisconsin. In that same decade a staggering 80 percent of all women engaged in paid household labor in New York City had come from Ireland.[35] By the 1860s numerous Irish servant girls had arrived in frontier communities like Jacksonville, Illinois.

Although Irish women refused to listen to the jibes hurled at servant girls in America, they did pay attention to a counter message, which asserted that the household worker, when "compared with her sisters in the industrial field . . . certainly is well compensated." Undoubtedly, young Irish female migrants did not bother to read the statistical studies issued by the various progressive organizations in the late nineteenth century analyzing comparative female earnings. Even if they could read, they did not have to pore over the various government reports that noted the relatively high earnings of domestic servants. More importantly, they could read the letters of women who had migrated, glowing with pride as they told relatives and friends back home that servant girls in America could earn and save. Guidebooks written for prospective Irish immigrants also noted that

> servant girls in America get from eight to sixteen dollars a month—sometimes they get as high as twenty. Now if they save half of that amount every year, and place it at interest, they will have acquired a considerable sum at the end of ten

years. Many of them, to my certain knowledge, have, in the course of twenty or thirty years, by faithful industry and moderate economy become owners of from three to five thousand dollars.[36]

Compensation for domestic service varied from city to city, responding in part to the supply of young women who were willing to work. Whereas in New York in the 1850s servant women could expect from $4 to $7 per month, in San Francisco, plagued by a shortage of women who would be either wives or servants, Irish women were reported to be earning between $50 and $70 per month from 1849 to 1853. Wages also differed within a given city, and employers of household workers had greater leeway in deciding on a salary than did the employer of garment workers or textile mill hands, who had to consider the cost of supplies and materials. Yet even given the wide regional variation and despite the capriciousness of the wage-setting system, domestic workers had an economic edge over women employed in industry and certainly over needle women.

In Massachusetts, for example, in 1906 the only group of women who earned more than domestic servants were schoolteachers. Domestic servants over the entire state averaged $9.08 per week, whereas textile hands earned $7.15 and saleswomen a mere $6.21. Since domestic workers generally lived with their employers, they had no expenses of food, shelter, transportation, or the like. Most employers preferred that their servants dress in some sort of livery provided by the employer, so that the servants did not incur any expense in clothing, something that cost women who worked in sales a great deal of money.[37]

Descriptions of nineteenth-century women who tried to make a living sewing stress the dirty, oppressive conditions under which they lived and the poor diet by which they attempted to sustain themselves. Servants lived in a strikingly more healthful environment, residing in the best neighborhoods of the city, eating the same food—albeit leftovers—as their employers. Descriptions of nineteenth-century women who tried to make a living in the textile mills and the canneries, in the laundries and in the factories, emphasized the high rates of accident and industrial disease they endured and the miserable hovels to which they returned after grueling hours tending the machines for low pay. Servants usually had their own rooms or shared with only one other servant and could do with their earnings as they wished—spend it on themselves, send it home, donate it to some charity, save it, squander it, invest it. What they did with their earnings became their own choice and was not dictated by the basic demands of survival. For women who had migrated for economic reasons, for women who had decided to leave their homes in order to fulfill certain material goals, domestic service basically provided an ideal forum. Unlike the Italian culture, which stressed both female supervision and early marriage, nothing in Irish culture worked against the young female migrants who had chosen to live in other peoples' homes and perform domestic duties. Irish women had been reared in an environment characterized by rigid sex segregation and late and infrequent marriage. To them, the idea of living apart from their communities, apart from Irish men, would not have appeared aberrant, and for many the economic rewards of domestic work provided a good reason to postpone or perhaps permanently swear off marriage.

Interestingly, Irish communal leaders and organs of public opinion expressed mixed feelings about the Irish servant girls. On the one hand, there was tremendous pride over their independence, their earning power, and their continued devotion to parents and kin back home as evidenced by the generous sums servant women remitted across the Atlantic. An Irish priest in Memphis in the 1880s unequivocally asserted that "the most faithful specimens of womanhood that ever crossed from the shores of Europe, are the Irish servant girls of America." John Francis Maguire reported back to Ireland that "in domestic service her merit is fully recognized. Once satisfied of the genuineness of her character, an American family will trust her implicitly; and not only is there no locking up against her, but everything is left in her charge." Church leaders took pride in the scattered cases that came to their attention of Protestant employers being so impressed by the religious zeal of their servant women that they converted to Catholicism. Almost all Irish-American observers united in asserting that regardless of other faults, the Irish domestic woman remained chaste and uncorrupted by sexual temptation.[38]

On the other hand, a whole range of complaints and criticisms arose at the same time. To some Irish apologists the persistence of Irish women in domestic service loomed as a symbol of Irish failure and their inability to rise. For those Irish leaders who believed the Irish would do better in the West, away from the congestion of big city life, the large numbers of Irish women in service bore testimony to the plight of the urban Irish. The founder of one Irish community in Iowa, in fact, wrote back to his fellows in the East exhorting them: "To every single man I would say: 'With or without money, move westward: Your labor is ample security for your living . . . marry some of those fine young girls buried alive in the basement kitchens of New York, and bring her West. She, in a business point of view, will pay." Similarly, Bishop Hogan of Kansas City declared in 1877, "Young people should have been kept in families with their own. We have suffered them to become hirelings, to die in damp kitchens and cellars."[39] While the Irish press complained that Irish women were discriminated against by employers who always preferred Protestant to Catholic help, these same newspapers were not above engaging in some of the same kind of mockery of the Bridgets of the American home, and frequently printed jokes that depicted the ignorance of their own women. The *Irish Miscellany* in 1858 somehow was able to include this item:

"How old are you, Bridget?" said a gentleman to his servant girl. "About fifty, sir," replied Bridget. "You are mistaken Bridget; you are not over twenty." "Yes sir, that is it. I'm about twenty or fifty. Somewhere along there."

This answer indicates about the same degree of intelligence as that of an old grey-headed negro.[40]

To some, domestic service was responsible for the low rate of Irish marriage and what was considered to be the abnormal family life of Hibernians transplanted in the New World. They felt that since women could make good money in service they eschewed marriage and therefore helped cause a lowering of the Irish birth rate. Finally, clergymen particularly believed that Irish servant girls spent far too much money on clothing and that their assertiveness on the job made Americans despise the Irish in general.

By far the most significant problem that the Irish community had with domestic service involved what was perceived as a threat to the religious life of Catholic girls who labored in Protestant families. Irish-Americans feared that employers exerted all sorts of pressure on their servants to hinder observance of Catholic ritual and often forced them to attend Protestant worship. Riots broke out in Boston in 1853 over one such young servant girl, Hannah Corcoran, and in Lawrence in the 1840s Bridget Horan's Catholic sisters abducted her from her employers, who had taken her to their Protestant church. The Irish press published possible answers that Irish girls might offer to employers who sought to lure them away from the Church, and novels, sermons, and special books all appealed directly to the thousands of servant girls to remain firm in their faith and unsullied by the values and life styles that surrounded them.[41]

Yet whatever Irish men may have thought about the respectability and morality of domestic service, they recognized that Irish women flocked to it as a way to make money and that the money earned by these servants provided much of the financial support for the Irish-American communities, for charitable and religious institutions. Irish male community leaders of all sorts recognized what a tremendous contribution Irish servants' earnings in America had made to the economy of Ireland. Thus, they responded vehemently and often violently to any threat to that earning power. Much of the Irish hostility against blacks in both the antebellum North as well as in numerous southern cities after the Civil War sprang from the fear that black women might challenge the Irish monopoly in domestic service. Similarly, when California employers in the 1870s began to employ Chinese men as servants the Irish, particularly in San Francisco, marshaled themselves to oppose this infringement. Led by an immigrant from Cork, Dennis Kearney, a massive anti-Chinese movement focused directly on the peril to women's employment, and as the crowds gathered they unfurled banners reading, "Our Women Are Degraded by Coolie Labor." Whether or not the Chinese newcomers really undermined the earnings of Irish women was less important than Irish male labor leaders, like Kearney or Frank Roney, recognizing how essential it was that Irish women hold onto their hegemony in the domestic marketplace. (Kearney turned his attention after the anti-Chinese agitation to running an employment bureau for Irish servant girls.)[42]

Domestic service provided the core of Irish female employment. It supplied the destinations to which millions of young Irish women went, choosing by themselves, and along female chains of family and friends, to leave Ireland and come to America. Irish women took these jobs for economic reasons and because the nature of the work did not jar their cultural patterns or the values they cherished. Most American women stressed that they objected to domestic work because it isolated them and denied them a meaningful social life that might lead to marriage. This objection, however, would not have struck a very responsive chord in Irish women, who were accustomed to functioning in a world where men and women shared few if any activities and matrimony was not the major objective. Similarly, though they might have felt isolated, tucked away in Protestant neighborhoods, they usually worked in the company of other servants, mostly other Irish women, with whom they could share both memories and aspirations. Although Irish women lived apart from their communities they continued to participate in church and church-related projects.[43]

The job itself was difficult. Servants, particularly live-in servants, as were most Irish immigrant women, lived at the beck-and-call of their employers. Employers had access to servants and could demand that they cook, clean, dust, iron, launder, scrub, and mind children around the clock. There was no standard since middle- and upper-class homes varied widely in terms of size, number of family members, amount of entertainment, and the like. All of these factors influenced the routine and schedule of chores for a servant.

Employers also differed widely as to pay, and the flexibility of wages in domestic service meant that servants could exercise some control over what they earned. An Irish girl, brought over by her sister, a domestic, was advised, "'Don't ax a penny more than you're worth. But know your own vally and ax that.'" Furthermore, Irish women, although unschooled and often illiterate, recognized that what they had to offer was highly sought after by Americans and that they had basically no competition. Therefore, they could take a role in setting the terms of their labor, quitting a job when it did not conform to their needs or their standards. James Michael Curley, a son of Irish immigrants, chuckled over the story of "the Back Bay maid who served a Thanksgiving turkey with one leg missing. Fired when she explained that she gave it to the cop on the beat, she picked the turkey up by the other leg and threw it at the dowager who had called her a 'dirty Irish pig.' 'I'm not fired,' she said, 'I quit.'" Less dramatically, Irish women served notice if they were not permitted to attend church or if they were forbidden to socialize during off-hours. Irish women rarely were willing to work in small towns where they had no Irish Catholic community to return to on their day off and where they would indeed be isolated. Similarly, they had come to America from such extreme poverty and their first-hand acquaintance with abject destitution was such that the room they had to themselves in their employer's house and the food that they could eat without fearing starvation made the jobs all the more attractive. Finally, by taking domestic service they avoided the quandary that plagued many other immigrant communities, where immigrant men and women, brothers and sisters competed for the same jobs. Irish women therefore could never be blamed by their men for depressing wages.[44]

While economic considerations as expressed through Irish values loomed largest in explaining why Irish women willingly and eagerly took what others rejected, one final factor must indeed be considered. Irish women had come to America as permanent immigrants. They knew that there was no going back to their beloved Ireland. They had to come to terms with their new home. Certainly, they had to begin immediately the process of acculturation on their own terms and domestic service provided perhaps the most intimate glimpse of what middle-class America was really like. Throughout the literature on Irish America the domestic servant emerges as the civilizer of the Hibernians in their new home. The servant girls in novels, sermons, and sociological studies provided the model to which the Irish were aspiring. They were the ones who set the tone that the immigrants were to emulate.

Robert Woods and Albert Kennedy, for example, asserted that among the Boston Irish, the young women who had been in domestic service were responsible for bringing "the family into larger and better quarters and add[ed] up-to-datedness in furniture."[45] From the kitchens and the parlors of Protestant homes Irish women were exposed to the "modern" world much more rapidly than were their sisters who, by necessity, labored in the factories or their brothers, married or single, who heaved their picks and shovels on construction crews. The American homes provided a school for the Irish women, a school where they could learn lessons that they would then pass on to their daughters, who might therefore be spared the necessity of being a Bridget.

With the economic orientation of the migration and the assertive determination of Irish women to actualize their goals, Irish women did experience a steady movement out of the ranks of domestic service into white-collar and semiprofessional positions. The persistence of Irish marriage patterns, highlighted by late and reluctant marriage, meant that Irish women could take advantage of opportunities in fields like teaching and nursing which essentially required that women choose between job or matrimony. Irish women often chose the former and as such demonstrated a fairly rapid rate of mobility. Sociologist E. A. Ross in the first decade of the twentieth century found the economic-professional rise of Irish women quite striking as he calculated, "Of the first generation of Irish, fifty-four percent are servants and waitresses; of the second generation, only sixteen percent. Whither have these daughters gone? Out of the kitchen into the factory, the store, the office, and the school."[46] Similarly, Rheta Childe Dorr and William Hard in 1909 surveyed factory employment for women and were struck by the paucity of Irish females. A Chicago labor leader observed that factory owners "can't get Irish-American girls any longer. . . . The girls of Irish descent are working, but they aren't working in factories."[47] Instead, they were streaming into offices as secretaries, typists, bookkeepers, and stenographers trained in both the public and Catholic schools to assume these cleaner jobs, which clearly carried with them greater status and higher pay. By the 1920s one survey of ethnicity and occupational stratification in Buffalo not only asserted that Irish women had done comparatively better in moving upward on the job ladder than had Irish men but "indeed the Irish women have a distinctly higher probability of becoming both ordinary and high grade office workers than the Native White Americans."[48]

Other Irish women of the first American-born generation gravitated toward nursing as a career. According to the 1880 Census, for example, nursing was the only profession for men or women which opened up for the Irish. In a variety of Boston medical facilities in the 1880s almost the entire nursing staff bore Hibernian surnames. The vast majority of students who enrolled in Boston Lying-In Hospital and Infirmary for Women and Children's course had either been born in Ireland or were first-generation Irish-Americans. Biographies of Irish-American women similarly demonstrated how common a career nursing was for them. For example, Margaret Sanger and one of her sisters were nurses. Ellen O'Keefe had immigrated to the United States and began working in a shoe factory in Lynn but very quickly gave that up to enroll in Bellevue's nursing training program. After having worked for decades as a registered nurse, she consecrated herself to a religious life.[49]

Numerous Irish-American women entered other prestigious occupations. Actresses and other theater personnel were highly visible examples of successful Irish women.[50] Female novelists, poets, and essayists dotted the Celtic-American literary landscape and individuals like Louise Imogene Guiney, Lola Ridge, Eleanor Cecilia Donnelly, Mary Anne Sadlier, Lelia Hardin Bugg, Rosa Mulholland, and Mary E. Blake combined Catholic piety, Irish nationalism, and late-Victorian sentimentality to produce many volumes, some of which sold widely in the Irish-American communities.[51] Similarly, a number of women of Irish birth or Irish descent made their mark in late-nineteenth-century journalism. Most of them, like Katharine Conway, Irene Kennedy, and Katherine O'Keefe, operated within the realm of Catholic publications, yet others established active careers in the general press in a number of cities.[52] Finally, in a number of other areas—charity work, librarianship, prison reform, medicine—Irish women demonstrated that they could succeed in the mainstream American competition for jobs. These women offered some degree of proof that the economic and occupational aspirations of the emigrating generation had been fulfilled—at least in part.[53]

The same assertiveness in the marketplace which had taken some Irish women from domestic service into office work, from factory to hospital, also helped others launch careers as entrepreneurs of various sorts. Even among the poorest Irish in Ireland and in the far-flung Irish settlements around the world hawking and peddling goods, such as fruit and vegetables and clothing, was the domain of women. The female peddler occupied a very important social rank in the Irish communities that were so poor that they could support very little in the way of small business. One such Irish woman, "Aunt" Arlie McVane, appeared daily selling sweets to the shipyard workers in New York. Married women with children could engage in this endeavor, as could widows, and some used their huckstering as a base for setting up grocery stores and other kinds of small shops. In New Orleans Margaret Haughery, an orphan in childhood and a widow in adulthood, established her reputation by selling milk in the streets. She saved enough money from this to set herself up in a bakery that eventually employed forty men and became the largest bakery in New Orleans. So successful was this former peddler that she emerged as the major philanthropist of Irish New Orleans and died in 1882 a very wealthy woman.[54]

Many Irish women, married and widowed, ran boarding houses as a means of support. Married Irish women could do so as well as sew on contract or help out in other kinds of family enterprise. The mother of Archbishop Williams of Boston had immigrated to the United States as a single woman and after marriage managed a boarding house while her husband worked as a blacksmith. When he died she ran both the boarding house and a grocery store in order to underwrite her son's education. Some of the Irish boarding houses run by women also expanded into hotels and restaurants.[55] Irish women also set up dressmaking shops, millinery shops, grocery stores, book stores, and even breweries and liquor stores.

Of all the possible paths that Irish women chose for self-support in the second generation, schoolteaching was the most important and certainly most popular. Schoolteaching for the second generation was what domestic service had been for the first. Like domestic service it tended to be steady work, untouched by the vagaries of the business cycle. Like domestics, female schoolteachers were expected and, in fact, often legally required, to remain single while they worked, a requirement that generally seemed not to have bothered these women who came from a culture that endorsed the notion of late marriage. The attraction of Irish women for schoolteaching grew out of the economic security such work provided. It also drew from the Irish strength in urban politics. Since public schools were part of any city's political apparatus, often controlled by the Irish during the last decades of the nineteenth century, it followed almost naturally that Irish stock women had easy access to these jobs. Political connections and acumen proved to be important assets for public schoolteachers, and as members of the Irish communities, women could expect this. When "Big" Tim Sullivan was growing up poor in New York's Bowery, he could not attend school because he had no shoes. His teacher, a Miss Murphy, however, "knew how to assist a poor boy promptly and without red tape. She took him around to Tammany District Leader Brennan, and when Tim went home that night he was wearing the first new pair of shoes he ever owned." Not surprisingly, Tim grew up to be district leader himself.[56]

Irish communal leaders as well as policy makers in the various Catholic dioceses recognized how important a role teaching played in the lives of Irish women. Parishes and dioceses introduced high school departments in their parochial schools precisely to prepare young women to enter normal schools, the standard route to a public schoolteaching career. Just as moral guidebooks for Catholic women addressed the particular problems of the women who served, as early as the 1870s special note was taken in the pious literature of schoolteachers, "the daughters of the people . . . Defenseless young women, who have spent all their years since early girlhood in fitting themselves for this important function." Many of the early supporters of Catholic college education for women justified such a radical proposal on the grounds that "a good college education is now a necessity to all our women who must provide for themselves and who would rise above the rank of clerks and domestic servants." Importantly, the ongoing debate within the Catholic church over the benefits of parochial, as opposed to public, education took on a new dimension when vast numbers of teachers in most urban public schools stemmed from the Irish Catholic communities. Many church leaders had asserted that the public schools represented Protestantism or godlessness, but this position became harder to maintain when "thousands of Catholic girls . . . had graduated from being pupils of public school into becoming teachers, and reflect credit alike on the race that produced them, the church to which they belong, and the country which afforded them and their Irish-Catholic parents the splendid opportunities which culminated in their education."[57]

It is no wonder that community leaders and institutions began to recognize the growing importance of public schoolteaching in the lives of Irish women. In city after city Irish women rushed into teaching. As early as 1870, twenty percent of all schoolteachers in New York City were Irish women, and since most were assigned to the heavily Irish neighborhoods, by 1890 Irish females comprised two-thirds of those in the Sixth Ward schools. In the first decade of the twentieth century, daughters of Irish parents made up the largest group of schoolteachers in New York City, with over two thousand out of a total teaching population of seven thousand women.[58] Similar strength demonstrated itself in Chicago, in San Francisco, in Albany, in various parts of Massachusetts—essentially, every place the Irish lived. Therefore, in 1908 American-born daughters of Irish parents made up 26.2 percent of all teachers in Buffalo, 26.4 percent in Fall River, 49.6 percent in Worcester, 29.9 percent in Lowell, 31.3 percent in Meriden, Connecticut, 24.0 percent in Providence, 38 percent in Scranton, Pennsylvania, and 15.5 percent in New Orleans. One study of a small industrial town in New England in the 1920s went so far as to assert that "with the exception of one young woman who is straight Yankee, all the teachers in the grammar school today, including the principal come from this [Irish] immigrant stock."[59]

E. A. Ross, who by the early twentieth century had come to celebrate the Irish as "good" immigrants, found everything about Irish women impressive, particularly their strong sense of self and their economic assertiveness. When he came to portraying Irish-American female schoolteachers in a number of popularized sociological works he seemed unable to contain himself. Irish girls, whom he saw as "swift climbers" in the public school bureaucracies, not only outnumbered women of every other group, but, he believed, made better teachers; he quoted "a city school superintendent" who confided to Ross that "'of two applicants . . . I take the teacher with an Irish name because she will have less trouble in discipline, and hits it off better with the parents and the neighborhood.'"[60] Whatever the veracity of this anecdote, Irish women in a number of places did, in fact, experience a certain amount of discrimination as they sought to enter and dominate the profession. During any number of anti-Catholic outbursts, Irish schoolteachers appeared as particularly appropriate targets, since nativists feared that these Catholic women operated directly on papal orders to undermine American religious tolerance. Incidents in a variety of places found Protestant-dominated school boards offering higher pay to Protestant teachers or directly resorting to the hackneyed "No Irish Need Apply." Thomas Beer related in his study of the 1890s that in a town "not far from Ralph Waldo Emerson's grave," a young Irish woman "had to take an oath that she was a Unitarian in order to teach. Returning from this humiliation to her lodging, she found a gang of Christian women rifling her trunk in search of a nun's veil or penitential emblems."[61] Despite what in the end amounted to minor, last-ditch efforts at holding back the floods, Irish women eagerly took work in public schools.[62]

The histories of Irish-American communities and the biographies of Irish Americans abound with references and descriptions of schoolteachers just as they abound with portraits of domestic servants and poor widows. While most Irish schoolteachers lived out their work lives in the classroom, year after year, some used public schoolteaching as a jumping off to other endeavors. Mother Jones was a schoolteacher before she became a labor activist. Myra Kelly, Eleanor Cecilia Donnelly, and Katherine O'Keefe moved from schoolteaching to literary-journalistic pursuits. Sister Leo Tracy, founder of the College of St. Theresa in Minnesota, taught school for four years, earning enough money to pay off the mortgage of the family farm. With her goal realized, she then entered the community of St. Francis. Irish-American women like Kate Kennedy, Margaret Haley, and Catharine Goggins who started out in the teaching profession left the classroom in order to organize teachers, while Kate Barnard, the "Good Angel" of Oklahoma, discovered in the public schools where she taught a first step in a life devoted to social reform.[63]

Schoolteaching, domestic service, factory work of various kinds, clerical occupations, and nursing all provided Irish women with sources of livelihood. Their move to America had been a migration for jobs. They had been reared in a culture that defined the worth of women in highly economic terms, and as such women often had to choose between economic aspirations and marriage. Within the marketplace Irish culture allowed women to be assertive and, if need be, to defy Victorian standards of respectable feminine behavior. This aggressiveness can help explain the extremely active involvement of Irish

Women delegates to the 1886 Knights of Labor Convention. Elizabeth Rodgers, an Irish immigrant, is seated in the middle holding the baby. (*Courtesy of the Library of Congress*)

"Mother Jones" (Mary Harris Jones) celebrating her one-hundredth birthday. Mother Jones emigrated from Ireland as a young girl. (*Courtesy of the Library of Congress*)

women in the American labor movement. Irish women provided much of the female trade union leadership in the last half of the nineteenth century.

Irish men also had a strong commitment to unionization and were well represented in the ranks of late-nineteenth- and twentieth-century organized labor. Irish men, however, differed less when measured against other male workers, native-born and foreign, than Irish women did. The real enthusiasm and involvement of women deviated sharply from that of most employed women. Kate Mullaney, who successfully organized the collar laundresses in Troy, New York, in the 1860s, for example, demonstrated that despite what male trade unionists might say, unskilled women could marshal themselves to put concerted pressure on their employer.[64] Leonora Barry, an immigrant from County Cork, found herself widowed at age thirty-two with two small children to support. The work she took in a New York State hosiery mill convinced her of the need for united worker action to upgrade starvation wages, and she joined up with the Knights of Labor. Barry eventually became a full-time organizer for the Knights, traveling around the country attempting to stimulate consciousness among women workers.[65] Augusta Lewis, whose parents had migrated to the United States from Ireland, was active in trade union work with women printers.[66] Mary Kenney O'Sullivan, the first woman organizer for the American Federation of Labor and also a daughter of emigrants from Erin, had begun her years with the labor movement among the women in the bookbinding industry.[67] Leonora O'Reilly, raised by her widowed mother, began work before she even entered her teens. Her mother, an active Knight of Labor, brought her into the world of trade unionism almost simultaneously with her introduction to the world of work. First Leonora served as an organizer for the United Garment Workers of America and later helped found the Women's Trade Union League and participated in numerous reform activities designed to ameliorate the economic status of working people.[68] Another Irish woman who participated actively in the Knights was Elizabeth Flynn Rogers, the mother of eight children, who held the highest ranking post of any woman in the Knights. In 1886 she served as a master workman of District Assembly 24, whose constituents included all Knights in Chicago and its surburbs.[69] Among glove workers Agnes Nestor emerged as a prominent unionist and her influence and reputation for assertively advancing the goals of the union extended beyond Chicago to a national sphere.[70]

All of these women engaged in what late-nineteenth-century America considered to be less than respectable behavior for women. Yet they and leaders of the movement to unionize public schoolteachers – Kate Kennedy in San Francisco, Margaret Haley and Catherine Goggins in Chicago – in essence ignored this particular social convention because it interfered with their quest for economic security.[71]

Irish-American women in all sorts of occupations agreed with this refusal to appear passive and pliant when it came to wages and work. Women of Irish origin in shoemaking, printing, meat packing, garment-making, and textile manufacture, waitresses in restaurants and operatives in steam laundries, bookbinders and button workers, retail clerks and telephone operators—all seemed willing to risk public disapproval and disdain in order to secure their economic lives.[72] The dedication of thousands of Irish women across the country to trade unionism was eloquently summarized by Leonora O'Reilly, herself so ardent in her commitment, as she described a young woman, Margaret Hinchey, who in 1913 was arrested and imprisoned during a strike action of the Panama Hat Workers:

> Margaret Hinchey is a young Irish woman, clean of thought, pure of heart, brave as truth itself. She understands that economic justice for the workers must come through the organization of labor. When the laundry workers of New York struck against inhuman conditions she threw up her position as forewoman saying "Good God no one could be so mean as to go to work in a laundry now!" Her first strike taught her that the workers have to fight the courts as well as the employers if they want justice. When she found herself blacklisted she came to the Women's Trade Union League saying "Use me in any way you can for the good of the cause . . ." Since then her strength her courage and big heart have been at the service of every group of girls struggling for the right to live and enjoy life.[73]

Agnes Nestor. Nestor, born in Ireland, was president of the International Gloveworkers'
Union. (*Courtesy of the Library of Congress*)

While a handful of Irish women crossed over from trade unionism to a
more radical economic analysis, like Populist Mary Lease or Mother Jones or
Elizabeth Gurley Flynn of the I.W.W. and then the American Communist
Party, the vast majority viewed their trade unionism instrumentally. They
worked because women worked if they did not marry. If trade unionism
improved their earning power, then the social stigma that it carried mattered
very little.

Irish women and men used different standards by which to measure
acceptable female behavior than did men and women produced by the Protestant American culture of the nineteenth century. Since the dictates of the
Irish world view judged the worth of a woman in part by her economic
prowess, then activities like trade unionism fit into a perfectly acceptable
pattern. Likewise, domestic service did not stigmatize the young woman who
spent the years before marriage tending someone else's home, and the money
she earned as a result of those long days cooking and cleaning compensated
for whatever degradation she might have felt. Irish men certainly valued the
economic activities of their women. Since the culture de-emphasized the
romantic aspects of male-female relations, the money a woman brought into

saving their money

marriage may have been a more important asset than good looks, a charming personality, or whatever other "ephemeral" characteristics went into romantic attraction. A small item in the *Irish World* in 1873 neatly summarized the importance of a woman's money as it told of one Maggie O'Brien, a dining room attendant at Donovan's Hotel in Omaha. Her aunt willed her a fortune, estimated between $25,000 and $50,000. "Miss Maggie has suddenly grown as beautiful as she is rich."[74]

The relative success of Irish women in their pursuit of economic security emerged in a variety of sources. They saved enough money to expend their resources for charitable causes and for family support networks. They also used it for themselves. Many saved money from domestic service so that when they married they could bring a sizable sum into their new home.[75] Others continued to eschew marriage yet saved and invested their money, sometimes buying land and, upon death, leaving significant estates. For example, in the Irish enclave of Dubuque, Iowa, in the 1860s the single largest property owner was a servant woman, Ellen Sullivan, who died at age thirty-five, leaving over $50,000 in property. In Detroit in the 1880s, Mary Doyle, a serving girl who earned a meager $2.50 a week, bought two lots on Woodward Avenue, preferring real estate to a savings bank.[76] The representative of the steamship and railway interests in Massachusetts testified to an 1871 Committee of State Charities in favor of "Freedom of Immigration at the Port of Boston." He cited this example of an Irish woman, his own servant:

> She is employed as a cook; not the ignorant cook of former days, but intelligent and skillful, one who regulates the economy of the family and contributes to our comfort. . . . At the end of a year she has received $260, and her maintenance. She is able to place $200 in the savings bank. At the end of five years she has a thousand dollars. Is not that woman worth a thousand dollars to the country, who can accumulate in the course of four or five years a thousand dollars? One or two days before I came to this hearing I was waited upon by a woman who had once been at service in my own family; who had been induced by me to purchase a house with her wages, and to live in it, keeping one room for herself and collecting rent from the remainder. She was able in a few years to pay for the entire estate, and she came with $6,000 to make a new investment in real estate.[77]

Given the large number of employed Irish females, their sharply tuned economic sense of self, and their generally successful movement from unskilled and domestic work into white-collar and professional occupations it is striking how almost universally historians have ignored them. This lack of attention is all the more surprising in light of the recent literature on comparative ethnic mobility in nineteenth-century America. Studies of economic successes and failures in Springfield, Newburyport, Waltham, and Boston, Massachusetts, as well as Buffalo and Kingston, New York, South Bend, Indiana, and elsewhere have all measured Irish rates against those of other immigrants and against

Mary Kenney O'Sullivan and three of her children. O'Sullivan, an Irish immigrant, was the first woman organizer for the American Federation of Labor. (*By permission of the Schlesinger Library, Radcliffe College*)

native-born Americans. Significantly, however, none of these studies has included the earnings of women; nor have they been able to consider the contribution women made to the material well-being of their families and their communities. Generally, the Irish have emerged from these studies as not only the poorest group initially but as having the most sluggish rate of movement out of the lower ranges of income, property holding, and occupational status. Had these historians analyzed female employment and wealth acquisition both in terms of aggregate group statistics or of comparison of Irish women with women in other groups, a different picture might indeed have developed.[78]

Irish women took their years in the labor force quite seriously. They viewed work as a way to secure personal goals and aspired to do better. Furthermore, judging from the millions of dollars that Irish women earned and sent to families in Ireland or that they contributed to the Catholic church and its various charitable projects, it would seem that not including Irish women's economic products into a study of comparative mobility renders the terms of those studies quite limited. Similarly, the ardent activism of Irish women in trade unionism in order to improve their wage-earning potential also indicates the centrality of work to their lives.

To further blur the employment picture of Irish women, the literature on the history of women and work, written primarily although not exclusively by women historians, has first and foremost sought to demonstrate the hurdles and obstacles endured by women as they sought admission to the professions and to the most lucrative forms of employment. As a result, the immigrant woman who did not aspire to be a doctor, who did not consider the possibility of a career in law, somehow emerged as a failure, due to the inherent sex discrimination in the market place. Yet within the contours of Irish female aspirations, viewed from their own perspective rather than from the professional, native-born, Protestant vantage point, a surprising pattern of fulfilled aspirations and job mobility appears. For some Irish women, in fact, the swift current of upward movement from domestic work to office work to nursing or schoolteaching in their own lives can be demonstrated. For the masses of Irish women mobility needs to be viewed across generational lines, and the mother who worked as a domestic or who held down a job in a textile mill before marriage might indeed have seen her daughter teach school.

For those Irish women who could take advantage of the opportunities in America, opportunities undreamed of in the small towns of Ireland, migration meant a tremendous improvement in income and status. The economic goals of migration could be fulfilled in the kitchens and parlors, shops, schoolrooms, and hospital wards of nineteenth- and twentieth-century America. To seize those chances women had to continue behaving in Irish ways and eschew marriage altogether or put off the decision for years. If the hundreds of thousands of single Irish women who earned and saved bore witness to the possibilities of success, the legions of widows and deserted women who lived in abject poverty and could not share in the bounty of American life underscored the differences between the married and single state.

FIVE  The Darker Side
of Migration: Social
Problems of Irish
Women

I have seen women—aye women—wives and mothers, in all the horrors of a
miserable intoxication. Oh what a ghastly spectacle it is to see a woman, whom
God ordained to be all that is noble and beautiful, under the powerful influence
of strong drink; to see a woman who was once pure and spotless as the snow . . .
suffering all the misery and degradation of sin and ruin arising from the use of
ardent spirits.
  "An Irish-American's Views"

The successes and fulfilled aspirations that many Irish women experienced, particularly those who remained single into their thirties or even
beyond, contrasted sharply with the plight of Irish women, abandoned and
widowed, orphaned and abused, who could not take advantage of the opportunities of American life. For some Irish women the lives of poverty they
had to endure in the teeming American slums demonstrated the differences
between being married and remaining single. The grim statistics on Irish
female crime, alcoholism, dependence on charity, and mental illness indicate
what marriage might hold in store for those who acted improvidently or for
the children of the poor. Importantly, the kinds of problems, the types of
"pathology," that engulfed Irish women grew out of Irish culture just as surely
as did their work patterns, their political behavior, or their family relations.
When Irish women deviated they did so by excess drinking or by engaging in
petty crimes, but they rarely indulged in sexual immorality. Few Irish women,
no matter how overwhelmed by the circumstances of life, crossed that line.
These patterns did not change markedly across the last half of the nineteenth

106

century, although with the middle-class status in postimmigrant generations, the intensity of the problem diminished.

Urban life favored the young women who could go off as domestics and live with employers. The problems endured by married women and widows may, in fact, have deterred single colleens from plunging into matrimony. They would have known those women who came married with children, those who arrived as burdened widows, for whom life in America was circumscribed by the poverty of slums and tenements. Whether the Irish female immigrant settled in New York or Boston or made her way to inland cities like Pittsburgh or Chicago, if she could not go into service because of family responsibilities, she entered the American economy at the very bottom, swelling the ranks of the poor and the destitute. The Irish arrived poor, poorer than other immigrants who came at the same time. Their overwhelming peasant background equipped them for only the most menial of work that commanded the most paltry of wages. The clearly articulated anti-Catholic, anti-Irish hysteria that swept America over and over again in the nineteenth century compounded their misery and constricted their chances for job mobility.

Almost all surveys of charity recipients and of almshouse residents, of inmates in the workhouses and occupants of the dilapidated shantytowns, indicate that Irish women—widowed, deserted, or married to poor men—were overrepresented among the needy. The single woman appeared less often in distress. Married and widowed Irish women far outnumbered all others in the annual reports of the various charity organizations from the 1850s through the century's end, and in some years natives of the Emerald Isle accounted for over 60 percent of all the inmates of the New York City almshouse. Even during the twentieth century they showed up in charity institutions and in need of relief more frequently even than the newest immigrants, for example, from Italy. Of the 44,950 people who accepted outdoor relief from the New York Association for Improving the Condition of the Poor between 1854 and 1860 a staggering 69 percent had been born in Ireland, whereas German immigrants accounted for a mere 10.8 percent of the total. Between 1879 and 1889, the Irish in Pittsburgh accounted for 35.4 percent of all charity recipients, as opposed to the Germans, who comprised 13.0 percent of the needy. In the ten years between 1885 and 1895, the Irish of New York furnished 60.4 percent of all almshouse residents, causing one statistician to speculate that "if all the inhabitants of the city were Irish-born, they would require eight such almshouses as the one now maintained for the whole city . . . Ireland does not make a great show on the map, but her existence is absolutely necessary in order to maintain in New York an almshouse of the present magnitude." According to a 1901 U.S. government report, the Irish had the highest ratio of inmates in all penal and charitable institutions in the country. Even in places where relatively few Irish had gone, like Indiana, this trend persisted; among incarcerated Hoosiers in 1902, forty-eight had been born in Ireland, twenty-seven in Germany, and seven in England. On a national scale, in 1910 sociologist Edith Abbott computed that among Americans of Irish birth, 1,048.5 paupers were found for every 100,000 population. Natives of Switzerland were the closest rivals, making up 410.9 per 100,000. Although the numbers might be skewed by the possibility that other immigrant communities provided relief to their own more extensively than did the Irish, Hibernians still encountered a deep and pervasive poverty in the United States.[1]

Irish women bore the burden of poverty, since the legions of widows with children and deserted wives without support helped create this lopsided overrepresentation of the Irish among the poor. The single woman really had no need to be destitute since domestic work could be had and she had no reason to refuse such work. No children kept her from living with an employer and no cultural barriers caused her to find such work demeaning. For a woman with children more limited options constricted her. She needed to earn enough to support her children and she needed a job where she could live with them. She most likely possessed no marketable skills other than sewing, and the fierce competition among needle women in the 1860s and 1870s had driven wages down below the point of sustenance.

The voluminous records of public and private charity societies indicate that Irish women, almost all of whom were supporting children by themselves, as a result of either abandonment or widowhood, accounted for the largest percentage of cases. In 1854 the New York Association for Improving the Condition of the Poor, for example, published the names of all individuals and families who had been aided by the association for three or more years. In the First District, 48 such entries bore Hibernian names. Three were men. Six were couples. The rest, 39 women, had been charity recipients for four or five years. In January 1877, 1,041 individuals applied for relief from this association. Eight hundred and eighteen of these were women, 658 of whom had been born in Ireland. Furthermore, of the 29 married women with children who received support from the Boston Children's Association in 1875, 15 were of Irish birth, while on the other side of the continent, in San Francisco, 59.2 percent of all females admitted to the almshouse in the years from 1860 to 1894 hailed from Ireland. The vast majority of these had been widowed, and Irish women far outnumbered Irish men who had also been driven to the point of desperation of living in a public almshouse.[2]

Even before the Famine migration, travelers and social commentators noted the desperate plight of destitute Irish women. Typically, Matthew Carey described in his *Essays on Public Charities* "a room in Shippen Street where the McGiffies lived, which contained no furniture, but a miserable bed, covered with a pair of ragged blankets. Three small chunks lay on the hearth. ... The occupant, a woman far too slenderly clad had two children, one about five years old, the other about fifteen months. Both were inadequately dressed for the season."[3] No Mr. McGiffie was present. The records of settlement workers in the predominantly Irish neighborhoods like the one served by Denison House in Boston confirmed the depths of destitution of women with children, and even as late as 1893 Emily Greene Balch jotted down a notation that she had seen an Irish "mother and baby die of starvation." Both had been abandoned. A young Irish woman, Eliza Flynn, found herself in 1850 so desperate after the death of her widowed mother that she wrote to Charles P. Daly, a successful Irish-American judge in New York, begging him for money since she now had to support herself and a sick younger sister. She wrote plaintively, "I am now left penniless and almost without resources."[4] Anne Sullivan, who grew up to world renown as the teacher of Helen Keller, endured a childhood of poverty. The details of her life reflected the forces many Irish women experienced. Born to poor immigrant parents, Anne was eight when her mother died, and two years later her father deserted Anne and two siblings. Anne spent a number of years in the Massachusetts State Almshouse in Tewksbury surrounded by dozens and dozens of other Irish females, many of whom brought their children with them into the unbelievable horror of this state institution. Few were lucky enough to leave and most lived out their lives in the stench and dirt of Tewksbury.[5]

Many Irish men and women made their home in yet another nineteenth-century American institution—the insane asylum. Figures on nineteenth-century admission to mental hospitals ought to be read with a degree of skepticism. Americans typically defined individuals with radically different values and behavior patterns as deviants who ought to be isolated from the rest of society. Irish men and women seemed particularly inappropriate by the standards of Yankee Protestants. Despite this cultural bias, the Irish not only found their way to these institutions more often than all other foreign-born individuals, but they entered insane asylums in large numbers every place they lived. In the United States, England, Canada, and in Ireland itself, the Irish up to the present day demonstrate an acute vulnerability to certain kinds of mental disorder, particularly schizophrenia and alcohol-related "insanities." In 1896, for example, one out of three inmates of the New York insane asylum hailed from Ireland. Irish individuals showed up twice as frequently as any other group at the Connecticut Hospital for the Insane from 1868 until 1901, although they comprised only 11.8 percent of the Connecticut general populace.[6]

Irish women contributed heavily to Irish statistics on mental illness. One physician at Blackwell's Island asserted that women from Ireland represented the single largest group there, noting that "'the combined moral and physical influences of their leaving the homes of their childhood, their coming almost destitute to a strange land, and often after great suffering,'" contributed to their· plight.[7] In the 1850s the *Boston Pilot* agreed with this assessment, since the writer believed that women experienced greater hardships as migrants and felt more homesick than did their brothers. In fact, as late as 1908 it was estimated that two-thirds of all Irish insane were women, and even at that late date the Irish made up the largest group of foreign-born in American insane asylums.[8]

That other immigrants had a lower rate than the Irish undermines the notion that mental instability grew directly out of the process of migration. Their high rates of hospitalization for insanity, therefore, cannot stem solely from Irish women moving more frequently than Irish men. Perhaps the ways in which Irish females migrated, without parents and without full community structures, compounded the usual problems. The kinds of jobs women took as domestic servants, living lives severed from their communities, as well as the kinds of marriages that they endured, clouded by poverty, desertion, and widowhood, all further exacerbated emotional problems that psychiatric analysts have discerned in the Irish wherever they live.[9]

In addition to the high rate of mental illness among the Irish newcomers, they generally were unhealthy. Measuring rates and causes of mortality in New York City in 1917, William Guilfoy discovered that Irish females between the ages of twenty-five and forty-four died younger on the average than all other women. Hibernian females forty-five to sixty-four suffered from degenerative diseases more than any other group of women at that age.[10] Significantly, however, Irish women in America lived longer on the average than Irish men. In Ireland women died at an earlier age than men. This reversal may have been due in part to the widespread involvement of Irish women in domestic work. Domestic service posed fewer safety and health problems than millwork or construction work, and living in with one's employer would have taken an Irish woman away from some of the dirtiest, most congested, most disease-ridden sections of any nineteenth-century city and situated her instead in upper- and middle-class neighborhoods.[11] The diet of a servant surpassed that of a mill hand and servants had less chance to imbibe than did Irish men and those women employed in other kinds of jobs.

While domestic work did provide a health benefit for Irish women, it also extracted a social price from those women who never married and spent all their work years in service. For such women illness posed a practical problem and old age presented a real crisis. They had no children or grandchildren to look after them when they could no longer work. They had been cut off from their communities and their support networks. In fact, almost all of the *single* women who inhabited the pauper institutions were elderly domestic servants who could no longer work.[12]

Irish immigrants not only added to the numbers of the chronically poor and mentally ill and provided many of the long-time residents of the state-supported institutions for the indigent, but they furthermore contributed heavily to the statistics on crime in nineteenth-century America. To be sure, figures on criminality, on arrests and convictions, are fraught with inconsistencies and are of questionable validity. Similarly, the lack of partiality on the part of police and courts when dealing with the poor and the immigrants has been well established by both contemporary observers and scholars of criminology and the history of crime. Yet even admitting the shortcomings of the available material, the figures on Irish female criminality indicate that some women lived disorganized lives in their new homes. Thousands of Irish women found themselves in prison in the last half of the nineteenth century. Irish women were arrested and convicted of crimes with much greater frequency than any other group. In Massachusetts in 1881, 336 women born in Ireland served prison sentences, with Canadian women, the next closest group of foreign born female convicts, totaling 71. The only women whose number (442) exceeded that of the Irish had been born in the United States, but many of them, in fact, were the daughters of Irish-born immigrants. Irish-born women served more time in Pennsylvania prisons than even native-born women between 1858 and 1872.[13]

Most observers of the impact of immigration on nineteenth-century American life remarked frequently on the predilection of Irish women toward crime and their excessive appearance as inmates of prisons. John White, a traveler from abroad who toured prisons in America in the 1870s, was struck at Blackwell's Island that "taking a row of cells at random I found that out of twenty female prisoners, no less than seventeen were Irish." Marie Thérèse Blanc in 1895 asserted that in Sherborn Prison for Women in Boston, four-fifths of the prisoners were Irish Catholics, "the only ones who retain any religion; some of them are very pious and partake of the Communion regularly every Sunday."[14] Similarly, American prison reformers and professional criminologists acknowledged the high incidence of Irish female criminality and almost universally chose an Irish woman as their "case study" of the deviant female. The archetype of the woman arrested and convicted for offenses against the public order was the Irish woman, who demonstrated the effects of poverty, drunkenness, and domestic violence which propelled women into lives of crime. Dr. Eliza Mosher chronicled the life of one such Irish woman, "Mary M.," in the *Boston Medical and Surgical Journal* in 1882. Mary M. had been married and had borne nine children, only three of whom survived. Her husband beat her, deserted her off and on, and Mary M. started drinking. She ended up in jail on a drunkenness charge. Almost all of the women that Caroline Woods wrote about in her 1869 narrative of *Women in Prison* bore Irish names and served time as a result of petty theft, drunkenness in public, and domestic violence. The Pauper Institution Trustees of the City of Boston included in its various annual reports family trees of deviance — tracing individuals, almost always with Irish-born mothers and fathers, and their crimes and prison records along to the next generation and its crimes and into yet a third generation, also dominated by poverty and criminality.

In 1899 it chose to document a family with an Irish-born mother who had been sent to Sherborn Reformatory four times and finally died in the almshouse in Charlestown. Her only daughter had served on Deer Island on twenty-six separate charges and had registered into the almshouse twenty-nine times.[15]

Contemporary observers believed that Irish women generally entered their lives of crime as a result of poverty and domestic discord, which drove them to drink. They also believed that the Irish personality, both male and female, tended toward violence because Irish society stressed fighting, aggressiveness, and combatitiveness. According to one turn-of-the-century analyst, they possessed "a tendency to lawlessness, a superabundance of unrestrained Celtic energy that makes for crime." This assessment of the Irish personality and its violent nature was noticed and expounded upon by the British as they sought to control their Irish subjects. It followed the Hibernians as they crossed the Atlantic and persisted well into the twentieth century. A psychological study of Irish children conducted even as late as 1923 noted that "the women as well as the men are great fighters. . . . with hand-to-hand encounters . . . hair-pulling, scratching, biting, tearing of clothes, and smashing of furniture." During the numerous riots in New York City in the last half of the nineteenth century, like the Draft Riot of 1863 or the Orange Riots of 1870 and 1871, Irish women figured into the bloody descriptions of street fighting. During the 1863 riot one reporter commented that the Irish women "ranged . . . their arms filled with reserve ammunition, their keen eyes watching for a break in the enemy's defense, and always ready to lend a hand or a tooth in the fray." (The violence of Irish women, which often brought them into trouble with the authorities and which landed them in jail, also sometimes served the interests of the Irish Catholic communities. In the early years of Irish settlement in a number of New England towns, Irish women physically defended the Catholic church building against the onslaught of an angry Protestant mob.) Obviously, this phsyical aggressiveness proved anathema to middle-class Americans in the nineteenth century, who venerated female passivity.[16]

The Catholic clergy and the Irish press recognized how much Irish women drank. They lamented the problem in maudlin lectures, sermons, and editorials that stressed the almost universal innocence and sobriety of women before migration. American life, they complained, brought women into greater contact with "whiskey, rum, groggeries, and spirit shops." Clergymen and community leaders spared no words in portraying the "saddest pictures . . . [are] when the woman who bears the sacred titles of wife and mother—whom all men respect and honor as the highest human type . . . —forgetting her sacred mission falls from her high place—and to what depths." The bishop of Newark in 1872 told with revulsion how he had been out on a sick call. A woman had asked him to come to a dying friend, and when he got there he found her drunk, as was the woman who had come for him. In a neighboring house he found "*four men and three women drunk!*"[17]

Irish antidrinking tracts blamed poverty for female drinking. They usually coupled this with a call for an Irish exodus from the cities to the rural areas. The clergy in particular almost always blamed men, in their roles of greedy saloon keeper, deserting spouse, faithless seducer, and brutal husband, for women's drunkenness. Men forced their wives and other women to accompany them down the besotten path. Although clerics outrightly condemned drink, they saw the grueling economic realities of the Irish in urban America and the breakdown of traditional Irish male-female gender boundaries as the root problems. In Ireland, where women and men lived such rigidly separate lives, a woman might tipple occasionally; but in America, where village controls seem to have been weakened, female drinking took a quantum leap upward.

That Irish community leaders willingly and openly discussed female drinking indicated how extensive and pervasive a phenomenon it was. Irish clerics naturally were embarassed by this "unladylike" behavior and were acutely uncomfortable with the Protestant American recognition of the problem.

Alcohol addiction did pose a major problem for the female immigrant from Ireland. Irish women, for example, made up 59 percent of all California almshouse inmates in the 1890s but they made up 72 percent of those female paupers who drank in excess—or at least who drank to the point that drunkenness kept them from being able to make a living and function outside the asylum. Yet of all women, regardless of nativity, who inhabited the California almshouses, only 13.4 percent were diagnosed as having a drinking problem. In a range of late-nineteenth-century studies that correlated arrest records with alcoholism and in other studies that examined the national origins of people who died of alcoholism, Irish men led all men and Irish women led all women. While Irish males drank more than did Irish women, Hibernian females in these studies exceeded other women more often than Irish men exceeded other men. In New York City in the six years between 1884 and 1890 3.08 Irish men per thousand died from alcoholism, while a fairly close 1.74 males per thousand from England and Wales and 1.35 per thousand from Germany suffered a similar fate. Yet among women the ethnic division was greater. Irish women died from alcoholism at a rate of 1.16 per thousand, whereas British and Welsh females totaled 0.42 per thousand and German women 0.12 per thousand. One study of Boston in 1890 found that Irish women actually suffered from alcohol-related liver illness more frequently even than Irish men.[18]

Irish women drank in the United States much more heavily and with much more serious consequences for their health than they had in Ireland. Irish men, to be sure, drank to excess more frequently in America, too, but for them it represented a reasonable continuation of a pattern of life funda-

drank more than in Ireland

mental to their culture. The conditions Irish women endured disrupted traditional patterns of authority and social control. Their long hard years of work, the grim realities of slum existence after marriage, the kinds of marriages they experienced fraught with poverty, domestic violence, desertion, and widowhood, all operated to strain the strength of even the hardiest of women. Certainly, not all or even a majority of Irish women were beaten by their husbands or found themselves deserted and needing to support a parcel of young children. Similarly, not all Irish women drank to the point of being a statistic that added to the high rate of Irish female alcoholism. However, a significant number in fact did endure the disorganizing effects of poverty and took to drinking, and the data clearly point to a strong continuity between the middle and end of the nineteenth century.

The kinds of deviant behavior that Irish women demonstrated were culturally acceptable within the Irish world view. Hard drinking among women, though condemned, did not go against the most fundamental elements of the social order. It might have been an embarrassment for a woman to be publicly intoxicated, but it did not violate those taboos that kept the social machine in gear. However severe their drinking problem, Irish women rarely crossed the line when it came to sexual deviance. In Ireland, illegitimacy was virtually unknown and prostitution extremely rare. In America, despite the breakdown of the tight control of sexual morality that dominated Irish village life, Irish men and women retained much of the sexual behavior they had exhibited in the homeland.[19]

Certainly, changes occurred and the almost universal adherence to sex segregation which typified Irish social life could not survive totally unaltered in the American city. Young men and women enjoyed much greater freedom of movement in America than they had in the traditional setting, and more institutions flourished where men and women could mingle freely in Boston or New York than in Killarney or Kilkenny. In America, Irish illegitimacy and prostitution did increase modestly, but their numbers remained small throughout the nineteenth century and the early twentieth century.

Even the same poverty that, in part, pushed so many Irish women to alcoholism and criminality did not propel a significantly large number into prostitution, as it did for women in other groups. Descriptions of the Irish enclaves portrayed a society still committed to both gender boundaries and sexual prudery, with the parish priest often acting as the primary enforcer. In New York's St. James parish, where Al Smith grew up, Father John Kean was famous for thrusting his head out of the rectory window at precisely nine o'clock, ordering all the boys and girls indoors. According to Smith's sister Mamie, everybody obeyed. Mothers in Irish families also exercised a strong role in the transmitting of Irish sexual values, and in Smith's family, his mother not only forbade him to walk along a certain stretch of Water Street where "hideously painted and bedizened" women plied their trade but went as far as removing from the parlor an ornate document, which proclaimed her husband's membership in a Volunteer Fire Company, because it included a partly clothed Neptune figure on its gilt-edged paper.[20]

The preponderance of Irish women in domestic work further limited the possibility of illicit romance, given how sharply curtailed the servant's hours away from her employer's home were. If anything, the Irish Catholic clergy tended to fear that the young servant girl might be forceably seduced by her Protestant employer or that disreputable employment agencies actually fronted for prostitution rings. This may explain why Irish women went to agencies less often than did other women seeking domestic positions and instead relied on word of mouth, personal contacts, or the bureaus set up by the Sisters of Mercy. Furthermore, given the relatively high wages of domestic service, a servant had less need to enter the streets than did a needle woman or a mill hand. Therefore, in the studies of late-nineteenth-century prostitutes, few had been live-in servants prior to turning to prostitution.

Some nineteenth-century commentators on Irish life did feel that Irish women fell from virtue no less than other women, and some even asserted that Irish women contributed more than their share of sexual deviants. Some of these statements seem to have been based on only the most superficial of observations and tended to link Irish prostitution with general anti-Irish diatribes. For example, George Kibbe Turner's 1909 exposé for *McClure's*, "The Daughters of the Poor," asserted that Ireland, "noted throughout Europe for the chastity of its women," furnished many of New York's prostitutes; he then hooked up prostitution with Irish dominance and control of Tammany Hall politics. British journalist William Stead chose an Irish-American girl, "Maggie Darling," daughter of a drunkard, as his prototypical fallen woman for *If Christ Came to Chicago*, just as he seemed to have chosen mostly Irish characters to represent all the dregs of American life. Finally, a cartoon that appeared in *Harper's Weekly* in 1873 connected a brothel (disguised as a "boarding house for young women") with Catholicism. The holy pictures on the wall indicated that the cartoonist believed that Catholics comprised many of America's prostitutes, and in the 1870s *Catholic* and *Irish* were synonymous in America.[21]

Scattered statistics gathered in a variety of places from the last half of the nineteenth century provide some evidence as to the prevalence of prostitution among Irish women. The classic survey of New York prostitution published in 1859, undertaken by William Sanger, asserted that among the women he sampled, 60 percent were foreign-born, of whom one-half were Irish women who operated in the lowest grade of establishment. Despite Sanger's pretenses of scientific objectivity in his survey, he exhibited his anti-Irish venom by decrying that "because of the lamentable manner in which the Irish have suffered in their own country, we must be taxed in New York for their support in hospitals, Almshouses, prisons of women whose poverty compelled their crime." Importantly, Sanger's was the only large-scale investigation to conclude that many prostitutes had emigrated from Ireland.[22]

The traditional Irish sexual code undoubtedly had weakened somewhat in America. In its annual reports the Boston Children's Services Association divided up the mothers who received aid according to marital status, and throughout the 1870s and 1880s unwed Irish mothers did indeed apply for help. For example, in 1877 twenty-six such colleens in distress sought relief for themselves and their infants, as did ten in 1878 and twelve in 1879. Generally slightly more women described as Irish-American, that is, American-born daughters of Irish immigrants, showed up in these dire straits than did women of the immigrating generation.[23]

Similarly, individual case histories of prostitutes and the memoirs of reformers who crusaded against vice cited the existence of an occasional Irish-born prostitute. Histories of the Irish in particular towns drew attention to some of these "fallen" women, for example, Maria Sullivan, who ran a brothel in Lawrence, and Mary O'Meara, "Bridget Fury," and "Irish Mary," who plied their trade in New Orleans at the same time that they engaged in robbery and other kinds of street crime.[24] More prevalent in much of the native-born, reformist literature are portraits of Irish girls, innocent and naive, who found themselves cruelly seduced and abandoned when pregnant. Typical was the case of "Carrie," described by Louisa Harris, a St. Louis prison matron. Carrie had been born in New York state, the daughter of Irish parents. "She had loved, and it had proved her downfall. As is so often the way, her lover betrayed her confidence in his selfish sensualism, then left her to bear the shame alone." This story underscores once again the generally more positive image of Irish women, even when they deviated. Carrie's lover had been an Irish man. He was to blame while Carrie, the quintessential Irish female, suffered.[25]

Most commentators on Irish America, however—including some of the most virulent anti-Catholic anti-Hibernians as well as most reformers—grudgingly admitted that Irish women "preserve the abstinence from sexual vice which distinguishes them so honorably at home." Charles Loring Brace, who viewed the Irish as perhaps the major blight on nineteenth-century America and who had almost nothing good to say about the Celtic newcomers, their religion, their social patterns, their drinking habits, and their family forms, actually found one thing in their favor. He believed that when it came to sexual purity, Irish girls behaved admirably, particularly when measured against young German women. Brace generally believed that Germans made better Americans, that they were "more honest and hopeful a class than the Irish," but "the young girls, however, coming from a similar low class were weaker in virtue than the Irish." At the other end of the spectrum, in the early twentieth century, E. A. Ross admired the Irish, particularly when he set them against the newer immigrants from Southern and Eastern Europe. He particularly admired the lack of sexual immorality on the part of the women and the men, noting that "rape, pandering, and the white-slave traffic are almost unknown among them." The notorious libertine Frank Harris, who titillated Victorian readers with descriptions of seductions and amorous trysts, admitted that when he tried to turn his charm on Irish women—on both sides of the Atlantic—he failed. He learned "what a terrible weapon the confessional is as used by Irish Catholic priests. To commit a sin is easy . . . to confess it to your priest is for many women an absolute deterrent."[26]

Among the stock attributes of the Irish that dominated nineteenth-century American caricatures and that acted themselves out upon the American stage, sexuality never appeared. As queen of the kitchen, Bridget might have been dirty and disorganized, ignorant and tempestuous, slightly dishonest and strikingly inebriated, but she was always chaste. Likewise, Pat drank and brawled. His simianlike face indicated his degraded level of both civilization and intelligence. Yet sexual abuse of women did not figure into his portrait.

Any number of late-nineteenth- and early-twentieth-century social analysts concerned with sexual problems in America and the prevalence of the "social evil" confirmed these more impressionistic comments on the lack of a real Irish presence among the ranks of sexual deviants. In Jane Addams's discussion of the subject in *A New Conscience and an Ancient Evil* the Irish never appeared. In the New England Female Moral Reform Society reports on prostitutes and other women with sexual problems in Boston no reference to Irish women surfaced in all the years from 1851 to 1868, despite the discussion in the reports of the nativity of the women who were aided. Generally, this antiprostitution, female-help society believed that native-born American girls were most active, saying that "the brothels of Boston are supplied by individuals of our sex from the country."[27]

Furthermore, statistical studies of various sorts underscored this phenomenon. Vice commissions in a number of cities in the 1910s, for example, were particularly interested in the ethnic make-up of prostitution, and in Boston, Philadelphia, and Syracuse few Irish women were included: in Boston in 1909, 3 out of 100 cases appeared; in Philadelphia 5 out of 185; and in Syracuse 1 out of 50.[28]

Slightly higher figures were cited in George Kneeland's 1917 study of 1,106 New York City prostitutes incarcerated in Bedford Reformatory. Ten percent of the foreign-born women had come from Ireland, and the parents of approximately 4.0 percent of the women had emigrated. Of all arrests of Irish females in Chicago between 1905 and 1908 only 1.1 percent were charged with prostitution; the Irish rated lowest of all Chicago ethnic and racial groups among those apprehended for "crimes against chastity." Likewise, in 1908-9 among Irish women serving in Massachusetts penal institutions for sex crimes, a mere 0.1 percent had been born in Ireland and 0.2 percent were the daughters of Irish immigrants.[29]

Irish women and men still emerged relatively innocent concerning sexual behavior in the nineteenth century. Of the 1,182 Irish females and males who served in Suffolk County (Boston) prisons in 1881, only 16 had been convicted on some type of sexual misconduct—adultery, fornication, keeping a house of ill fame, indecent exposure, or polygamy. Similarly, in both Massachusetts and New York fewer Irish men were sent to prison for "crimes against chastity" than any other group of men. In the forty years from 1840 to 1880 the Lowell Irish contributed less to that city's statistics on illegitimacy than did native-born Americans, and of the 15,000 Irish men and women in the City of Spindles in 1845, most of whom were young and single, only 4 found themselves in prison on charges of fornication.[30]

To say the least, Irish community leaders were thrilled to peruse these figures and to hear the praises offered to their women. Bishops and newspaper editors, priests and publicists, found political ammunition not only in the low rates of Irish prostitution (evidence to be set against the other staggering figures on Irish criminality) but in that native-born Americans, Protestants, had to admit that the Irish woman bore a "pre-eminent reputation for purity and honour." Ella McMahon, speaking of her sister emigrants from the "Virgin Isle," admonished her readers to "consult the public records, seek the testimony of facts, question the people among whom they live in America as elsewhere, it will be clearly manifest that weaknesses are almost unknown among them, that vice does not venture to appear." In 1872, for example, the *Irish World* sneered at the "892 unfortunate Protestants—from the Census taken by the police of the fallen women of Chicago, we find that out of 926 unfortunates, 892 were born Protestant, 26 Catholic; while of this 26 only 3 had come from Ireland." Any number of Irish commentators asserted that employers of domestic servants, particularly in hotels and other commercial establishments, sought out Irish girls because they trusted them and knew that if they hired colleens there would be no sexual improprieties.[31]

Yet the more they proclaimed the chastity and honor of their women, the less community institutions felt called upon to offer services of any kind for females. Since the sexual code of behavior played such an important role in the Irish world view and in the Irish sense of self, if their women did not break that code, then their situation could not be so bad and resources need not be expended in their behalf. Alcoholism could be understood. Mental illness could be explained away. Deserted wives could learn to cope. Widows with small children might solve their own problems. All of these social ills were part of life as the Irish understood it, and as such they required little expension of energy and resources. Had Irish female rates of sexual deviance been higher, had Americans generally condemned Irish women for sexual promiscuity, the development of social services for Irish women might have had a very different history.

Immigration to the United States generally raised the status of Irish women and improved the quality of their lives. However, not all women were lucky enough to escape the dangers and pitfalls of uprooting oneself from one's ancestral home and attempting to transplant in a new environment. Some could not make it. Certain Irish women—the alcoholics, the "insane," the widowed and the deserted, the inhabitants of the pauper houses and the workhouses, the recipients of charity, the beggars, and the criminals—illustrated the dark side of Irish-American life, which contrasted with the cheerful servant girl and the aspiring clerk, the successful schoolteacher and the devout, pious Catholic housewife. Their presence in the Irish communities may indeed have served as a clear warning to unmarried women that perhaps they ought not exchange a job in service for a husband.

For those women who could not seize the new opportunities, disarray and disorganization were facts of American life. The kinds of service and the types of resource which they could tap during periods of crisis reflect how the Irish-American communities were structured and indicate the persistence of Irish gender segmentation.

SIX  The Web of Support: Sisters of Service

Some in the struggle for existence in America will escape, their successes will be blazoned forth; those who fail and die, silence will cover them . . . who cares for a few children of the poor more or less—who cares for a few girls more or less, surrendered to infamy . . . ?
Charlotte Smith O'Brien, "The Emigrant in New York"

Without a community of Sisters, no parish, no Catholic community is properly provided for.
John Francis Maguire, *The Irish in America*

In choosing to leave the ancestral villages, with their intricate patterns of kinship support and communal cooperation, the young Irish women who streamed to the American shore in 1850 or in 1900 required new sources of social service. They not only needed to restructure traditional patterns of female support that had sustained women in the old setting during periods of crisis—illness and death, widowhood and old age, childbirth and domestic strife—but the realities of American life confronted them with new problems and new opportunities. The resources provided by the larger American society, by the government, and by private non-Catholic charities could be of no real help because of the cultural barriers that kept the Irish newcomers from using non-Catholic institutions.

Importantly, the traditions of rigid gender boundaries meant that the all-male Irish secular organizations could also not render effective aid to needy women. Even within the Catholic Church, which provided most of the help to the Hibernian newcomers, the male and female spheres were so sharply set

Help from the nuns

off from one another that the only source of real service and sustenance for the widows, the abandoned, and the abused women came from the nuns, most of whom belonged to either Irish orders or orders that attracted many Irish women. The strong emphasis that these religious women gave to economic security as the key to female well-being confirmed the Irish female world view.

Irish women, devout Catholics fiercely committed to their own cultural traditions, could hardly have been expected to take advantage of the charitable resources available in American society. The evangelical Protestant mission that underlay most nineteenth-century charity made these sources of aid unacceptable. The strongly anti-Irish ideology, to which even public institutions subscribed, also made government-sponsored help seem odious to the Irish. With the possible exception of the settlement houses, such as Hull House in Chicago, which consciously sought to minimize the ethnocentric bias of Protestant America, Irish women availed themselves of the various services only when driven to the point of desperation.

Like emigrants from elsewhere, the Irish in the United States actively worked to create an internal community structure of organizations of all kinds—mutual aid and benefit societies, insurance and charitable organizations, temperance lodges, nationalistic societies, fire companies, military units, building and loan associations, "county-based clubs" (what Yiddish-speaking immigrants would later dub "landsmanshaftn"). Irish men, in fact, proved to be among the most ardent organizers of clubs and associations. The process of building a separate Irish community structure replete with organizations had begun well before the great Famine influx. Al Smith, as a young man in New York, actively participated in one such club, the St. James Union, which although part of the parish structure actually operated on a secular level, offering a potpourri of recreational and political activities. Smith recognized the benefit that membership in the union brought him and the other young men, remembering "a strange thing about it was that it became known in the neighborhood, and business, and trades people recruited their employees from the Union because they were sure that the boy was leading the kind of life that met with the approval of the pastor."[1]

The Irish-American press reported extensively on the doings of local and national societies, boasting proudly of new ones while lamenting the demise of others. The press and the Catholic clergy viewed the existence of a well-developed communal network of organizations as a barometer of the health and prosperity of Irish America. Editorials in the press stressed the position that organizations were needed to help fulfill the Irish political mission in the United States and that clubs, societies, and lodges should provide the nucleus for increased Hibernian power in American politics, keeping in mind the pressing goals of national liberation across the sea. The *Irish World* in July 1873 asserted its sense of communities priorities, as it declared:

The Irish American element can lay claim to being thoroughly and efficiently organized in so far as temperance and purposes of mutual aid are concerned. This is a fact to be proud of, for these movements tend to make and keep us compact and strong. But we regret to say that one species of union, and a most essential one, is sadly neglected. We refer to organizations on a military basis. Temperance and benevolence associations are very good as far as they go, but, after all, it is firm ranks and shining weapons that most disarm hostility and win respect. It is a very singular thing that a people, with such martial instincts and such a brilliant record as the Irish, should be so backward in this matter.[2]

In light of the extensive economic suffering of Irish widows and children in the United States, however, as well as the staggering numbers of Irish females who had no alternatives other than the pauper house or the insane asylum, such assertions appear strikingly incongruous.[3]

This is not, however, to say that the members and leaders of the Irish-American societies, all of whom were men, were unconcerned or unmoved by the plight of immigrant Irish women. To be sure, societies did expend resources to help destitute women. Some Irish societies as well as philanthropic Irish on their own devised schemes to help bring Irish women over to the United States, like Vere Foster's Irish Pioneer Emigration Fund, which claimed responsibility for facilitating the passage of fifteen thousand Irish women.[4] In the various port cities, where the ships dumped their human cargo, Irish societies made some effort to assist the newly arrived Irish men and women who often landed with scarce resources, little explicit knowledge of American ways, and a minimum of marketable skills. Individuals like these, women in particular, could be the ideal targets for the tricksters, fleecers, and frauds who infested the ports. In the 1850s the Hibernian Society of New Orleans requested that city officials station two Irish police officers at the notorious dock to stand guard against the procurers who preyed on single Irish women. The society also set up an intelligence office, manned by one Peter Kavanagh, to make sure the young girls circumvented the dishonest employment offices in the city.[5] An Irish society in New York attempted to provide similar services for unprotected women, but even well into the 1860s it never had enough money to really do the job.[6]

Other Irish societies labored to direct immigration girls away from the cities immediately; for example, the Women's Protective Emigration Society of New York in the late 1850s believed that the best service it could provide for the green colleens was to transport them West for their own protection.[7] Yet other organizations directed their efforts at assisting the most destitute and wretched immigrant women on a case by case basis, like the Hibernian Society of Baltimore, which raised money to send women deemed unable to cope with America back to Ireland.[8]

The Irish themselves recognized how feeble these efforts were and acknowledged that other immigrant groups made a better showing when it came to rendering meaningful services to the poor and bewildered new arrivals. In 1871 the Charitable Irish Society of Boston had painfully to admit how far below the other groups it fell, as one member pointed out, "I would also call your attention to the want of a fund to temporarily assist distressed Irishmen arriving in this city. The Scotch, and the British, and Welsh, and other nationalities, have their homes where a poor strange wayfarer can be accommodated . . . but the friendless Son of Erin, has none to shelter or give him food!"[9] Had this unnamed Irish-American ventured to comment on or ponder the extent of services available to the "friendless *Daughter* of Erin" his picture indeed would have been even more grim. Particularly striking in the development of services for Irish female immigrants was that even after the 1860s, when female arrivals began to outnumber males, and even after the clergy in Ireland had begun to raise a great hue and cry about the lack of protection of women, the established Irish societies in the United States paid little heed. Beginning in the late 1870s, Charlotte Smith O'Brien, the daughter of the nationalist patriot William Smith O'Brien, who happened to be Protestant, launched an almost single-handed campaign to provide real services for the streams of arriving women. Not until 1883 could she convince the New York archdiocese to establish a center to greet the incoming females, provide them with shelter, and conduct an employment office to match them up with potential employers. This center, Our Lady of the Rosary, located at 7 State Street, flourished under the directorship of Father John Joseph Riordan and between 1884 and 1894 harbored over fifty thousand young women. The idea of such a center took hold and was actualized just about at the point when the massive Irish influx was slowing down. When O'Brien first began her campaign, the Irish-American press questioned her motives, suggesting that she might be a British agent, and her Protestant religion also made Church officials skeptical.[10]

The extent of the services that Irish women could draw upon when in need did not increase substantially even after establishing themselves in Irish neighborhoods, where women lived as impoverished widows faced with the support of small children. Although it is impossible to ascertain exactly how many Irish men belonged to mutual aid and benefit societies, dozens of such organizations functioned in each city, creating a vast array of benevolent groups that provided some sort of widow and orphan pension program. Organizations such as these, however, tended to be short-lived, so that even knowing how many men had joined would not help in finding out how many of their widows were actually able to avail themselves of this critical service.

The amount of money paid out to survivors varied from association to association. The Limerick Men's Benevolent and Social Association, founded in New York in 1890, paid $75 to the survivors, whereas the Irish Catholic and Benevolent Union in 1878 could pay, on the average, $125 to the bereaved widow. Some of the more well heeled groups might make a separate payment for funeral expenses; others assumed that the widow would cover the cost of the last rites. Undoubtedly, the money a widow might get from any one of the hundreds of such organizations that sprang up in Irish America would be useful to her, but if she still had young children to support, the money could hardly protect her from the need to go out and work or send children into the labor force. Furthermore, a strikingly small number of Irish men actually joined and consistently paid their dues in order to allow their future widows to reap the benefits. The Limerick Association, for example, estimated that even at its height no more than 1 percent of all Limerick men belonged.[11]

Irish communal and Church leaders recognized the paucity of resources a widow could draw upon and understood that even if her husband had faithfully paid his dues to any one of the dozens of societies that existed in the large and medium-sized cities, she still "was compelled to seek for some such employment as washing and scrubbing in order to pay her rent and support her orphan children." Recognizing this, Archbishop Feehan of Chicago in 1883 began planning for a more systematic benefit organization, the Catholic Order of Foresters. Although the C.O.F. proved to be quite popular, it took at least a decade until it had enough members to really begin to account for substantial survivor support.[12] Similarly, the Knights of Columbus, founded in New Haven, Connecticut, in 1882 by Father Michael J. McGivney of St. Mary's Parish, attempted to provide some sort of security to Irish widows based on sound actuarial principles while it also sought to offer men "something more . . . a Catholic social center; a club for the Catholic men, young, middle-aged and old."[13]

These two organizations did offer much more extensive relief than the small, scattered societies, but the late date of their founding reveals much. They did not begin to function until the very end of the nineteenth century. For decades before, poor widows, the deserted, or women whose husbands could not find work existed in poverty while the clubs and lodges seemed unable to address their plight.

Any number of factors can account for this lack of support. For one thing, the tremendous and widespread poverty of the Irish meant that many men did not have enough money to set aside even a few cents a month for membership in a mutual aid society. Although the newness of the urban experience might have required a few decades before the newcomers began to think in terms of support systems necessitated by a new environment, those Irish men who actively participated in formalized voluntary associations tended to be very politically oriented. The associational life they created reflected their concerns about politics both in the United States and back in Ireland. As such, Irish men often appeared less involved in the plodding, mundane concerns of an organization that did not promise to drive out the hated British from Ireland or that did not throw itself into the wheelings and dealings of some urban political machine. Overlaying all these factors, the cultural patterns that put women and women's concerns in one sphere and men and their interests in another inhibited the all-male societies from thinking about women, even sisters, wives, and daughters. The tradition of gender segmentation and the culture of gender animosity that the Irish brought over with them as they set up families in America closely resembling those of Ireland also fed into a community structure that separated men and women and kept them from seeing each other's plight as part of their own. Irish men in their American homes did keep alive a tradition of sociability and as enthusiastic joiners, they created a vast array of clubs and societies, lodges and groups. Yet their world view and their own sense of priorities fashioned a web of voluntary associations that did not place the problems of women high on the agenda.[14]

If Irish women could not turn to the established organizations in their communities for assistance in illness or poverty, where could they go? Naturally, informal networks provided a tremendous amount of assistance to individuals. Descriptions offered by social workers and other commentators noted repeatedly the tendency of the Irish to assist kin. E. A. Ross saw a connection between the fact that the Irish "are free givers, and no people are more ready to take into the family the orphans of relatives" with their generally sluggish rate of economic progress, citing "a Catholic educator" who "accounts for the scarcity of Irish millionaires by declaring that his people are too generous to accumulate great fortunes."[15] In the Irish enclaves few single individuals lived alone or found themselves isolated in rooming houses; instead, unmarried Irish "young" men and women lived with family.[16] Biographies of "famous" Irish-Americans stress the sacrifices that brothers and sisters, in particular, made for each other as they learned to cope with American life.[17]

Yet some problems were too great and some families were too poor to provide the assistance that would make a real difference. If Irish women could not turn to the men's organizations for sources of support because of traditional gender barriers, they could rarely turn to all-female Irish societies, because for all practical purposes, such groups did not exist. A literal handful of beneficial societies of Irish Catholic women, such as the St. Mary's Mutual Aid Society in Brattleboro, Vermont, or the Catholic Female Beneficial Society of Philadelphia, provided sickness benefits for a small number of women members.[18] Toward the nineteenth century's close some of the nationally based male Irish Catholic organizations began to authorize the formation of female auxiliaries, which allowed women members to reap certain sickness and death benefits. The C.O.F. established such female units in the 1890s and Elizabeth Flynn Rogers, who had been active in the Knights of Labor in Chicago, assumed a major position in this all-female benefit society. The Women's C.O.F. was organized into "courts," each of which had twenty members, to whom specific tasks had been assigned. Margaret Haley, pioneer organizer of public schoolteachers, belonged, as did her mother and widowed sister. Although Haley disliked Rogers and opposed her political control of the organization she believed that such societies for women played crucial roles in both their economic and social lives. According to Haley, the C.O.F. "let the old women who couldn't get insurance in. That was wonderful; they'd be worth one thousand dollars when they died. You can see that these old women that never had any feeling of value, financial value on their time—and just think of what they could give to their children. . . . With these women, all it meant was a thousand dollars when they died."[19] Despite their benefit, these organizations did not address the problems of widespread destitution of Irish women in any fundamental way. Too few women belonged and the societies developed quite late in the history of the Irish in America.

Aid and support at times of crisis certainly derived from the informal channels of community and neighborhood where Irish women lived. From all accounts—personal, journalistic, literary—Irish women did in fact rely on their extensive female social networks, and their friendships with each other played important social roles in Irish communities. Irish women valued their neighborhood contacts and extensive friendships, which also often led to assistance. Because of the urban friendship networks, Irish women balked at the idea of moving to farms, and most of the Irish proponents of colonization pointed to the reluctance of women as a major factor keeping the Irish trapped in cities.[20] American observers also recognized the informal supports that thrived in the Irish enclaves. Helen Campbell told of Irish women who helped each other out during illness and periods of their husbands' drunken rages, and Ruth True's study of *Boyhood and Lawlessness* on New York's West Side detailed how Irish neighborhood mothers spied for each other on their male offsprings, reporting any delinquent behavior. Similarly, the many vignettes of Jacob Riis detail the extensive aid that Irish women provided to each other and the profound female friendships that flourished among the Hibernian poor. So obvious was the comradeship among these women to writer William Dean Howells that in his short story "An Imperative Duty" he described the young Irish women "going about Boston Common with their arms *around one another,* and not around any 'gentleman friend.'"[21]

Much female socializing involved visiting and talking, exchanging information, seeking advice in hallways and in backyards while performing domestic functions. Many Irish men and women of the "lace curtain" classes found the social life of the female Irish poor a source of embarrassment, an indication of how little the poor women had Americanized. Mary E. Blake, a Boston Irish novelist, for example, shared her disgust with her readers in 1883 as she asked, "Haven't you seen in driving through some of our Celtic suburbs, two frosy-headed Irish women with sleeves rolled above their red elbows exchanging confidences over a rickety fence, while the open door of the cheerless cottage discloses a vista of general untidyness beyond?" An 1862 Irish traveler to America painfully described a summer evening in the tenement district, where "all were out of doors . . . numbers of the females would be sitting on the 'stoops' their chins in their hands, their elbows on their knees, conversing in the brogue of the Emerald Isle; large numbers were Irish, but with very little Irish fun left in them; death, languor, listlessness, and disease hovering around and over them." Despite the negative image of stoop-life socializing, the neighborhoods of Irish America provided for women the forums for female friendship networks and informal support systems.[22]

The Church provided the only formal institution in which women participated on any regular basis. Like everything else in the Irish communities, Church and Church-related clubs maintained very separate activities for men and for women. Few Irish parishes sponsored any kind of activity for "frivolous" socializing by young men and women together, and dancing was discouraged.[23] The idea of an organization or club that catered to males and females at the same time seemed anathema to the Irish. When the Y.M.C.A. in Newark, New Jersey, admitted women, the *Irish World* sneered:

> If we are not mistaken, to the Young Men's Christian Association of Newark belongs the honor of practically proclaiming in favor of Women's Rights. They have amended their constitution so as to admit ladies to membership. But will this not necessitate another amendment—the altering of their name and title. Of course they cannot expect the young women to unsex themselves and call themselves "young men." Just fancy a young lady telling her friends that she was one of the Young Men's Christian Association! Clearly the title will have to be amended to be read "Young Mens and Womens Christian Association." We are glad to see that the association is not disheartened by its discouraging experience the past season in this way of public entertainments.[24]

Some of the Irish men's clubs—charitable, recreational, political, nationalistic, temperance—made an effort to invite "lady friends" to an occasional picnic or banquet, even though men and women usually remained physically separate during the festivities. So unusual was an Irish event where men and women rollicked together that a writer for Boston's *O'Neill's Irish Pictorial* in 1859 told his readers with wonder:

> We were surprised, upon calling at Warren Hall, South and Beach Streets, on Wednesday evening, the 27th inst. We had anticipated a small party got up for some benevolent purpose, but were much surprised to see the hall crowded to overflowing, by the members' wives and friends of the "Shamrock Society," who were, to the strains of harmony, displaying ankles unsurpassed, in jig or polka on any stage. We understand the party was got up to please the women who feel themselves "excluded from a participation" (by usage) in the "National Anniversary." To them, we suppose, may be attributed the extraordinary success of

the affair, for it was really a pity they had not procured a larger hall. We . . . never saw tables better provided with the "fixings." Our conclusion was, and is, that this was "Sheelah's Night." We are advocates of such Women's rights.[25]

Even the Catholic Total Abstinence Unions operated through much of the nineteenth century as all-male clubs in most parishes and cities, though organized efforts to curb Irish drinking on both sides of the Atlantic addressed an issue that was as much a female as a male problem.[26] Furthermore, the organized effort to achieve home rule in Ireland and the various societies constituted for that purpose also set up women's branches or ladies' auxiliaries only sporadically. Beyond a few scattered cases in which Irish women banded together to form a short-lived Ladies' Land League or a Fenian Sisterhood to collect money to help the brotherhood, few Irish-American women participated in the effort to rid the Emerald Isle of the hated British oppressors.[27]

The Ancient Order of Hibernians, probably the most important Irish-American organization and certainly the one with the greatest longevity, also waited and did not authorize the formation of a female unit until the 1890s, the first one being chartered in Grand Rapids, Michigan, in 1894.[28] Finally, Irish women got together for very specific communal purposes: to raise money for the "Irish Brigade" from Chicago during the Civil War, to organize boycotts of particular New York City merchants, to rally to the defense of Catholic and Irish interests in Lowell.[29] None of these efforts, however, led to the establishment of permanent, formalized organizations that could have produced support for women.

A few individual Irish laywomen in America recognized the plight of their "sisters" and sought to institute services and reforms for them. Mary Lunney, who had immigrated by herself to the United States at age twenty in 1850, married well and used her money to endow such philanthropic projects as the Temporary Home for Working Women and the New England Home for Intemperate Women which attempted to address the needs of Irish female immigrants. Frances Dolan, a native of Fermanagh, worked feverishly in New York throughout the peak years of Famine migration to set up protective services for freshly arrived colleens.[30] Ellen O'Grady, a probation officer and later the first women deputy police commissioner in New York, founded the Friend in Need Day Nursery where Irish Catholic working women could leave their small children.[31] Here and there, Irish women undertook similar projects, but generally they hardly were in the position to initiate and sustain social services for their less fortunate sisters. Married and widowed Irish women tended to be poor and burdened with responsibility, and single Irish women with a steady income continued well into the twentieth century to send most of their extra money back to Ireland. Furthermore, most Irish women, like Irish men, viewed public organizational work as the proper sphere of men and therefore avoided it.

Irish people generally agreed that social service work and charitable endeavors belonged to the Church and only the Church. Individual Irish Catholics who could donate money to a day nursery or a home for abandoned women were most likely to choose a church-sponsored enterprise.

Since the Church in America, particularly in the industrial cities of the North and Middle West, was staffed almost entirely by Irish clerics, it should hardly be surprising that it accepted traditional Irish gender segregation. The male church leaders in New York, Boston, Philadelphia, Chicago, and elsewhere, like other Irish men, did not see the needs of women as something of immediate concern to them. Despite the cry of the clergy on both sides of the Atlantic as to the great dangers that innocent Irish girls faced as migrants and new American urban dwellers, it instituted hardly any projects or services to counteract the negative side effects of migration. Guidebooks written by clerics during the heyday of the Irish exodus scarcely acknowledged the numerical predominance of women and dispensed advice on jobs almost completely from a male point of view. Only occasionally did priests in their own parishes set up places of refuge for women who had no home or who were looking for work.

The various bishops and other hierarchical officials gave more attention to the care of orphans than to the care of women. Church leaders feared that poor homeless children were the perfect targets for Protestant missionaries, who prowled the Irish neighborhoods offering shelter and food (and ultimately Protestantism) to the street waifs. Thus, among the Irish as late as 1856 a New York charitable society reported that "the Roman Catholics of this city, excepting the relief of a few orphans, make no corresponding provision for their poor, neither by their churches or otherwise." Church officials accepted the logic that women's problems ought to be addressed by other women, and the various orders of nuns therefore were able to do what men could not.[32]

The only men within the Church to provide relief for women were the members of the St. Vincent de Paul Society, whose leaders asserted that the plight of widows equaled that of orphans. This male lay Catholic society attempted to address their needs by providing money, food, and fuel to poor widows and by helping women find jobs. In the 1890s it also employed a woman, Miss McGurty, in Boston to greet female Catholic newcomers at the port. In 1896, for example, she made contact with over three thousand Irish immigrant girls, helping them find either work or relatives. In Brooklyn, the society sponsored a number of projects specifically for women. It established visiting programs for incarcerated women facing re-entry to society. The vast bulk of these women were of Irish origin as was the paid agent of the society, Anna Connolly. The Vincentians, however, generally also recognized the special roles of nuns and tended, like the clergy, to act as a referral service, sending women with particular problems to the appropriate religious order for help.[33]

It was from the nuns representing the female religious orders that Irish women, faced with poverty, alcoholism, domestic violence, and illness could expect aid and support. It was to these religious women that they did, in fact, turn when in crisis. Since all involved were women, the line of gender segregation was not crossed. Since they were all Catholics, the line of religious faith was not broken. Since the vast majority was Irish, too, recipients and dispensers of charity understood each other.

Some of the most important orders to service Irish women in the United States had originated in Ireland, such as the Sisters of Mercy, the Presentation Sisters, and the Sisters of Charity of the Blessed Virgin Mary, whereas others like the Sisters of Notre Dame de Namur, the Sisters of the Good Shepherd, and the Sisters of the Holy Cross had initially been constituted elsewhere but attracted large numbers of recruits in Ireland. Orders from around the world, and particularly those that in the nineteenth century operated in the United States and served Irish women, tended to launch major drives in Ireland to gain new members. Thus, for example, when Mother Angela Gillespie of the Sisters of the Holy Cross in 1870 needed to replenish the ranks for her female educational projects, she journeyed to Ireland, where she actually encountered some difficulty because "the Dominican Sisters first, then the Sisters of Mercy and their Bishop . . . have thoroughly gleaned the country." Not entirely unsuccessful, however, she did manage to bring nineteen new women to St. Mary's in Indiana. Similarly, whenever a priest in a particular Irish parish or the officials of a particular diocese came to recognize the depths of the problems of women, both young and old, they almost invariably sent off to Ireland to try to induce an order to come and help them in the United States.

The presence of large numbers of nuns from Ireland may have played a very important role in convincing significant numbers of Irish-American girls to take vows themselves and enter some of the same religious communities. The option of entering an order seems to have been a very important part of Irish-American girlhood, and biographies of Irish Americans note many women family members who did, in fact, choose this. For example, Sister Mary Joseph Dempsey, born in 1856 in New York state, was one of four daughters in an Irish immigrant family, three of whom entered orders.[34] Nuns provided role models of women engaged in a variety of educational, charitable, and social welfare activities, often doing work deemed inappropriate for women. Yet the nuns' celibate life harmonized with the high rate of nonmarriage that characterized Irish-American family life. An Irish young woman who chose to enter a religious community did not break with accepted expectations.

Nuns provided an amazingly wide range of services for Irish women in the large Catholic cities. In Boston, the hub of Gaelic America, the Franciscan

Sisters organized St. Joseph's Home for servant women who were out of work or who were sick and had no one to care for them, and the Sisters of Notre Dame de Namur established an industrial school in 1858 to upgrade the employment opportunities of working girls. This particular order, which usually tended to emphasize the higher education of women, also sought to address the needs of impoverished women in Boston and in 1860 called together the poor Irish mothers

> who stood most in need of instruction, direction, and special assistance in the management of their homes . . . teaching the untaught and overworked creatures how to make everything clean, tidy, and bright about them; helping them to have the children regular in their attendance at school, neatly dressed, with their clothes mended and all marks of degrading poverty removed . . . aiding every wife and mother to be herself, to husband and children, a model of sobriety, thrift, and gentleness.[35]

The so-called "gray nuns" ran a working girls' home in Boston, almost all of whose residents were young Irish women, and the massive influx of Hibernian females created such a serious problem that the Sisters of the Third Order of St. Francis in 1868 established St. Elizabeth's Hospital specifically designed to treat women's diseases. Starting in 1898 the Sisters of Saint Joseph taught working girls such marketable skills as typing, bookkeeping, and accounting in the evenings at the Daly Industrial Home for Girls, and the Sisters of St. Francis ran a nursing school under the ausipices of the Boston Lying-In Hospital and Infirmary for Women and Children.[36]

Although Catholic New York was less overwhelmingly Irish, Irish nuns there played a very important role in Catholic social services for women and tended to serve a predominantly Irish clientele. Just as in Boston, New York communities established employment bureaus and medical facilities, homes and training schools, to provide for women what others would not. The Irish Presentation Sisters set up classes for adult women in St. Michael's, a West Side, almost all-Irish parish, and also sheltered some four thousand women in their lodging house, which functioned from 1877 to 1885. Almost all the residents at St. Joseph's Catholic Home for the Aged were Irish women who had been domestic servants in New York, who in their old age turned to this institution founded and run by the Sisters of Charity in 1871, as were the young women who took advantage of St. Elizabeth's Industrial School, which in the 1890s offered the chance of more lucrative employment. Ellen O'Keefe, an immigrant herself from Ireland, founded the Sisters of Reparation of the Congregation of Mary and established St. Zita's House, where women who had been in prison found shelter, food, and job training. O'Keefe, who became Sister Mary Zita Dolorosa, not only labored primarily with these unfortunate Irish women, but like other directors of Irish Catholic charities in America, she went back to Ireland to inspire others to join her order, dedicated to "the reclamation of unfortunate women who have been committed to the island for intemperance or other cause, receiving them on their discharge and introducing them to a life of industry and self-respect."[37]

In Chicago, 97 of the 104 inmates of the home for the indigent aged of the Little Sisters of the Poor in 1880 were Irish women as were the vast majority of the employed women who sought a respectable and clean place to live at the St. Joseph Home and the St. Francis House of Providence established by the Sisters of St. Joseph.[38] The Mullanphy family, the wealthiest, most famous Irish family in St. Louis, arranged for the Ladies of the Sacred Heart to set up a training school for "indigent girls of the better class" as well as a widows' home, and the Sisters of St. Joseph, working primarily with the St. Louis Irish maintained a night refuge, which in the 1890s cared for over fifteen hundred girls a year and operated an employment bureau for domestic servants.[39] The *Irish World* reported in 1874 that the Holy Cross Sisters in Baltimore had established a training school where poor girls could prepare for teaching jobs. The small Irish community in nineteenth-century Washington, D.C., boasted St. Rose's Industrial School, directed by the Sisters of Charity, and stressed teaching older girls dressmaking and domestic skills.[40]

An extensive national network of this kind sustained Irish women from childhood through old age, providing training schools and employment services, houses of refuge and shelters for the homeless, medical facilities and day nurseries for the children of working women. In fact, because of the fairly rigid gender division, which defined nuns' work as that which involved women, the services available to women exceeded those available to men. In New York, for example, there was one Catholic old age home for men but three for women, and nuns organized women's hospitals, women's industrial training schools, and women's employment bureaus without comparable services for Irish men.[41]

Nowhere did the nuns' bias in favor of their own gender emerge more strongly than in the field of education. Many orders were expressly forbidden by their charters to teach boys or at least boys above a certain age. Others merely preferred to teach girls and as such did not open up their services to boys. Since parochial education rested almost completely in the hands of the sisters (except at that point in a parish's history when it had not yet invited an order of nuns to take over its educational program), frequently the school for girls opened many years before the school for boys in the same parish, and many more girls attended than did their brothers. For example, the first Catholic girls' school opened its doors in Brooklyn in 1847, whereas the boys' school commenced in the mid-1850s. In Providence, Rhode Island, St. Patrick's parish decided on a school for girls in 1843 but waited six years until an equivalent institution for boys began in this all-Irish parish. In 1871 St. Rose's in Chelsea, Massachusetts, provided education for its girls, yet fifteen years elapsed until the boys were also accommodated.[42] Therefore, more girls received parochial education than boys in the predominantly Irish parishes, with a substantial difference in numbers. For example, at St. Ann's, an East 12th Street parish in New York in the late 1870s, 250 boys and 560 girls enrolled in the parish school, and in Lawrence, 400 boys as opposed to 600 girls attended the city's Catholic schools.[43] In 1872 and 1873 the *Irish World* surveyed the vast array of Catholic institutions in American cities and found that though 87 educational institutions of various sorts operated for young men, a lopsided 209 served young women.[44]

The differential in educational services became even more striking at the postelementary level. High school departments were added in Catholic schools primarily for girls in order to prepare them for teaching careers.[45] Facilities for girls provided by the nuns tended to be slightly better than those for boys. When the Sisters of Notre Dame de Namur opened the doors of Saint Aloysius's parish school for girls in the Washington, D.C., Irish "Swampoodle" neighborhood, they found solace in that the boys' school was in significantly worse repair than theirs.[46]

The concern of nuns for the education of girls in the Irish communities also provided a major stimulus for the development of Catholic female higher education. Some of the first Catholic women's colleges in the United States — Trinity in Washington, D.C., founded in 1900 by Sister Julia McGroarty; Marymount in Tarrytown, New York, established in 1919 by Mother Marie Joseph Butler; and St. Elizabeth's in New Jersey, begun by Mother Xavier Mehegan in 1880 — all attracted predominantly Irish students and were staffed primarily by nuns of Irish origin. These colleges, which tended to be quite vocational in their emphasis, inspired a great deal of controversy at the time of their founding. In fact, a heated debate questioned the propriety of higher education for women, yet all parties to the controversy admitted that if Catholic higher education were not provided, many Irish-American women would go to college anyhow but would attend Protestant or public institutions.[47]

Nuns likewise provided care for young orphan girls before they did so for orphan boys. The first Catholic children's charity in New York, St. Patrick's Asylum, founded in 1817, served Irish girls only, while St. Vincent's in Boston, founded in 1831, similarly was the first Catholic orphanage in the city and catered just to girls. In Troy, New York, an orphanage connected with St. Peter's parish in 1847 sheltered little girls, yet little boys had to wait until 1850.[48]

Two orders in particular worked for the care of women and served a population that almost entirely hailed from Ireland: the Irish-founded Sisters of Mercy and the Sisters of the Good Shepherd, whose sole objective was the reclamation of "fallen women." In both cases these nuns not only labored among Hibernian females—immigrants and their daughters—but they defined their role in a mixture of spiritual and economic terms. Looking at the Sisters of Mercy one can see how the Irish female self-conception, which stressed the economic value of women, came to be combined with the nuns' "otherworldly" emphasis. This order, founded by Catherine McAuley in Dublin in 1831, grew out of the same social dynamic that propelled the hundreds of thousands of young Irish women to the United States. McAuley was appalled at the lack of services of any kind for the young country girls who streamed into the city looking for work and she found it particularly ironic that poor girls with "unblemished" records had fewer resources than did those who had "fallen" and could turn to the Magdalen Asylums. The order she created dedicated itself to acts of mercy for the sick and the incarcerated, for the orphans and the aged, but its most distinctive mission targeted women—homeless women and women without jobs, women with virtuous reputations who without special efforts might indeed lose that virtue. The rules laid down by Mother McAuley to govern the order that would eventually spread around the globe underscored the convergence of the spiritual and the material as she laid out:

> Distressed women of good character admitted to the House of Mercy, shall if necessary, be instructed in the principal mysteries and required to comply with their religious obligations. . . .
> Suitable employment shall be sought for, and great care taken to place them in situations for which they are adapted, in order that they may continue such length of time in them as shall establish a character on which they can depend for future support. Many leave their situations, not so much for want of merit as through incapacity to fulfill the duties in which unwisely engaged. They shall not be encouraged to remain long in the House of Mercy, as in general, it would be better for them soon to enter on that state and employment by which they are to live.[49]

The first Sisters of Mercy came to the United States in 1843 led by Frances Warde from their mother house in Carlow, Ireland, starting their initial foundation in Pittsburgh and rapidly spreading to New York, Chicago, Baltimore, Providence, San Francisco, St. Louis, Rochester, Manchester, Philadelphia, and scores of other cities where their services were requested. Wherever they went they established the same kinds of institution: Mercy Houses, where women in distress could seek refuge; employment agencies, particularly for domestic servants; training schools for young women looking to move into clerical and nursing work; Business Girls' Clubs, which provided housing for single women and served as an alternative to the lodging houses; and day nurseries for the children of working mothers.[50]

Although the original group targeted by the Sisters of Mercy for special care was respectable females, the nuns often found themselves called upon to succor all kinds of women, including prostitutes and delinquent girls. Although this deviated from the order's specific purpose, it was consistent with their female orientation, and these women as well as those who were *merely* poor, homeless, or abandoned received the same kinds of vocational and emotional support. Literally thousands of Irish and Irish-American women availed them-selves of the services of the Sisters of Mercy, and the presence of their community in a city provided a focal point for an Irish female sense of pro-tection. John Francis Maguire related, for example, the story of

> a young and handsome Irish girl who was lately trapped into hiring, in a Western city, with a person of infamous character. She was fortunately observed by a poor old Irish woman, who, knowing the peril in which the young creature stood, boldly rushed to her rescue, and, at personal risk to herself, literally tore the prey from the grasp of the enemy. The rescued girl was taken to the Refuge in the Convent of Mercy, where she was at once in safety: and though she lost all her clothes, save those in which she then stood, she congratulated herself that she had never crossed the threshold of a house of ill-fame.[51]

This story, or variations on the basic theme, repeated itself every place the Sisters of Mercy went and everywhere the Irish found themselves in some degree of distress. In New York, one of the most important of the Mercy Foundations, the stress on service to women by providing protection and the tools for economic security could be seen by sheer number. During the first year that the House of Mercy operated (1849-50), over twelve hundred Irish women were placed in jobs, and the number of women actually living with the sisters and receiving food and clothing from them averaged two hundred a night. By 1853, 7,356 "were placed in respectable situations." Furthermore, surveying their work up to 1864, Maguire counted 9,504 women who had lived with the sisters and 16,869 who found jobs through their offices.[52]

In Rochester, Buffalo, and other towns in upstate New York Irish immigrant women could count on the Sisters of Mercy to help teach them a marketable skill or take care of their children when they went to work.[53] Carpet mill women in Thomsonville, Connecticut, could attend evening classes run by these religious in the 1870s, and working girls in Worcester, Massa-chusetts, could feel safe in the lodging house there, since it was run by Sisters of Mercy.[54] The Sisters of Mercy who directed the employment bureau in Harrisburg, Pennsylvania, not only helped Irish girls secure positions but they "safeguarded the right of the girls by laying down the rules for their employers in respect to hours of work, wages and a demand to treat these girls with respect and consideration."[55]

The Sisters of Mercy, almost all of whom were Irish, recognized that the women, almost all of whom were Irish, standing in such desperate need of help required job training and placement as well as spiritual sustenance. These Irish nuns believed that unless women could support themselves and live in dignity, their souls were in danger, just as surely as was their virtue. The distinction for them between the economic and the religious therefore blurred as they sought to take care of the multitudes of Irish women who had abandoned their homeland and were attempting to succeed in urban America.

So, too, the Sisters of the Good Shepherd perceived that poverty and prostitution were intimately linked together and that to redeem a woman from the latter, one also had to elevate her from and protect her from the former. Although the order was not Irish in origin, having begun in France in 1641 as the Sisters of Our Lady of Charity of the Good Shepherd, by the time it spread to the United States in 1843, Irish and Irish-American women made up the bulk of the professed. These sisters worked only with women and divided up their charges into three categories: the Preservation Class, made up of "orphans and destitute girls, who have been rescued from surroundings that might prove harmful to their moral well-being"; the Penitent Class, comprised of "wayward girls and unfortunate women," some of whom had been brought to the sisters by the courts or by their families; and finally the Magdalens, women who had been so totally reformed and converted after their "fall" that they formed themselves into a sisterhood to "consecrate their services to the welfare of their wayward sisters." The smallest percentage of the women who were cared for by the Sisters of the Good Shepherd actually became Magdalens, and in the fifty years from 1857 to 1907 that the order functioned in New York

> it has received 13,108 girls, of whom 8,581 were committed from the courts; and 4,457 came of their own will.
>
> Of these, 7,274 have been returned to family and friends; 4,672 have been otherwise discharged; 251 have been transferred to other institutions; a few have left without permission or been sent out of the State; 369 have died peaceful and edifying deaths in the Home in which they found refuge and mother's welcome when the world had forsaken them; 491 are in the house at present writing.[56]

While being sheltered in the home, women and girls not only received daily religious instruction but were taught skills and trades that would allow them self-support and make it no longer necessary for them to prostitute for a living. The thousands of Irish women who found themselves under the care of these nuns in New York, Boston, Philadelphia, Chicago, Baltimore, St. Louis, Providence, and elsewhere learned to sew and prepared for domestic jobs in advent of their eventual return to their communities.[57]

These orders of nuns, which attracted many Irish to their ranks, worked among Irish women in America and confirmed the Irish values that viewed as central a woman's economic function and that saw the salvation of souls and the eradication of poverty as inseparable goals. Importantly, in the vast literature written as reminiscence and record of the Sisters of Mercy and the Sisters of the Good Shepherd, the nuns did not see their purpose as preparing women to becoming good wives. No place in their statements of purpose did they define the role of the order as that of helping poor young women enhance their prospects for successful matrimony. Instead, they sought to make these immigrant women and their daughters economically self-sufficient as part of the mission to heighten their spirituality.

A similar combination of spiritual and economic purpose underscored the writings and activities of Mary Frances Cusack, the "Nun of Kenmare." A sister in the cloistered convent of the Poor Clares in Kenmare, she was a radical and something of a gadfly in Ireland. After failing in her efforts to start a training school for girls in Knock, she turned her spirited efforts to the welfare of Irish immigrant girls in the United States, publishing her *Advice to Irish Girls in America* in 1886 and striving, in vain, to establish homes for Irish laboring women there. Cusack openly condemned the hierarchy in America for its insensitivity toward, even exploitation of, the immigrant women, and she took on bishops in a number of cities for the paucity of resources they allocated for the poor Irish girls now in America.[58]

Despite Cusack's charges against the Church, Irish-American women remained deeply committed and thankful to their parishes as well as to the sisters. Their gratitude was demonstrated by the large number of young Irish women who chose to become nuns themselves. It can be measured by the vast sums of money that they donated to their parishes and to the projects directed by the sisters. They donated because of their general attitude toward the Church; in fact, the histories of the Roman Catholic Church in Boston, New York, Philadelphia, Washington, D.C., Chicago and every city where the Irish settled indicate that women contributed the vast bulk of financial support for both parish maintenance and Catholic charitable work generally. The religiosity of Irish women was sustained and strengthened by the services the Church offered these women. Ladies' fairs proved very popular as ways for women to raise money to support any number of church activities, and the funds raised became critically important as the Church sought to cope with the floods of poor Catholic immigrants inundating the cities. The Catholic New York Foundling Asylum, for example, received $71,500 in donations raised by such a fair in New York City in 1870, and one woman, a Mrs. R. B. Connelly, personally collected over $20,000 of that. Such events had a social as well as a charitable function and they became the backbone of funding for parishes, parish charities, and charitable projects run on a diocesean level as well as for the humanitarian activities directed by the various Catholic sisterhoods.[59]

Many women made outright gifts of money to the Church and the chronicles of one Irish-American parish after another contain the names of legions of such women. Four young Irish women pooled their resources in 1851 in West Roxbury, Boston, to pay for the lot on which Sacred Heart Parish arose. The official history of St. Paul's Parish in Buffalo told of a house-keeper, a Miss Elizabeth McKee, who served the same Protestant family for thirty years. In successive years she donated the money to put up a black walnut memorial front in the church, helped underwrite the Parish House building fund, and gave one thousand dollars in 1888 for parish maintenance. Judge Thomas McManus, active in the Irish Catholic community of Hartford, Connecticut, noted that when money was being raised to build St. Joseph's Cathedral, servant girls opened their hands and demonstrated that they were "the best of Catholics, and the most liberal supporters of the church." So important were the individual donations of Irish servants that one Irish resident of Dorchester in Boston reminisced that "Father Ronan used to go round to the back door of all the houses and talk to the living-in girls—they're the ones that really started St. Peter's Church." Miss Catharine Brennan gave St. Mary's in Providence its 340-pound bell and also adorned the church with its largest stained glass window. Some Irish women waited until death to share their resources with probably the most important institution in their lives and legacies from servant women and women in other occupations provided both large and small sums to the Church.[60]

The services that Irish women accepted from the Church reflect the convergence of cultural traditions with the realities of the new life in America. That Irish women found support and aid through the efforts of female religious orders emerged from the tradition of gender segregation and from the sympathetic bonds that united women with one another. That Irish women frequently banded together into formalized networks for economic and for religious purposes, but rarely for recreational, social, or political, underscored what women deemed both important and appropriate. The problems Irish women faced grew out of the soil of America, although their roots had sprouted in Ireland. Similarly, the solutions to problems took on American forms, but their fundamental nature was quintessentially Irish. From the earliest years of Irish settlement in America through the opening decades of the twentieth century, Irish women's behavior reflected fundamentally Irish values, while solutions to their problems were offered in consistently Irish ways.

 SEVEN Irish Men / Irish Women:
The World View from
the Nineteenth Century

I n this century of revolutions, not only political but social when women of
almost all nationalities were to be found in the pulpit and on the rostrum
howling for imaginary rights which once obtained must necessarily degrade the
sex and deprive them of that God-like influence which they now possess over
their husbands and brothers, be it to the eternal praise of noble Irish woman,
recorded, that not a single instance can be found, where she has so far forgotten
her native dignity—so far forgotten her native modesty as to put herself forward
as a champion of a movement.
Irish World

To throw aside the tiresome details of home-keeping; board, or live in a flat; to
slaughter the unborn innocents; to have a free foot, unfettered by duty to house,
husband, or children, are not the crying demands of *fin de siècle* women?
Eleanor Donnelly, "The Home Is Woman's Sphere"

Irish women as migrants, as new Americans, and as members of an
aspiring middle class behaved aggressively and valued their economic prowess.
They often migrated without men. Sometimes by choice, sometimes by default,
many led lives independent of men and relied heavily on female networks for
support and sustenance. All of these characteristics might have made them
excellent recruits for the feminist struggle to improve the status of women in
America and to expand their political, social, and economic vistas. Irish men,
in fact, profoundly feared that their women might succumb to the rhetoric of
the movement, a rhetoric that differed radically from Irish-Catholic culture.
The Irish press, as one eloquent voice in Irish America, went beyond mocking
the women's movement to portraying it as a major threat to the Irish-Catholic

lifestyle. Importantly, fears of Irish men, as expressed in their sermons, lectures, and editorials, greatly exceeded the danger. They believed, incorrectly, that their sisters' and wives' economic sense of self reflected a latent feminism. Yet Irish women turned a cold shoulder to the organized women's rights movement despite their marketplace assertiveness and economic independence. The reasons they did so tell a great deal about how they viewed themselves and how they defined their aspirations in their new home.

Migration had been a "liberating" experience for Irish women. They consciously had chosen to leave a society that offered them little as women to embrace one that proffered to them greater opportunity and expended greater resources upon them. Because of these opportunities single Irish females migrated in increasingly large numbers from the 1860s on. Irish women affirmatively chose domestic work, a job that others would not take, not only because it blended in with their views of marriage and family but because it offered them a chance to earn money and save as well as providing them with a first-hand peek at how Americans lived. They consciously *chose* domestic service because it fit in with their needs and aspirations. The high rate of Irish female employment and the vast sums of money that women accumulated and donated to kin and Church or spent on themselves demonstrate that as women in America they had many options.

Observers both within and without the Irish communities agreed that women in families, as wives, daughters, and sisters, brought the family "up," civilized them by introducing the manners and accouterments of the middle class. Women spearheaded the push upward, and Irish men resented this effort to make them over into refined Americans. Many an Irish-American man might have winced in recognition of Mr. Dooley's Hennessey, who on Christmas morning turned to his wife with muffled annoyance: "How thoughtful iv ye Mary Ann, to give me th' essays of Emmerson. I wuz sayin' on'y la' week to a friend iv mine in th' pork pit that iv all th' fellows that iver hurled the pen Emmerson f'r me money.'"[1] The resentment stemmed not just from being the object of an uplifting campaign but that women carried on the campaign.

In America Irish women could go to school and prepare themselves for careers, most importantly, for schoolteaching, but also nursing. Whereas in Ireland, more boys attended school than girls and stayed longer, in America the tables had turned. Irish girls outnumbered their brothers in parochial and public schools, particularly in the more advanced grades. Studies of Irish-American educational achievement in a number of nineteenth-century towns point to this trend. In Waltham, Massachusetts, among Catholics (which meant Irish in this New England mill town in the 1860s and 1870s), female high school graduates outnumbered males four to one. In Trempeleau County, Wisconsin, in the 1860s, "of all the groups only the Irish sent more girls than boys" for a high school education. The first graduating class of Gardner (Massachusetts) High School in 1876 included ten children from the Irish immigrant community there: all girls. In 1893 in the same school eight young people from the Irish enclave graduated and of them six were females. At Pittsburgh Central High School in the decade from 1855 to 1865, 20 percent of all the male student body were Irish boys, whereas Irish girls made up 37 percent of the female student body. The differential in boy-girl public school attendance is all the more striking given the hostility of the organized Irish community toward public education and the frequent condemnations of American education by the Roman Catholic clergy. Despite the plethora of sermons and religious tracts that linked common schooling with Protestant-ism, atheism, sexual depravity, and social unrest, Irish girls continued to flock to the American classrooms because of what those classrooms promised for their future.[2]

The defiance of Irish girls as they rushed to the American high schools and normal schools to train themselves for respectable and secure jobs com-plemented their generally assertive behavior and underscored their eco-nomically aggressive sense of self. These factors, along with their profound attraction toward American culture, caused Irish men to fear that their wives and sisters and daughters would also be attracted to the feminist movement, which was in its heyday during the years of Irish migration and adaptation.[3]

In America Irish women, particularly domestic servants, could work for wages and spend their surplus earnings as they wanted. They could, for example, spend it on *themselves*. Religious tracts and pious novels condemned servant girls squandering money on finery (money that the writers believed should have been going to the Church), but the women continued to spend their money on themselves when they wanted. Although statistics on the amount of money Irish women spent on clothing are hard to come by, the very fact that clerics decried the women's self-indulgence suggests that it must have been quite widespread. Moreover, late-nineteenth-century writers com-monly described Irish women as well dressed. One early-twentieth-century settlement worker, Mary Simkhovitch, of New York's Greenwich House, surveyed the lives of women in a variety of ethnic groups and concluded that although "tastes varied, the Irish girl had the greatest refinement in her dress." Half a century earlier, Charles Dickens had compared the Irish newcomer with the one already Americanized: "she [the new immigrant] has not yet acquired the grand *notions* of dress and independence which the Irish girl long resident is apt to have picked up."[4] Another British traveler in the 1860s, Thomas Nichols, also found the taste and clothing of Irish women noteworthy and after documenting how women sent back to Ireland a lion's share of their monthly earning, he described how they then turned to satisfying their own wants:

When these helpful young ladies from the Emerald Isle have done their duty to their relations, they are free to indulge in their own tastes, which are apt, I must say, to be a little extravagant. I have been amused, on a Sunday morning, to see two Irish girls walking out of my basement door dressed in rich *moire antique*, with everything to correspond, from elegant bonnets and parasols to gloves and gaiter-boots—an outfit that would not disgrace the neatest carriage in Hyde Park. These girls had been brought up in the floorless mud cabins covered with thatch, and gone to mass without shoes or stockings very likely, and now enjoy all the more their unaccustomed luxuries.[5]

Servant girls might very well have picked up tips about American styles and fashions from their employers but even the Irish mill girls in Lowell had a reputation for being good dressers in contrast to their more slovenly brother operatives.[6]

Irish men believed that in America their women had become altogether too self-involved, too self-centered, and too imitative of the Yankee Protestant women around them. The issue of dress and the money women spent on it underscored this heightened sense of self, which many men feared represented a short step from embracing the women's movement's selfish "new woman," whom they despised so much.

Irish men resented the women's movement for a number of reasons. From a very practical point of view Irish men who had come to America and had learned to operate the machinery of politics and government genuinely worried that women—be they native-born or Irish—could undermine the base of their power. Women activists boldly asserted that if given the opportunity they would clean up the corruption fostered by city machines. Irish men took these claims seriously and opposed women's suffrage out of the fear that women would actually do what they promised—or threatened—to do. Importantly, it would have been in the Irish politicians' interest to support women's suffrage, since enfranchising females would have increased the numbers of Irish Catholic voters, loyal to the same machines and committed to the same issues. Irish men, however, did not know that extending the vote to women would in the end do little to harm the structure of politics as they knew it. They incorrectly feared that Irish women would seek to displace them and join the feminist-reformist crusade.

In a few isolated nineteenth-century Irish Catholic communities, leaders decided that suffrage for women *could* work to the advantage of their own interests. In places like Boston, Worcester, and other Massachusetts towns, the large pools of Irish women could be tapped to vote in ways harmonious with those of Irish Catholic men and to help shore up any weaknesses in Irish political control. More importantly, the votes of Catholic women could be useful as weapons in the incessant religious friction that dominated, for example, the Boston school committee. Church officials and community leaders, like *Boston Pilot* editor John Boyle O'Reilly, were put in a very difficult spot because of their outspoken opposition to women's suffrage and their belief that the ballot box belonged to men, while at the same time they felt it was essential to promote Catholic interest in the schools as decisions were made on textbook choice, teacher assignment, treatment of "sensitive" subjects, and the like.[7]

Ironically, Irish men demonstrated tremendous shrewdness and political savvy as well as flexibility as politicians. They skillfully managed to wield power over ethnic groups that eventually outnumbered the Hibernians. They managed to manipulate progressive reforms that had been designed to undermine the machines. Yet they could not see that women's suffrage represented no real threat. In fact, it could have been an opportunity for them, but cultural values were too deeply ingrained. The fear that the suffrage movement would bring with it the collapse of social life as it ought to be was too great for even these perceptive political operatives.

To Irish male immigrants the idea of women crossing over the boundary into men's activities appeared ludicrous as well as threatening. The idea of women organizing into clubs and associations and tackling issues that men ought to handle seemed outlandish, bizarre, perhaps a fit subject for joking and satire. The Irish press reported women's suffrage activities as humorous at best. Suffragists were "cackling" or "crowing" hens and also "strong-minded shriekers" attempting to change the essential nature of human relations. The correspondent for the *Irish World* in Washington, D.C., reported in January of 1873 that "the female 'Suffrage Convention' has met in the city and the cackling of the hens is loud and extensive." In another piece, titled "Crowing hens: or women's rights," the *Irish World* satirized the movement:

"Why shouldn't *we* crow?" said the speckled hen.
"Why not?" said the white hen.
"Why not?" said all the hens as the question went round.
"We are as clever, as strong, as handsome, as good in every way as that domineering old cock; in my opinion we are superior!" said the speckled hen.
"And mine," said the white hen.
"And in mine," said the red hen.
"And in mine" said all the hens, much impressed and excited by this new view of things.
So they practiced and stretched out their necks and stuck their heads on one side, all in imitation of the old cock; and a very remarkable noise they made.
"Hey day!" said the rooster, stopping to listen as he ran through the yard.
"My dear creatures, what are you at? Give up this nonsense. While you keep to clucking you are highly respectable—when you take to crowing, you can't think what ridiculous figures you all cut. Keep to clucking, dears, keep to clucking!"[8]

The Irish organs of public opinion reveled in what they perceived as the humor of the women's rights movement, and undoubtedly readers of the

Irish World chuckled heartily over "a Brooklyn women's rights woman" who "named her three boys Susan, Mary, and Kate." When a female doctor was appointed city physician for Springfield, Massachusetts, during a rampaging smallpox epidemic, a male "poet" for the newspaper could not contain himself and jotted down:

Old golly, come and hear my ditty
As I will sing of Springfield city
The small pox goes like all creation
Since Mrs. Williams goes on vaccinating
When other cities do not but wishin'
Springfield has her "she" physician
Weak-kneed men who did this duty
Must now make way for female beauty
Free love now in all its branches
Judges clear away your benches
Lawyers quit and leave the forum
Before your pants and vest are torn
For women's rights will surely dock us
Of pants and vests as well as office
Come all bands both men and women
Fill your glasses till they are brimming
We have one officer yet alive
To handcuff Martha's seven thirty-five
Halaloojah. Praise de lord
For dis good news poor sinners heard
And brother physician don't you scoff us
For giving sister Williams an office.[9]

Later in the nineteenth century and in the early years of the twentieth, few aspects of life on Archey Road seemed as ridiculous to Mr. Dooley as when the "new woman," Molly Donahue, one of Dunne's most memorable characters, tried to learn to ride a bicycle, joined a political club, believed that she and her daughter ought to vote, and donned bloomers. The same Molly who assertively brought middle-class genteel culture into her home also heralded the age of the "new woman" as she announced to husband Malachai, "'the' new woman . . .'ll be free from th' opprision iv man . . . she'll wuriukout her own way, without help or hinderance . . . she'll wear what clothes she want . . . an' she'll be no man's slave."[10]

Dunne in this portrayal of Molly articulated the essential Irish male disdain of the women's rights movement. In order to work out their "own way," young Irish women had left their native land in the hundreds of thousands to take jobs by themselves in the United States and to live out lives often independent of "th' opprision iv man."[11] American feminists held up a model of womanhood that squared well with the actual behavior of Irish-American women. Irish men, long critical of their own women's independence, profoundly feared that Irish women could be sucked into the feminist move-ment. Feminism not only threatened the political power of Irish men, it threatened the very foundations of Irish culture and its delicate balance between the sexes.[12]

The division of the sexes into rigidly discrete categories, each with its own locus, each with its own tasks, made the world rational and orderly, while the feminist cause demanded that separate spheres for men and women be obliterated. It argued that women be allowed to enter all the places heretofore reserved for men, be they the political party or the medical school, the pulpit or the classroom.

Irish-American leaders in the late nineteenth century believed that in America the feminist had actually already won the day and that it was be-coming increasingly difficult for men and women to live properly. The *Irish World* asserted that the women in America had entered in droves almost every area of employment that "would be considered unfeminine in Europe" and particularly that female "physicians without number" had taken over.[13] "Society as now organized," lamented *O'Neill's Irish Pictorial* "takes them [women's rights activists] by the hand and embraces them, while the Irish women earning bread by labor, attending their religious duties, and paying a portion of their wages to the building of churches, and supporting schools, are despised and lectured against as dangerous."[14] John Boyle O'Reilly was con-vinced that feminism undermined morality:

> Women's suffrage is an unjust, unreasonable, unspiritual abnormality. It is a hard, undigested, tasteless, devitalized proposition. It is a half-fledged, unmusical promethean abomination. It is a quack bolous to reduce masculinity even by the obliteration of feminity . . . it is the sediment, not the wave of the sex. It is the antithesis of that highest and sweetest mystery—conviction by submission, and conquest by sacrifice.[15]

To O'Reilly, a champion of almost every other liberal cause of the day, the widespread success of the suffrage movement bespoke the "degeneracy of the times."[16]

That degeneracy, spawned by the breakdown of traditional gender barriers, inevitably led to sexual immorality and deviance, according to Irish men. In the middle and late nineteenth century they believed that the ad-vocates of suffrage worked hand in hand with the advocates of free love "and its accompanying abominations." The writers and editors of the Irish press inevitably linked feminist ideology with sexual license, polygamy, abortion, birth control, divorce, and the like—all being supported by "demoralized females, who have outraged every instinct of womanly decency, and every truth of Christianity." According to the Irish-American male world view, the convergence of feminism and sexual vice flowed naturally from the fact that the vast majority of activists in the women's movement were native-born

Protestant women of Anglo-Saxon stock who subscribed to a religious ideology allowing divorce and greater sexual freedom than did that of Catholic Ireland. Articles on divorce and editorials against sexual deviance inevitably drew the connection both with feminism and Protestant Anglo-Saxonism. For example, in October 1872 the *Irish World* noted that in the previous year the state of Connecticut had granted 409 divorces, or one divorce for every 12 marriages, and with horror at the high statistics the editors concluded, "Such evidence of 'progress' must be gratifying to all Protestants, who rejoice over the fact that Connecticut is one of the most Protestant states in the union." In a very similar vein, in June 1859 *O'Neill's Irish Pictorial* editorialized that "'freelove' in all its hideousness, with all brutalizing and demoralizing doctrines, finds its advocates and adherents even in the land of the Puritan. A town of the rigidly righteous State of Vermont, furnishes the trysting place where the devotees of free love and free lust hold disgusting orgies."[17]

The sexual tendencies of Protestants contrasted sharply with the Irish Catholic self-perception of a sexually chaste people, untainted by the "isms." "The teachers of women's rights, or hearers of crazy women's lecturers, are not to be found amongst the Irish people, who, it is admitted stand aloof from such crazy poisonous contagion. The said crazy women sowing more immorality in the community than any other source."[18]

The ethnic-religious contrast in terms of divorce and involvement with the various social movements of the day including feminism, not only helped the Irish men justify their own cultural traditions but became a rallying cry for the preservation of Irish-Catholic distinctiveness, directed particularly at the younger, Americanizing generation. Differences between Irish Catholics and Anglo-Saxon Protestants on "moral" issues merged through much of the literature as a justification for keeping children out of public schools at the same time that they were intended to inspire pride and strength in group loyalty.

In both England and America the Irish believed that practices like "baby-farming" (where infants, commonly born out of wedlock, were given away to a wet nurse who would care for them and then place them in homes) prevailed among Protestants and bore directly on the kinds of plans and proposals advocated by feminists. When a "baby farm" was uncovered in Boston the *Irish World* made the comparison noting that

> no wonder the old New England stock . . . is thinning out and a new one budding and growing and spreading continuously until it promises to cover every inch of soil, and desecrate the rock. No wonder, Mr. Yankee that with your factories, your secret drugs, and female physicians, your lying in hospitals, your baby farms and your baby farmers, your family is growing small and becoming beautifully less on the land.[19]

Even more devastating was the Irish condemnation of abortion in America.

The newspapers splashed across their pages violent enunciations of "this festering sore, abortion, which has been fed and inflamed by the loose notions of marriage and motherhood prevailing among Protestants." The writers cited the declining birth rate among native-born Protestants as evidence of the popularity of abortion and consistently asserted that feminist ideology justified, even celebrated, abortion as a key to women's emancipation. As Catholics, they viewed it as a form of murder, pure and simple, and pointed with pride to the fact that "*not one of those barbarous mothers was a Roman Catholic.*"[20]

The Irish not only found the message of the suffragists odious and out of tune with their own cultural values but quite bluntly they did not like the suffragists as people. These women behaved in ways that Irish men deemed unwomanly. They talked about things that women ought not to talk about in public. Further intensifying the Irish feelings against them, feminists seemed to be anti-Irish and anti-Catholic. The Irish men linked them with female charity workers and missionary evangelicals who worked to undermine Catholicism in America and with the middle-class clubwomen in whose homes many an Irish girl cooked and cleaned. These women, who believed that the ballot box belonged to them as well as to men, were the same ones who at best patronized the Hibernian newcomers and more frequently vilified them, discriminated against them, and sought to hamper them in every way possible. James Michael Curley went on record against the women reformers, as he asserted, "no land . . . was ever saved by little clubs of female faddists . . . what we need . . . are men and the mothers of men and not grabbing spinsters and dog raising matrons in federations assembled."[21]

To a certain extent, the Irish perception of the feminists' cultural biases was rooted in reality. A strongly worded anti-Irish, anti-Catholic message ran through much of the nineteenth-century women's rights campaign. The middle-class Protestant women who swelled the ranks of the movement did not stand aloof from the prevailing prejudices of their class and their day and they disliked the Catholic newcomers and feared papal influences as intensely as most Americans at the time. Suffrage newspapers, for example, indulged in the same stereotyping and labeling of Irish men and women as did the general American press, commenting in a variety of ways on their ignorance, lack of common sense, volatile tempers, and total submission to ecclesiastical authority. Importantly, most of the suffragists' negative portrayals of the Irish centered on Irish men, depicting their drinking and their violent natures. For example, the *Women's Journal,* which ran many Irish jokes, typically told this one:

> *Judge:* Murphy, you are drunk again.
> *Murphy:* Yes Your Honor.
> *Judge:* Didn't you solemnly promise me, when I let you off the last time, that you would never get drunk again?
> *Murphy:* Yes, Your Honor; but I wush drunk at the time. Your Honor, I wushn't 'sponsible for what I shaid.[22]

Irish women, less often poked fun at in the suffrage newspaper, were still the subjects of occasional jokes when it came to the perennial Bridget. "A Brooklyn woman said to her girl, a fresh arrival on the latest boat from Cork: 'Bridget, go on, and see if Mr. Bock, the butcher on the corner, has pigs' feet.' The dutiful servant went out and returned. 'Well, what did he say?' asked the mistress. 'Sure, he said nothing mum.' 'Has he got pigs' feet?' 'Sayeth, I could not see, mum—he had his boots on!'"[23]

More seriously, women's suffrage writers saw Irish men as violent and brutal particularly when it came to their wives, confirming the feminist position that Irish men bore the responsibility for much of the oppression of women. Gruesome news items of drunken husbands beating their wives echoed the *Women's Journal* position that women needed protection through suffrage.[24] The feminists, in fact, repeatedly contrasted their voteless status with that of the enfranchised Irish man, who, no matter how tempestuous, inebriated, or irrational, could exercise his right to vote and hold office.

The Catholic church was also condemned as a prime agent in the effort to keep women powerless and subordinate, opposing suffrage, because, as Lucy Stone noted in 1888, "We know that whatever tends to broaden women's minds and to interest them in public affairs renders them less blindly submissive to ecclesiastical influence."[25]

In a number of specific incidents Irish Catholics, as an organized group, and feminists clashed directly over some issue of public policy and these battles tended to exacerbate each side's negative feelings about the other. The suffragists in Boston, for example, took on with a vengeance John Boyle O'Reilly because of his opposition to the extension of the vote to women, claiming that the poet-editor "will soon enjoy the distinction of having called women suffrage more bad names than any other man of his day and generation." The *Boston Pilot,* O'Reilly's newspaper, became a storm center of controversy as the Hub City struggled with the issue of women's suffrage in municipal elections. Because of incidents like these, and since the backbone of the feminist movement came from Protestant, native-born American women who subscribed to a world view so strikingly different than that of the Irish, the male newcomers interpreted almost every act of the women's movement as hostile. By inference they assumed that any time women organized themselves for some purpose it would immediately jeopardize Catholic interests. These women, they believed, had to be feminists. The controversy did not limit itself to Boston. In Hartford, Connecticut, Philadelphia, and elsewhere, Irish men jumped to the conclusion that anti-Catholic actions by organized groups of women grew directly out of the suffragists' diabolical schemes against the Irish and their church.[26]

It did not matter to the Irish that not only did many of the antisuffragists indulge in the same anti-Catholic rhetoric as those who would enfranchise women but that many "anti's" purposely opposed enfranchisement of women because it would grant the ballot to Irish females as well. Margaret Deland, an active Bostonian, a reformer, and a novelist, went so far as to exclaim, "We have suffered many things at the hands of Patrick and now the New Woman would add Bridget!"[27] The Reverend Thomas Van Ness justified his opposition to women's suffrage because "in Colorado, the Irish men lay shillelahs on their wives to compel them to vote as they wish. Can we afford to bring another bone of contention into married life? . . . The Irish husband can compel his wife to vote as he pleases; the educated man in Brookline cannot."[28] While this Protestant minister may have known very little about the power relations in the Irish family, he did represent an important segment in the antisuffrage bloc. In an analysis of the forces in Massachusetts that worked in tandem to defeat women's suffrage, Thomas Wentworth Higginson drew out the irony of an alliance that brought together "the Roman Catholic wing of the Democratic Party" and the "Federalist half of the Republican Party." Higginson found this a "singular coalition," suggesting:

> The Federalist Party of the coalition joines in it not for the love of the other half but absolutely and literally for the fear of it. The one thing that makes the whole women's suffrage movement terrific to "society women" is not so much the fact that it would require them to vote—for in voting, if thus limited, there would be something rather well-bred and English—but the fact that Bridget and Nora will in this country, have to vote also. And the oddest thing of all is that, in order to prevent this undesirable result, the religious prejudices of Bridget's husband and Nora's brother are called into recognition to keep her out. Through fear of the Irish women they ally themselves politically speaking with the Irish man.

Justin D. Fulton, an active Boston nativist, ranted throughout the 1880s and 1890s that the enfranchisement of women amounted to handing over power to priests and the Pope. Since Irish women, he believed, slavishly followed the dictates of the church, they would vote only according to Romish doctrines, to the detriment of American liberty and freedom.

Irish men and women, needless to say, had no love for anyone who insulted Hibernian pride or who declaimed against the Church of Rome, but the feminists posed a more fundamental threat to Irish culture than did the "anti's." The feminists dreamed of a world where gender differences would blur to a minimum. The Irish fiercely believed in a world where gender differences gave order, balance, and rationality to human relations. The Irish profoundly feared that the feminists could succeed in convincing Bridget and Norah to share in that dream and in the process shake the foundation of the Irish world.

The suffragists did actually attempt to appeal to Irish Catholic women, trying to convince them that suffrage, and the wider extension of women's rights, could operate in their interests. The suffragists frequently drew the analogy between the movement for home rule in Ireland and the movement for granting political rights to women in America. Newspapers like the *Women's Journal* trumpeted loudly any statement by a Catholic cleric or prominent male Hibernian in support of giving women the ballot and demonstratively sought to link Irish traditions of strong and assertive womanhood with the needs for enlarged spheres for women. Father Thomas Scully of St. Mary's, Cambridge (Massachusetts), emerged as a hero to the suffrage women. This priest labored extensively among the women in his parish, urging them to vote in Cambridge elections, particularly because of his support for a "no-license" ordinance that he hoped would help curb Hibernian drinking. Furthermore, feminists recognized the economic dimension to female subordination, and the cry of "equal pay for equal work" reflected in part a feminist strategy to win over women of the working classes. Surely, they reasoned, this demand of the movement should strike a responsive chord to the hundreds of thousands of laboring women of Irish origin. The sympathy of the feminists toward Irish wives as victims of domestic violence impoverished by their husbands' drinking was sincere. They truly believed that Irish women needed help to break out of this mire. Importantly, in this recognition they did not differ from many Irish community leaders and Catholic clerics who blamed Irish men for the sorrow of their wives and the misfortune of their children.[30]

After describing a fair run by Irish women for a Catholic charity in Boston in 1886, the *Women's Journal* asked pointedly, "In all this Catholic assemblage the women were equals of men, speaking and voting for its success. Without women it would have been a failure, just as politics today. Why not invite women Catholic and Protestant into politics?"[31] In any number of ways Irish-American women answered this question for the suffragists and rejected their overtures. Running a church bazaar as well as earning money, saving it, and spending it, were one thing; politics was another. That Irish men and women enjoyed a relative equality in certain events and activities did not imply a meshing of spheres. That Irish women had an upper hand in family matters and could shape critical life decisions did not therefore mean that they wanted to enter activities reserved for men. In fact, almost the opposite situation developed. Irish women defined the economic sphere as the one in which *they* operated. They felt no need for politics and political games. That turf belonged to men, and with hardly any exceptions Irish women believed that it constituted a less important sphere than their own.

The Irish female resistance to feminism in its various phases represented a puzzling problem and a historic irony. On the one hand, Irish women lived lives quite apart from men and never passively followed male authority. They were also economic creatures competing in the scramble of the marketplace.

Even Irish traditions of gender segregation and reliance on female networks could have been a basis for the support of the movement. Like "new women," Irish women understood the differences between the married and the single state. They recognized that economic success and matrimony might be mutually exclusive. Yet, Irish women emphatically rejected the message of the movement, the ideology of feminism.

The number of Irish women who involved themselves in the women's suffrage movement amounted to a virtual handful. Cora Scott Pond lectured for the Massachusetts Women's Suffrage Association in the 1880s, and nationally, only Lucy Burns, in the early twentieth century, took a formidable role in the movement. Also in the 1910s, Eleanor O'Donnell McCormick in Memphis worked for the passage of the suffrage amendment.[32]

A much larger group of Irish women emphatically went on record against the ideas of the "new women" or remained totally uninterested in issues raised by the organized suffrage campaign. Mother Jones, for example, thought that the feminists essentially concerned themselves with trivial matters when compared to widespread economic suffering under industral capitalism. Augusta Troup and Kate Mullaney, active women trade unionists, believed that the differences in goals and values between working women and the women's rights advocates created a vast gulf in understanding and a massive barrier to cooperation. Some Irish women actively worked against the suffrage movement and Katherine Conway, a journalist and Irish community figure of note, participated actively in the Massachusetts Association Opposed to the Extension of Suffrage to Women. Conway missed no opportunity to criticize the women's movement, although she noted somewhat grudgingly, "The woman's suffragist, we must admit in the face of notable example, is often a most admirable woman, whom we are compelled to like personally, however little out of sympathy to her cause." Despite this, Conway believed, "It seems so beyond question that woman, as woman, can have no vocation to public life . . . it cannot be necessary, or even useful, that she should try to do what she cannot do." Ironically, Irish women who themselves pursued active careers rejected the notion that no fundamental differences existed between men and women or that separate spheres should not exist. As Katherine Mullaney, yet another journalist, exclaimed, "Let Catholic women be true children of Mary unsullied in their purity. . . . Oh! if men and women, instead of quarreling over a superiority which does not exist, would only recognize, acknowledge, and admire in each other the gifts, so different yet so equally balanced in worth, which God has given them!"[33]

Poet Eleanor Donnelly chose more lyrical language, as she asserted:

They dressed like men, they talked like men, they forced themselves into the manliest avocations of men, loud-voiced and aggressive, to the criminal neglect to their own bounden duties. Eve was content with one of Adam's ribs. Her daughters of today want (what the Irish men called) 'his entire system.' . . . All that is gentle, attractive, womanly withers under the hot sun of publicity and notoriety.[34]

The paucity of Hibernian female names among the ranks of the movement further testifies to the lack of interest that Irish women demonstrated for its aims, methods, and ideals. Given their assertiveness and fierce commitment to things they believed in, this absence loudly proclaimed hostility.

The opposition of the Church to the enfranchisement of women does not in and of itself explain away the small amount of Irish female support. The Church expressed ambivalent sentiments about trade unionism, particularly the Knights of Labor, yet Irish women participated enthusiastically and joined the labor movement in large numbers because it offered a realistic way to advance economic goals. Similarly, the Church consistently opposed Catholic attendance in public schools, but this did not stop the tens of thousands of young Irish women who flooded the public high schools and normal schools to prepare themselves for good jobs. Clerical opposition to higher education for Catholic women posed little problem for the Irish-American girls who sought college education as an important prerequisite for a career.

Nor can traditional Irish notions of women's inferiority give sense to the Irish female hostility for the feminist crusade. Irish women never accepted the subordinate and submissive role that the culture assigned to them, and when it came to things that *they* deemed important, they flexed their muscle and acted. Like their brothers, husbands, and fathers, they accepted the notion that separate spheres for men and women operated for everyone's benefit. The cultural traditions of gender segregation and the resulting patterns of gender hostility created a situation in which women had no interest in participating in men's activities, had no yen to join male company. Like Irish men, they seized on those aspects of the feminist argument which seemed the most antithetical to Catholicism and Irish culture as a justification for opposing feminism. The movement spoke to issues that did not interest them and addressed questions they found offensive, particularly those of divorce, abortion, birth control, and sexual freedom. The woman's movement had a cultural outlook and a religious orientation that differed profoundly from that of Irish women. The middle-class basis of the organization for the expansion of women's rights drove an additional wedge between them and the legions of working-class Irish women who had immigrated to America for economic goals and saw no reason to expend energy on causes and crusades that brought them no closer to fulfilling their goals.

The feminists actually had a great deal to offer Irish women. Their vision of economic justice certainly could have fit into the Irish female world view. The feminists correctly recognized that married Irish women lived lives of poverty, oppression, and victimization. Yet in the final analysis ethnicity and cultural values proved to be more significant than gender. Despite the strides Irish women had made toward acculturation, their commitment to their Irish heritage remained intact. Their economic assertiveness and strong sense of self did not jar with those cultural traditions but proved instead to be the mechanism for blending old-world ideals with American needs.

A Note on the Sources

Historians have long claimed that it is impossible to write a full-scale book on immigrant women or on any group of women from the ranks of the so-called inarticulate. By using recent quantitative social histories, however, as well as looking at other wide-ranging sources, doubt can be cast on that claim. A number of different kinds of sources went into making this book possible. The major problem, in fact, that I encountered in putting together this study of immigrant Irish women was that the mountains of material from government, charity, and church sources, particularly on a local level, seemed almost insurmountable. The number of federal, state, and municipal documents that dealt with Irish women in terms of work, education, family, deviance, and the like ran into the thousands. The number of predominately Irish parishes that wrote anniversary booklets, which chronicled the activities of women—lay and religious—similarly provided me with more materials than could intelligibly be worked through. More charity and settlement houses left records, published and unpublished, about Irish women than any one study could encompass with real care.

This book considers Irish women as migrants, family members, laborers, and participants in the life of their church and community. It could have been organized differently. It could have traced patterns of Irish female migration and adaptation chronologically and therefore would have looked for and stressed patterns of change. Had I opted for such an analysis, I would have focused on different kinds of sources. Such a thematic organization would more appropriately have been based on original quantitative research. The data for such a project are there and have been digested in part by many recent works in the "new social history." I chose, however, to paint the broad canvas, trying to depict the widest panorama. Others hopefully will pick up the brush and fill in the details through quantitative and qualitative research yet to come.

The starting point for the research on Irish immigrant women naturally ought to begin with those women before they left Ireland and this rich literature, produced particularly by anthropologists, provides a cogent basis for analysis. Most importantly here, Solon Kimball and Conrad Arensberg's *Family and Community* (Cambridge, Mass.: Harvard University Press, 1940) and Conrad Arensberg's *The Irish Countryman* (New York: Macmillan, 1937) examined the nature of the single-inheritance system and its wide-ranging impact on Irish men and women. More recent ethnographic work, such as John Messenger's *Inis Beag* (New York: Holt, Rinehart, & Winston, 1969), and Hugh Brody's *Inishkillane* (Harmondsworth: Penguin, 1973), confirmed this pattern. Nancy Scheper-Hughes linked these classical anthropological studies with the psychiatric literature on Irish schizophrenia in her study *Saints, Scholars, and Schizophrenics* (Berkeley and Los Angeles: University of California Press, 1979).

Historic studies of Ireland also contributed significantly to the attempt to understand the role of Irish women. The raging debate among historians over the nature of the Irish demographic shift proved particularly revealing and despite criticism, the works of Kenneth H. Connell, such as *Irish Peasant Society* (Oxford: Clarendon Press, 1968) and his numerous articles that appeared particularly in *Past and Present* and *Economic History Review* in the 1950s and 1960s, furthered my understanding of male-female relations in the Emerald Isle. No study compares in importance to Robert E. Kennedy's *The Irish* (Berkeley and Los Angeles: University of California Press, 1973) as a tool in the analysis of emigration from Ireland and the attraction of women to that exodus.

Certain primary sources ought particularly to be highlighted as they influenced this study. Parliamentary reports and papers issued by the Devon Commission shed light on marriage patterns among the Irish and how the Irish felt about them, and the official Census of Ireland, when viewed in light of probable error and miscalculation, offered a beginning point for analyzing population trends. Popular magazines in Ireland, like the *Gael* and the *Irish Monthly*, provided me with a convenient way to sample literary images of women and family life. Furthermore, the details that can be gleaned from biographies and autobiographies of Irish women and men—both those who stayed in Ireland and those who migrated—provided details about age at marriage, rates of nonmarriage, patterns of migration, attitudes about the opposite sex, and the like. These qualitative sources are useful in confirming the accuracy and fleshing out the vast collections of statistics from both primary and secondary accounts.

Official sources in the United States were also indispensible in painting a portrait of Irish women. Many of the forty-one volumes of the Immigration Commission (1911) provided data on the Irish, both men and women, and states like New York, Massachusetts, Rhode Island, Illinois, Pennsylvania, and California, which housed massive Irish enclaves, issued voluminous reports of all kinds to add to the knowledge of Irish women's work, family life, and deviance. Municipal reports chronicled particularly the problems of poverty, crime, and intemperance that plagued the Irish. Perhaps the most important source of statistics and descriptions of Irish females came from the various state labor commissions. Although these bodies were primarily interested in factory workers, the kinds of questions they asked and the number of women that they interviewed made them invaluable for this project. The Massachusetts Bureau of the Statistics of Labor, the first of its kind, took a tremendous interest in the conditions of women's work, particularly in the years it was directed by Carroll D. Wright. The annual reports yielded a great deal of information as did many of the bureau's special reports. Maine, Minnesota, Rhode Island, and Pennsylvania also had active and productive labor departments that collected material on women, work, and ethnicity.

This study also made ample use of traveler's accounts, which need to be treated with a great deal of care because of the highly personal nature of the evidence and the selectivity of perceptions. Foreign travelers to nineteenth-century America tended to focus on the bizarre and the outlandish in the new American setting. British travelers especially posed an interesting problem because many brought to their accounts of American life their own deep-seated anti-Irish prejudices. If they found the Irish to be volatile, criminal, incorrigible, disorganized, and priest-ridden in the Emerald Isle, they tended to look for those very traits in the immigrants. Despite these problems, such accounts, when used in tandem with a spectrum of other kinds of sources, were useful.

Similarly, studies of crime and drunkenness in the nineteenth century offered a peek at the netherside of Irish-American female existence. These observations stressed the deviant behavior of maladjustment of Irish women. These observations, hardly objective, had a tendency to define the Irish "character" or the ignorance fostered by the "Romish" church as causes of the problem. Despite such important *caveats,* however, the fact that widows and abandoned Hibernian wives made up the vast majority of cases helped confirm patterns that emerged from less subjective accounts.

Journalists and reformers have left a wide array of observations about Irish life and the status of Irish women in their communities. Settlement house residents in New York, Chicago, and Boston, furthermore, labored most extensively among neighborhood women, and the papers of the North Bennett Street Industrial School, Denison House, and Rutland Corner House, which are kept at the Women's Archives of the Schlesinger Library, chronicle the individual problems of Irish women in late-nineteenth- and early-twentieth-century Boston. Memoirs of settlement workers like Jane Addams, Lillian Wald, Emily Green Balch, and Mary Kingsbury Simkhovitch add numerous anecdotes about Irish women they knew. These details, when added to a stockpile gleaned from the writings of Jacob Riis, Robert Woods and Albert Kennedy, Frances Kellor, and Helen Campbell, flesh out the statistical material from state and municipal records.

Probably the most important role Irish women played in America, according to native-born American women, was as domestic servants, and the voluminous literature on the servant question provides one perspective on Irish female behavior. Ladies' periodicals such as the *Ladies' Home Journal* gave an idea how employers felt about Irish domestics. Similarly, a number of "scientific" studies of service such as Lucy Maynard Salmon's *Domestic Service* (New York, 1897), sought to present the complaints and aspirations of both employee and employer. Recent secondary studies of domestic work, most importantly David Katzman's *Seven Days a Week* (New York: Oxford University Press, 1979) presented invaluable information about the nature of the occupation. Significantly, Katzman, like most recent historians who have studied the subject, could not or chose not to view domestic work as a nineteenth-century Irish girl would have—a reasonable occupation that by the standards of the day paid well, and that by the standards of her own needs and experiences provided a reasonably acceptable life style.

The attempt to view domestic service and other issues—family, religion, politics, education—from the vantage point of Irish women themselves is, to say the least, a difficult undertaking. The scores of autobiographies of Irish women or Irish men take one step toward that, but only a small step because of the highly selective nature of autobiographical writing. Similarly, so few Irish women in fact wrote autobiographies they are therefore not necessarily representative and provide too small a base of data. However, internal community sources, church bulletins, parish commemorative histories, and lists of donors to charitable projects provide a somewhat broader picture of mass behavior. The records of the Fenian movement, in the O'Donovan Rossa Collection at the Archives of the Catholic University of America, indicate that women rarely donated money to that cause. On the other hand, the rolls of contributors to many Catholic charitable projects—the Home of the Guardian Angel in Cambridge, Massachusetts, as one small example (the records of which are in the Archives of the Roman Catholic Archdiocese of Boston) —reveal that women donated significantly more money than did men. This was not a random circumstance. Irish Catholic women found the nationalist movement uninteresting and unworthy of their largesse partly because politics was a man's province and partly because that movement did not speak to their needs, concerns, and aspirations. Not so the Church, which provided Irish-American women with shelter, schooling, employment bureaus, vocational training centers, day nurseries, hospitals, social clubs, and the like.

The histories of various religious sisterhoods in a variety of American cities, most written as testimonials or chronicles by nuns themselves, others written as historic pieces (frequently in the form of masters theses at Catholic universities), contributed mightily to this study. Besides providing a massive amount of detail about who the nuns were (Irish-American women) and how they functioned in the Irish Catholic communities, they offer a view of what Irish women deemed important. The fact that the Sisters of Mercy and the Sisters of the Good Shepherd emphasized vocational training as a first step toward salvation underscored the economic priorities of Irish women—nuns and laywomen alike. That the orders did not stress preparation for marriage, but preparation for the marketplace, provides an insight into the value hierarchy of these women.

Like most ethnic communities in America, the Irish enclaves of many cities have attempted to write their history as a legacy to posterity. These filiopietistic studies have many drawbacks. To say the least, they seek to deflect attention from problems and pathologies while they attempt to portray the heroic, the noble, and the solidly respectable. Yet even here the basic outlines of social life and family structure, employment choices and educational patterns, can be discerned. A privately published study of the Irish in Gardner, Massachusetts, for example, written for the benefit of the Irish in Gardner, Massachusetts, is nonetheless a rich source of social history. Such a history describes who migrated first and whom they brought over, and which young Hibernians graduated from high school every year. A slim, celebratory volume like this also describes Catholic charitable projects and who took advantage of them. Successful businesses are painted in glowing colors, with biographies of schoolteachers and young people who entered religious orders. Taken in this context, and multiplied for dozens of Irish communities across the country, one can consider these as rich resources.

Furthermore, Irish-American newspapers—the *Boston Pilot,* the *Irish World* (New York) and *O'Neill's Irish Pictorial* (Boston) as well as the *Catholic World*—not only provided a plethora of details of immigrant life, particularly in the newspapers' "Information Wanted" columns, but provided a chance to see how the Irish saw themselves. Fiction, particularly of the sentimental, mass audience type, further mirrored group priorities and group pressures.

The Irish in America have been studied well. No analysis can compare to Oscar Handlin's *Boston's Immigrants* (Cambridge, Mass.: Harvard University Press, 1941). One might venture to say it created ethnic-immigration history and set a standard of excellence that all subsequent attempts in the field need to measure up to. Thomas Brown's *Irish-American Nationalism* (Philadelphia: J. B. Lippincott, 1966), William Shannon's *The American Irish* (New York: McMillan, 1963), George W. Potter's *To the Golden Door* (Boston: Little, Brown, 1960), and Carl Wittke's *The Irish in America* (Baton Rouge: Louisiana State University Press, 1956) all stand as solid works that emphasize different aspects of the Hibernians in America. What is so striking in all of these works, though, is that none of the historians made much of the numerical preponderance of women as migrants and as residents of the Irish enclaves. The fascination that historians have had with the Irish (men) in politics has obscured the Irish female economic drive and has meant that the massive involvement of Irish women in trade unionism, the rapid movement of Irish women in schoolteaching, nursing, and other occupations, and the low rates of Irish marriage have gone virtually unnoticed and unexamined.

The fields of the "new" social history and family history with their extensive use of statistical techniques and quantitative sources helped me make the jump from the "older" histories of the Irish to this analysis of Irish women. Works by Tamara Hareven, Richard Sennett, Herbert Guttman, Allen Dawley, Don Doyle Harrison, Daniel J. Walkowitz, Elizabeth Pleck, and Carol Groneman, to name but a few, collected vast amounts of statistical-interpretive material on Irish-American marriages, family arrangements, work patterns, and educational achievements. In the light of these efforts the gaps in older studies can be filled in to help shift the focus from Irish men to Irish women and the nature of Irish male-female relations. These studies also have limitations. Many of the works in the recent spate of mobility studies, like those of Stephen Thernstrom, Michael Frisch, Howard Gitleman, and others, by necessity studied Irish male earnings, occupational status, and property accumulation through census records and other readily available statistical sources. How those studies would have looked had the earnings of Irish servant girls in Newburyport, Irish female schoolteachers in Waltham, and the Bridgets, Norahs, and Hannahs who worked as bookkeepers, nurses, and stenographers in Springfield been included, one only can speculate.

A study like this could be repeated for Italian women, German women, and French-Canadian women as well as for internal female migrants who abandoned the rural South to make their way to the urban North. That immigrant women have not been studied is not because the material was not there. That poor, working-class women have not been studied is not because they were "inarticulate." It may be more accurate to say that historians, with their own biases of gender, class, and culture, have been basically deaf to the voices of such women and have assumed that they could not be studied. A creative use of the best of the old descriptive histories and the best of the new quantitative studies, cemented together with internal community sources that help one view these women as they viewed themselves, can go a long way toward filling this gap.

Notes

The following collections are contained in the Archives of the Schlesinger Library, Radcliffe College, Cambridge, Mass.:

Consumers' League of Massachusetts Papers
Domestic Reform League Papers
Denison House Papers
Ellen Martin Henrotin Collection
Harriet Jane Hanson Robinson Papers
Leonora O'Reilly Papers
North Bennett Street Collection
Rutland Corner House Papers
Women's Educational and Industrial Union (WEIU) Papers

INTRODUCTION

1. J. Hector St. John de Crevecoeur, *Letters from an American Farmer* (London: Everyman's Library, 1971), p. 41.

CHAPTER 1

1. "Jessy Darling, or the Emigrant's Farewell," in *O 'Neill's Irish Pictorial*, March 5, 1859, p. 65.

2. Robert Dudley Edwards and T. Desmond Williams, eds., *The Great Famine: Studies in Irish History, 1845-1852* (Dublin: Irish Committee of Historical Sciences, 1956); Cecil Woodham-Smith, *The Great Hunger* (London: H. Hamilton, 1962).

3. J. C. Beck, *A Short History of Ireland* (New York: Harper & Row, 1952), p. 144.

4. John Francis Maguire, *Father Matthew: A Biography* (London: Longman, Green, Longman, 1863), p. 424.

5. "Foreign Immigration" *American Review* 5 (1847):639.

6. 1851 Census, quoted in E. Estyn Evans, *Irish Folk Ways* (London: Routledge & Kegan Paul, 1957), p. 295.

7. According to John Murphy, "Priests and People in Modern Irish History," *Christus Rex* 23 (4):235-59, 5,000 priests and nuns ministered to 5 million Catholics in 1844. By 1900, when Ireland's population had dropped to 3 million, 141,000 religious were serving Ireland.

8. Robert E. Kennedy, *The Irish: Emigration, Marriage, and Fertility* (Berkeley and Los Angeles: University of California Press, 1973), p. 27; Oscar Handlin, *Boston Immigrants* (Cambridge, Mass.: Harvard University Press, 1941) pp. 42-43, 242.

9. Kennedy, *The Irish*, pp. 2-3.

10. Kenneth H. Connell, "Population," in *Social Life in Ireland: 1800-1845*, ed. R. B. McDonald (Dublin: Cultural Relations Committee of Ireland, 1957), pp. 85-97; Thomas Walter Freeman, *Pre-Famine Ireland: A Study in Historical Geography* (Manchester: Manchester University Press, 1957), pp. 38-39.

11. Gale Edward Christianson, "Population, the Potato, and Depression in Ireland," *Eire-Ireland* 7, no. 4 (1974):70-95; Kenneth H. Connell, "The Potato in Ireland," *Past and Present* 23 (1962):57-71; L.M. Cullen, "Irish History without the Potato," *Past and Present* 40 (1968): 72-83; *Parliamentary Papers*, 1835, 32:229; Kenneth H. Connell, *The Population of Ireland, 1750-1845* (London: Oxford University Press, 1850); idem., *Irish Peasant Society* (Oxford: Clarendon Press, 1968); Brendan Walsh, "A Perspective on Irish Population Patterns, *Eire-Ireland* 4, no. 3 (1969):3-21; Michael Drake, "Marriage and Population Growth in Ireland, 1750-1845," *Economic History Review* 16 (1963):301-13; "A Few Words on the Census of Ireland," *Fraser's* 64 (1861):300-307.

12. Quoted in Joseph Lee, "Marriage and Population in Pre-Famine Ireland," *Economic History Review* 21 (1968):283-95.

13. Thomas Naughten, "The Exodus of the Irish," *Westminster Review* 157 (1902):85-88; Richard J. Kelly, "Emigration and Its Consequences," *New Ireland Review* 21, no. 5(1904): 257-267.

14. "Some Results of the Irish Exodus," *Irish Monthly* (1873) pp. 117-20.

15. "Survey of Ireland from 1840 to 1886," *Journal of the Statistical and Social Inquiry Society of Ireland* 68 (1888):321-61; "Irish Progress during the Past Ten Years, 1881-1890," *Journal of the Statistical and Social Inquiry of Ireland* 71 (1891):453-507; T. W. Russell, "Lessons of a Decade," *Nineteenth Century* 32 (1892):581-93.

16. Kennedy, *The Irish*, p. 214.

17. Edward Cayne, "Irish Population Problems," *Studies* 21 (1954):151-67; R. C. Geary, "Some Reflections on Irish Population Trend Questions," *Studies* 21 (1954):168-77; James J. Walsh, "Shy Irish Bachelors," *America*, March 29, 1930, p. 593.

18. Kennedy, *The Irish*, p. 72-73.

19. Kenneth H. Connell, "Peasant Marriage in Ireland after the Great Famine," *Past and Present* 12 (1957):76-91.

20. "The Grand Match," *Gael*, 1899.

21. Connell, "Peasant Marriage in Ireland."

22. See the following works by Kenneth H. Connell: *Irish Peasant Society*, pp. 113-21; "The Land Legislation and Irish Social Life," *Economic History Review*, 11, no. 1 (1958):1-7; "Potato in Ireland," pp. 57-71; "Peasant Marriage in Ireland."

23. Conrad Arensberg and Solon Kimball, *Family and Community in Ireland* (Cambridge, Mass.: Harvard University Press, 1940).

24. Freeman, *Pre-Famine Ireland*, p. 40; Kennedy, *The Irish*, p. 12.

25. Conrad Arensberg, *The Irish Countryman* (New York: Macmillan, 1937), p. 86.

26. Alf MacLochlain, "Social Life in Country Clare, 1800-1850," *Irish University Review* 2, no. 1 (1972):55-78; L. M. Cullen, *Life in Ireland* (London: G. T. Batsford, 1968).

27. Edward Wakefield, *An Account of Ireland, Statistical and Political*, 2 vols. (London: Longman, Hurst, Rees, Orme and Brown, 1812), 2:751.

28. Arensberg and Kimball, *Family and Community*, pp. 45-58.

29. John C. Messenger, *Inis Beag: Isle of Ireland* (New York: Holt, Rinehart & Winston, 1969), pp. 40-41; Arensberg, *Irish Countryman,* pp. 42-52; *Irish World* (hereafter cited as *I.W.*), December 3, 1879, p. 8.

30. Robert M. Sillard, "The Social Side of Irish Character," *Westminster Review* 161 (1904):82-89.

31. Nancy Scheper-Hughes, *Saints, Scholars, and Schizophrenics: Mental Illness in Rural Ireland* (Berkeley and Los Angeles: University of California Press, 1979), pp. 95-100; Richard Stivers, *The Hair of the Dog: Irish Drinking and the American Stereotype* (University Park: Pennsylvania State University Press, 1979), pp. 72-74.

32. Quoted in Kennedy, *The Irish,* p. 65.

33. Eileen Kane, "Man and Kin in Donegal: A Study of Kinship Functions in a Rural Irish and Irish-American Community," *Ethnology* 1, no. 1 (1974):91-108; Arensberg and Kimball, *Family and Community,* p. 196.

34. Evans, *Irish Folk Ways,* p. 36; Scheper-Hughes, *Saints, Scholars,* pp. 99-107; Sean Gaffney and Seamus Cashman, *Proverbs and Sayings of Ireland* (Rathgar, Ire.: Wolfhound Press, 1974), pp. 103, 106.

35. Robert F. Bales, "The Fixation Factor in Alcohol Addiction: A Hypothesis Derived from a Comparative Study of Irish and Jewish Social Norms," Ph.D. diss., Harvard University, 1944, pp. 189-92; Kennedy, *The Irish,* pp. 139-72; Connell, "Peasant Marriage in Ireland."

36. George Birmingham, *Irishmen All.*

37. John Francis Maguire, *The Irish in America* (New York: D. & J. Sadlier, 1868), p. 203; Scheper-Hughes, *Saints, Scholars,* p. 99-102; Connell, "Peasant Marriage in Ireland," pp. 514-18; Michael Anderson, *Family Structure in Nineteenth-Century Lancashire* (Cambridge: Cambridge University Press, 1971).

38. Kennedy, *The Irish;* Arensberg and Kimball, *Family and Community,* pp. 66, 133.

39. Hamilton Holt, *The Life Stories of Undistinguished Americans as Told by Themselves,* (New York: James Pott, 1906), pp. 143-49.

40. Ibid.

41. Arensberg and Kimball, *Family and Community;* Kennedy, *The Irish,* pp. 66-85; Elise de la Fontaine, "Cultural and Psychological Implications in Case Work with Irish Clients," in *Cultural Problems in Social Case Work* (New York: Family Welfare Association of America, 1940), pp. 21-37; Scheper-Hughes, *Saints, Scholars.* See also Marvin K. Opler, "Cultural Differences in Mental Disorders: An Italian and Irish Contrast in the Schizophrenics," in *Culture and Mental Health* (New York: Macmillan, 1959), pp. 425-42; "Cultural Perspectives in Research on Schizophrenics," in *Culture and Social Psychiatry* (New York: Atherton, 1967), pp. 282-303; with Jerome Singer, "Ethnic Difference in Behavior and Psychopathology: Italian and Irish," *International Journal of Social Psychiatry* 2, no. 1 (1956): 11-23.

42. "Irish and English Peasantry," *Irish Penny* 1, no. 1 (January 5, 1833):8.

43. Kennedy, *The Irish,* pp. 51-65; Evans, *Irish Folk Ways,* pp. 65-66.

44. F.M.F. Lovibond, "Women and Hygiene," *New Ireland Review* 21, no. 2 (1904):74-82.

45. Arland Ussher, "The Boundary between the Sexes," in *The Vanishing Irish: The Enigma of the Modern World,* ed. James A. O'Brien (New York: McGraw-Hill, 1953), pp. 156-69.

46. Kenneth H. Connell, "Illegitimacy before the Famine," in *Irish Peasant Society,* pp. 51-86; Gustave de Beaumont, in *Ireland: Social, Political, and Religious,* trans. William Cooke Taylor, 2 vols. (London: R. Bentley, 1839) 2:35.

47. Connell, "Illegitimacy," p. 83; Kenneth H. Connell, "Catholicism and Marriage in the Century after the Famine," in *Irish Peasant Society,* pp. 119-21;

48. Albert Leffingwell, *Illegitimacy and the Influence of Seasons upon Conduct: Two Studies in Demography* (London: Sonnenschein, 1892); A. C. Haddon, and C. F. Browne, "The Ethnography of the Aran Islands, County Galway," *Proceedings of the Royal Irish*

Academy, 1891-1892, p. 800; "Clipping, May 5, 1880," *Post,* papers of Sir Thomas Askew Larcom, National Library of Dublin; James F. Cassidy, *The Woman of the Gael* (Boston: Stratford, 1922), p. 267; *I.W.:* December 3, 1870, p. 8; May 9, 1874, p. 5.

49. Connell, "Catholicism and Marriage"; Kennedy, *The Irish,* pp. 158-59; David W. Miller, "Irish Catholicism and the Great Famine," *Journal of Social History* 9, 1 (1975):81-98.

50. *I.W.,* August 19, 1871, p. 6.

51. "Irish Song," *Living Age* 35 (1852):1; *Gael* 23, no. 6 (1904):210-11, 269.

52. John C. Messenger, "Sex and Repression in an Irish Folk Community," in *Human Sexual Behavior: Variations in the Ethnographic Spectrum,* ed. Donald S. Marshall and Robert C. Suggs (New York: Basic Books, 1971), pp. 3-37; James Macauly, *Ireland in 1872: A Tour or Observation with Remarks on Irish Public Questions* (London: Henry S. King, 1873), pp. 243-44.

53. James Clarence Mongan, "The Woman of the Three Cows," in *Proud We Are and Irish,* ed. James M. Cleary (Chicago: Quadrangle, 1966).

54. James Lyman Molloy, "Kerry Dances," in *One Thousand Years of Irish Poetry,* ed. Kathleen Hoagland (New York: Devin-Adair, 1947), pp. 532-53.

55. Robert T. Anderson and Gallatin Anderson, "The Indirect Social Structure of European Village Communities," *American Anthropologist* 64 (October 1962):1016-17; Messenger, *Inis Beag,* pp. 61-62, 76-78.

56. Lawrence J. McCaffrey, *The Irish Question, 1800-1922* (Lexington: University of Kentucky Press, 1968).

57. Arensberg and Kimball, *Family and Community,* pp. 65, 68-69; Messenger, "Sex and Repression," p. 9; George Gmelch, *The Irish Tinkers: The Urbanization of an Itinerant People* (Menlo Park, Calif.: Cummings, 1977), p. 18.

58. Marguerite Moore, "Dawdlings in Donegal," *Catholic World* 62, no. 368 (1895):167-78; quoted in Cullen, *Six Generations: Life and Work in Ireland from 1790* (Cork: Mercer Press, 1970), p. 51; Alf MacLochlain, "Social Life in County Clare, 1800-1850," *Irish University Review* 2, no. 1 (1972): 55-78.

59. Connell, *Irish Peasant Society,* p. 18; Marie Harrison, *Dawn in Ireland* (London: Andrew Melrose, 1917), p. 27.

60. William Carleton, "The Irish Matchmaker," *Irish Penny* 1, no. 15 (October 10, 1840):116-20; "The Irish Midwife," *Irish Penny* 1, no. 26 (December 26, 1840):202-4; Sean O'Sullieabhain, *Irish Folk Customs and Belief* (Dublin: Cultural Relations Committee of Ireland, 1967), pp. 50-55; Macauly, *Ireland in 1872,* pp. 1-2; Brody, *Inishkillane,* p. 83.

61. J. J. Lee, "Women and the Church since the Famine," in *Women and Irish Society: The Historic Dimension,* ed. Margaret MacCurtain and Douncha O'Corrin (Westport, Conn.: Greenwood Press, 1979); Marguerite Moore, "A New Woman's Work in the West of Ireland" *Catholic World* 64, no. 382 (1897):451-59; Connell, *Irish Peasant Society,* pp. 113-61; Patrick William O'Ryan, *The Plough and the Cross* (Point Loma, Calif.: Aryon Theosophical, 1916).

CHAPTER 2

1. U.S. Immigration Commission, *Statistical Review of Immigration, 1820-1910: Distribution of Immigration, 1850-1900* (Washington, D.C., 1911); John R. Commons, *Races and Immigrants in America* (New York: Macmillan, 1907), p. 122.

2. Frances Morehouse, "Irish Migration of the 'Forties,'" *American Historical Review* 33 (1928):579-92; S. H. Cousens, "Emigration and Demographic Change in Ireland, 1851-1861," *Economic History Review* 14, no. 2 (1961):275-88; Gerald Shaughnessy, "A Century of Catholic Growth in the United States: 1820-1920," Ph.D. diss., Catholic University of America, 1922; S. H. Cousens, "The Regional Patterns of Emigration during the Irish Famine, 1846-1851," *Institute of British Geographers, Transactions and Papers* 27 (1960):119-34.

3. Maldwyn Alan Jones, "The Background of Emigration from Great Britain in the Nineteenth Century," *Perspectives in American History* 7 (1973):3-92; James Meehan, "Some Features of Irish Emigration," *International Labour Review* 69, no. 2 (1954):128-39.

4. Cousens, "Regional Patterns," p. 309; Meehan, "Irish Emigration"; John Archer Jackson, *The Irish in Britain* (London: Routledge & Kegan Paul, 1963), p. 18; "The Irish in America," *Westminster Review* 129 (1888):713-32.

5. Census data in Robert E. Kennedy, *The Irish* (Berkeley and Los Angeles: University of California Press, 1973), pp. 67-68, 77-78. London *Times,* quoted in Richard J. Kelly, "Emigration and Its Consequences," *New Ireland Review* 21, no. 5 (1904):257-67. See also G.R.C. Keep, "Some Irish Opinion on Population and Emigration," *Irish Ecclesiastical Record* 84 (1955):377-86; A. M. Sullivan, "Why Send More Irish out of Ireland," *Nineteenth Century* (1883);

6. Richard J. Kelly, "Emigration and Its Consequences," *New Ireland Review* 21, 5 (1904): 257-67.

7. John Verschoyle, "The Condition of Kerry," *Living Age* 171 (1886): 552-67.

8. Oliver MacDonagh, "The Irish Catholic Clergy and Emigration during the Great Famine," *Irish Historical Studies* 5, no. 20 (1947):287-302.

9. Terry Coleman, *Going to America* (New York: Pantheon, 1972), pp. 180-92; Cousens, "The Regional Pattern," p. 309.

10. Quoted in Edith Abbott, *Historical Aspects of Immigration* (Chicago: University of Chicago Press, 1926), pp. 662-63.

11. Ibid.

12. Robert F. Clokey, "Irish Emigration from Workhouses," *Journal of the Statistical and Social Inquiry Society of Ireland* 25 (1863):416-35; Robert Ernst, *Immigrant Life in New York City: 1825-1863* (New York: Columbia University Press, 1949), p. 243; R. Denny Urlin, "Remarks on the Middle Class (Female) Emigration Society," *Journal of the Statistical and Social Inquiry Society of Ireland* 25 (1863):439-46.

13. Maurice O'Sullivan, *Twenty Years A-Growing* (New York: Viking Press, 1933), pp. 219-23.

14. "The Life Story of an Irish Cook" in *The Life Stories of Undistinguished Americans as Told by Themselves,* ed. Hamilton Holt (New York: James Pott, 1906), pp. 143-47.

15. "The Philosophy of Immigration," *Catholic World* 9 (1869):399-405.

16. Katherine Conway and Mabel Ward Cameron, *Charles Francis Donnelly: A Memoir* (New York: James T. White, 1909), p. 10.

17. Some of the sources on migration patterns of individual Irish-Americans include Dale Fetherling, *Mother Jones: The Miners' Angel* (Carbondale: Southern Illinois University Press, 1974), p. 3; James Michael Curley, *I'd Do It Again: A Record of All My Uproarious Years* (Englewood Cliffs, N.J.: Prentice-Hall, 1957), p. 17; Sisters of Reparation of the Congregation of Mary, *"Blessed are the Merciful": The Life of Mother Mary Zita, Foundress* (Patterson, N.J.: St. Anthony Guild, 1953), p. 18; James J. Walsh, "Mother Xavier Mehegan and Her Work," *Catholic World* 121, no. 725 (1925):624-32; Elizabeth Gurley Flynn, *The Rebel Girl: An Autobiography* (New York: Masses and Mainstream, 1955), p. 26; Miriam Allen deFord, *They Were San Franciscans* (Caldwell, Id.: Caxton Printers, 1941), pp. 136-37; Marie M. Grearson, *The Early Irish Settlers in the Town of Gardner, Massachusetts* (Author, 1932), p. 14; Joseph I. C. Clake, *My Life and My Memories* (New York: Dodd, Mead, 1925), pp. 2-6; Rev. William Byrne, "One Hundred Years of the Catholic Church in Boston," 1880, archives of the Roman Catholic Archdiocese of Boston; Mary C. Donelin, "American Irish Women 'Firsts,'" *Journal of the American Historical Society* 24 (1925):215-21.

18. Brendan MacAodha, "Letters from America," *Ulster Folklife* 3, no. 1 (1957):64-69; "Irish Poor Laws and Irish Emigration," *Quarterly Review* 157, no. 314 (1884):440-72; "An Irish Emigrant's Letter," *Living Age* 32 (1852):422; Arnold Schrier, *Ireland and the American Emigration, 1850-1900* (Minneapolis: University of Minnesota Press, 1958), pp. 24-25, 29, 31-

38, 75, 115; Gordon Stables, "With the Irish Emigrants," *Potter's American Monthly* 18 (1882):512-16; Charles Dickens, "The Irish in America," *All the Year Round* 1, no. 22 (1869): 510-14.

19. Quoted in Franklin E. Fitzpatrick, "Irish Immigration into New York, from 1865 to 1880," Master's thesis, Catholic University of America, 1948, p. 42.

20. "Immigrant Women and Girls in Boston: A Report," 1907, box 7, folder 49, WEIU Papers.

21. Quoted in John F. Maguire, *The Irish in America* (New York: D. & J. Sadlier, 1868), pp. 203-4.

22. Dickens, "The Irish," p. 510.

23. *Boston Pilot,* 1850-53; *I.W.,* 1870-77.

24. *Report of the Temporary Home for Women,* 1890, folder 52, Rutland Corner House Papers.

25. Ibid.

26. Kennedy, *The Irish,* pp. 66-85; Frederick A. Bushee, "The Growth of the Population of Boston," *Quarterly Publications of the American Statistical Association* 7, no. 46 (1899):239-74.

27. Thomas D'Arcy McGee, *A History of the Irish Settlers in North America, from the Earliest Period to the Census of 1850* (Boston: American Celt, 1851), p. 139.

28. William J. Onahan, "Irish Settlements in Illinois," *Catholic World* (1881):157-62.

29. John J. Hogan, *On the Mission in Missouri, 1857-1868* (Kansas City: J. A. Heilmann, 1892), p. 6.

30. Edward Everett Hale, *Letters on Irish Immigration* (Boston: Phillips, Sampson, 1852), p. 33.

31. Ibid.

32. Patrick J. Blessing, "West among Strangers: Irish Migration to California, 1850-1880," Ph.D. diss., University of California, Los Angeles, 1977; Caroll D. Wright, *The Slums of Baltimore, Chicago, New York, and Philadelphia: U.S. Bureau of Labor Seventh Special Report of the Commissioner of Labor* (1894), pp. 38-39; Oscar Handlin, *Boston's Immigrants* (Cambridge: Harvard University Press, 1941), p. 62.

33. Hogan, *On the Mission,* p. 82.

34. Homer L. Calkin, "The Irish in Iowa," *Palimpsest* 45, no. 2 (1964):33-96.

35. *I.W.,* October 21, 1871, p. 8.

CHAPTER 3

1. Oscar Handlin, *Boston's Immigrants* (Cambridge, Mass.: Harvard University Press, 1941), p. 117; Philip H. Bagenal, *The American Irish and Their Influence on Irish Politics* (London: K. Paul, Trench, 1882), pp. 71-72; R. R. Kuczynski, "The Fecundity of the Native and Foreign-born Population in Massachusetts," *Quarterly Journal of Economics* 15 (1901):4, 11-14, 17-19; F. S. Crum, "The Marriage Rate in Massachusetts," *Publications of the American Statistical Association* 4 (1895):322-39; "Immigrant Women and Girls in Boston: A Report Based on Five Hundred Schedules for the Intermunicipal Research Committee during Their Recent Investigation of Immigrant Women in the Cities," box 7, no. 49, WEIU Papers; "Report of an Investigation of 500 Immigrant Women in Boston Conducted by the Research Development of the WEIU," box 4, no. 48, WEIU Papers.

2. Howard P. Chudacoff, "Newlyweds and Family Extensions: The First Stage of Family Cycle in Providence, Rhode Island, 1864-1865 and 1879-1880," in *Family and Population in Nineteenth-Century America,* ed. Tamara K. Hareven and Maris A. Vinovskis (Princeton: Princeton University Press, 1978), pp. 179-205; Morgan Myfanwy and Hilda H. Golden, "Immigrant Families in an Industrial City: A Study of Households in Holyoke, 1880," *Journal*

of Family History 4, no. 1 (1979):59-68; Albert Gibbs Mitchell, "Irish Family Patterns in Nineteenth-Century Ireland and Lowell, Massachusetts," Ph.D. diss., Boston University, 1976, pp. 289-91; Daniel J. Walkowitz, "Working-Class Women in the Gilded Age: Factory, Community, and Family Life among Cohoes, New York, Cotton Workers," *Journal of Social History* 5, no. 49 (1972):464-90; Donald Barnard Cole, "Lawrence, Massachusetts: Immigrant City, 1845-1912," Ph.D. diss., Harvard University, 1956, p. 412; *Representative Young Irish-Americans of Troy, New York* (Troy: E. H. Lisk, 1889).

3. Mary Catherine Mattis, "Irish Mobility in Buffalo, New York, 1855-75: A Socio-Historical Analysis," Ph.D. diss., Washington University, 1975, pp. 175-80; Mitchell, "Irish Family Patterns," pp. 289-90; Walkowitz, "Working-Class Women," pp. 469-90; Frances E. Kobrin and Calvin Goldscheider, *The Ethnic Factor in Family Structure and Mobility* (Cambridge, Mass.: Ballinger, 1978), pp. 20, 48.

4. Elizabeth Gurley Flynn, *The Rebel Girl: An Autobiography* (New York: Masses and Mainstream, 1955), pp. 26-29; Mary Harris Jones, *The Autobiography of Mother Jones* (Chicago: Charles H. Kerr, 1925); Alice Clare Lynch, *The Kennedy Clan and Tierra Redonda* (San Francisco: Marvell, 1935); Lucille Rogers, *Light from Many Candles: A History of Pioneer Women in Education in Tennessee* (Nashville: McQuiddy, 1960), pp. 139-41; *I.W.*, May 10, 1873, p. 8.

5. John C. Messenger, *Inis Beag: Isle of Ireland* (New York: Holt, Rinehart & Winston, 1969), p. 130; Susan Kleinberg, "Technology's Stepdaughters: The Impact of Industrialization upon Working-Class Women, Pittsburgh, 1865-1890," Ph.D. diss., University of Pittsburgh, 1973, p. 240.

6. *Reunion: St. Mary's Parochial School, 1875-1895; Twenty-fifth Anniversary of the Founding of St. Mary's Parochial School: Cambridgeport, Massachusetts, 1875-1900* (Cambridge, Mass.: Frank Facey, 1900); Robert Woods and Albert Z. Kennedy, eds., *The Zone of Emergence: Observations of the Lower, Middle, and Upper Middle Working-Class Communities of Boston, 1905-1914* (Cambridge, Mass.: MIT Press, 1962), p. 109.

7. Arnold Schrier, *Ireland and the Irish Migration* (Minneapolis: University of Minnesota Press, 1958), pp. 130-31.

8. The data are complicated by the possibility that if an Irish woman married an American-born child of Irish immigrants the marriage would appear as an out-group marriage for purposes of registration of vital statistics.

9. Mitchell, "Irish Family Patterns," pp. 299-301; Julius Draschsler, *Intermarriage in New York City* (New York: Columbia University Press, 1921), p. 33; Bessie Bloom Wessel, *An Ethnic Survey of Woonsocket, Rhode Island* (Chicago: University of Chicago Press, 1931), p. 117.

10. John T. Cumbler, *Working-Class Community in Industrial America: Work, Leisure, and Struggle in Two Industrial Cities, 1880-1930* (Westport, Conn.: Greenwood Press, 1979), p. 123; Judith A. McGaw, "The Sources and Impact of Mechanization: The Berkshire County, Massachusetts, Paper Industry, 1801-1885", Ph.D. diss., New York University, 1977, p. 349; Clyde Griffen and Sally Griffen, *Natives and Newcomers: The Ordering of Opportunity in Mid-Nineteenth-Century Poughkeepsie* (Cambridge, Mass.: Harvard University Press, 1978); Constance McLaughlin Green, *Holyoke, Massachusetts: A Case History of the Industrial Revolution in America* (New Haven: Yale University Press, 1939), p. 370.

11. Schrier, *Ireland,* p. 109.

12. Harold J. Abrahamson, "Ethnic Diversity within Catholicism: A Comparative Analysis of Contemporary and Historical Religion," *Journal of Social History* 4, no. 4 (1971):359-88.

13. Lelia Hardin Bugg, *The People of Our Parish* (Boston: Callannan, 1900) p. 91.

14. George Deshon, *Guide for Catholic Young Women, Especially for Those Who Earn Their Own Living,* (New York: Catholic Book Exchange, 1897), pp. 270-303.

15. Ibid.

16. Elizabeth Gurley Flynn, *Rebel Girl* (New York: International Publishers, 1955), p. 113.

17. Joseph A. Hill, "Comparative Fecundity of Women of Native and Foreign Parentage of the United States," *Quarterly Publications of the American Statistical Association* 8, no. 104 (1913):583-604; Stephen Thernstrom, *The Other Bostonians: Poverty and Progress in the American Metropolis, 1880-1970* (Cambridge, Mass.: Harvard University Press, 1973) p. 166; R. R. Kuczynski, "The Fecundity of Native and Foreign-born Population," pp. 141-86; Laurence A. Glasco, "Ethnicity and Occupation in the Mid Nineteenth Century: Irish, Germans, and Native-born Whites in Buffalo, New York," in *Immigrants in Industrial America*, ed. Richard L. Ehrlich (Charlottesville: University Press of Virginia, 1977), pp. 151-75; Massachusetts Bureau of Statistics of Labor, *Ninth Annual Report* (Boston: Rand Avery, 1878), pp. 102-3; Jesse Chickering, *Report of the Committee Appointed by the City Council, and Also a Comparative View of the Population of Boston in 1850, with the Births, Marriages and Deaths, in 1849 and 1850* (Boston: J. H. Eastburn, 1851).

18. Tamara Hareven, "Family Time and Historical Time," in *The Family*, ed. Hareven, Alice Rossi, and Jerome Kagan (New York: W. W. Norton, 1979), p. 61; Hareven and Maris Vinovskis, "Marital Fertility, Ethnicity, and Occupation in Urban Families: An Analysis of South Boston and the South End in 1880," *Journal of Social History* 3 (1975):69-93; Hareven and Vinovskis, "Patterns of Childbearing in Late-Nineteenth-Century America: The Determinants of Marital Fertility in Five Massachusetts Towns in 1880," in *Family and Population in Nineteenth-Century America* (Princeton: Princeton University Press, 1978), pp. 85-125; Howard M. Gitleman, *Workingmen of Waltham: Mobility in American Urban Industrial Development, 1850-1890* (Baltimore: Johns Hopkins University Press, 1974), p. 33; Joseph J. Spengler, *The Fecundity of Native and Foreign-born Women in New England* (Washington, D.C.: Brookings Institution, 1930).

19. Woods and Kennedy, *The Zone of Emergence*, pp. 144-45.

20. Caroline H. Woods, *Women in Prison* (New York: Hurd & Houghton, 1869), pp. 120-21; Benjamin O. Flower, *Civilization's Inferno* (Boston: Arena, 1893), pp. 120-21; Helen Campbell, *Prisoners of Poverty: Wage-Workers, Their Trades, and Their Lives* (New York: Roberts, 1887), p. 164; North Bennett Street Settlement, *Report, 1904-1905*, pp. 27-28, North Bennett Street Collection; quoted in Earl F. Niehaus, *The Irish in New Orleans, 1800-1860* (Baton Rouge: Louisiana State University Press, 1965), p. 61; *A Report of the Labors of John Augustus, for the Last Ten Years in Aid of the Unfortunate* (Boston: Wright and Hasty, 1852), p. 10; Katherine B. Anthony, *Mothers Who Must Work* (New York: Survey Association, 1914), pp. 7-8.

21. Woods, *Women in Prison*, p. 34; Louisa Harris, *Behind the Scenes; or Nine Years at the Four Courts* (St. Louis: A. R. Flemming, 1893), p. 79.

22. Charles John Paul Bourget, *Outre-Mer (Notes sur l'Amérique)* (Paris: A. Lemerre, 1895), p. 217.

23. Mary Constance Smith, *A Sheaf of Golden Years: 1856-1906* (New York: Benziger, 1906); *I.W* : March 14, 1874, p. 7; March 28, 1874, p. 7; Charles Fanning, ed., *Mr. Dooley and the Chicago Irish* (New York: Arno, 1976), p. 164.

24. North Bennett Street Industrial School, "Duplications," I-20 Book, North Bennett Street Collection; *Annual Report of the Board of Managers of the Temporary Home for the Destitute*, 1848 (Boston: Andrews & Prentiss, 1849); Leslie G. Ainley, *Boston Mahatma* (Boston: W. M. Prendible, 1949); James Michael Curley, *I'd Do It Again: A Record of All My Uproarious Years* (Englewood Cliffs, N.J.: Prentice-Hall, 1957); James J. Corbett, *The Roar of the Crowd* (London: Phoenix House, 1925); quoted in Daniel Patrick Moynihan, "The Irish of New York," *Commentary*, August 1963, p. 97.

25. Vincent Edward Powers, "Invisible Immigrants: The Pre-Famine Irish Community in Worcester, Massachusetts, from 1826 to 1860," Ph.D. diss., Clark University, 1976, p. 164; *Niles Weekly Register* 40 (July 16, 1831):338-39; *Boston Pilot*, September 8, 1860, p. 4; George Svejda, *Irish Immigrant Participation in the Construction of the Erie Canal* (Washington,

D.C.: Division of History, National Park Service, 1969), pp. 29-30.

26. Massachusetts Commissioner's Report on the Pauper System, *Report of the Commissioners Appointed by an Order of the House of Representatives, February 29, 1832, on the Subject of the Commonwealth of Massachusetts* (Boston, 1833); "Report of Aid Given to Destitute Mothers and Infants, 1875," Collection of the Boston Children's Services Association; Associated Charities of the District of Columbia, *Second Annual Report, October 1883* (Washington, D.C.: Associated Charities, 1884), pp. 29-31; Kate Holladay Claghorn, "Immigration in its Relation to Pauperism," *Annals of the American Academy of Political and Social Sciences* 24, no. 1 (1904):200; Zilpha Smith, *Deserted Wives and Deserting Husbands: A Study of 234 Families Based on the Experience of the District Committees and Agents of the Associated Charities of Boston* (Boston, 1901); Lillian Brandt, *Five Hundred and Seventy-Four Deserters and Their Families: A Descriptive Study of Their Characteristics and Circumstances* (New York: Charity Organization Society, 1905).

27. Louis Sheaffer, *O'Neill: Son and Playwright* (Boston: Little, Brown, 1968), pp. 26-27.

28. Catherine J. Ross, "Society's Children: The Care of Indigent Youngsters in New York City, 1875-1903," Ph.D. diss., Yale University, 1978; Martha Van Hoesin Taber, "A History of the Cutlery Industry in the Connecticut Valley," *Smith College Studies in History* 41 (1955):1-138; William Geary, "Limerick Men's Benevolent and Social Association, Inc.: 1890, Record of Its Accomplishments," in *Remember Limerick: Limerick Men's Benevolent and Social Association, 75th Anniversary Book* (Author: n.p. 1965); *I.W.*, May 6, 1871, p. 5.

29. New York Association for Improving the Condition of the Poor (hereafter cited as NYAICP), *Report: 1868* (New York: Trow and Smith, 1868), p. 69; Mary R. Smith, "Almshouse Women," *Quarterly Publications of the American Statistical Association* 4 (1895):219-62; Jeremiah O'Donovan, *A Brief Account of the Author's Interview with His Countrymen, and of the Parts of the Emerald Isle whence They Migrated, Together with a Direct Reference to Their Present Location in Travels through Various States of the Union in 1854 and 1855* (Pittsburgh, 1864), pp. 45-46, 72, 167; Lillie B. Chance Wyman, "Studies of Factory Life: Among the Women," *Atlantic Monthly* 62, no. 371 (1881):315-21; *I.W.*, June 10, 1871, p. 3.

30. Oscar Handlin, *Al Smith and His America* (Boston: Little, Brown, 1958), p. 12; Jones, *Autobiography;* Elizabeth Gurley Flynn, *I Speak My Own Piece* (New York: Masses and Mainstream, 1955), p. 25; M. Schwertner, "Eleanor Donnelly: The Singer of Pure Religion," *Catholic World* 105 (June 1917):352-60; "Henry McCloskey and Some of His Contemporaries," *Journal of the American-Irish Historical Society* 28 (1930):119-30.

31. Frank F. Furstenberg, Jr., Theodore Hershberg, and John Modell, "The Origins of the Female-Headed Black Family: The Impact of the Urban Experience," *Journal of Interdisciplinary History* 6, no. 2 (1975):211-33; William B. Sullivan, "Celtic Danvers," *Historical Collections of the Danvers Historical Society,* 1913, pp. 74-85; Tamara K. Hareven and John Modell, "Urbanization and the Malleable Household: An Examination of Boarding and Lodging in American Families," *Journal of Marriage and the Family* 35, no. 3 (1973):164-86; Amos G. Warner, "The Causes of Poverty Further Considered," *Quarterly Publications of the American Statistical Association* 4, no. 27 (1894):50-68; Maurice F. Parmelee, "Inebriety in Boston," Ph.D. diss., Columbia University, 1909, p. 33; "Home of the Angel Guardian, Register Book, June 1851-December 1860," Archives of the Roman Catholic Archdiocese of Boston; St. Joseph's Home, *Report: From 1870 to 1880 Inclusive* (Boston: Learned, Thompson, 1881), pp. 13-15; *St. Vincent de Paul Quarterly* 4, no. 2 (1899):156-61.

32. Samuel Busey, *Immigration: Its Evils and Consequences* (New York: DeWitt and Davenport, 1856), pp. 82-89; Charles Cowley, *Illustrated History of Lowell* (Lowell, Mass.: B. C. Sargeant and Joshua Merrill, 1868), p. 203; Francis A. Walker, "American Irish and American German, *Scribner's Monthly* 6, no. 2 (1873):172-79.

33. Esther G. Barrows, *Neighbors All: A Settlement Notebook* (Boston: Houghton Mifflin, 1929), pp. 16-17.

34. *I. W.,* October 12, 1871, p. 3; Richard J. Kelly, "Emigration and Its Consequences," *New England Review* 21, no. 5 (1904):257-67.

35. James J. Walsh, "Are Irish Catholics Dying Out in This Country?," *America* 13 (August 5, 1922):365-66; "The Disappearing Irish in America," *America* 17 (May 1, 1926):56-57; M. V. Kelly, "The Suicide of the Irish Race," *America* 19 (November 17, 1928):128-29.

36. *Ibid.*

37. "The Irish in America," *Catholic World* 6, no. 36 (1868):765-76; "Irish in America," *Brownson's Quarterly Review* 3, no. 4 (1855):538-47; *I. W.:* November 15, 1872, p. 8; October 5, 1872, p. 6.

38. Joan Bland, *Hibernian Crusade: The Story of the Catholic Total Abstinence Union of America* (Washington, D.C.: Catholic University of America, 1951).

39. Bernard O'Reilly, *The Mirror of True Womanhood: A Book of Instruction for Women in the World* (New York: Peter F. Collier, 1878), pp. 179-81; John Lancaster Spalding, *The Religious Mission of the Irish People and Catholic Colonization* (New York: Catholic Publication Society, 1880); J. H. Tuke, "Irish Emigration," *Nineteenth Century* 2 (1881):358-71.

40. Hibernian Society of Cincinnati, *First Annual Report for 1850* (Cincinnati: Wright and Ferris, 1850), p. 6; Alice Henry, "Mrs. Winifred O'Reilly: A Veteran Worker," *Life and Labor,* 1911, p. 132-36; Nella Braddy Henney, *Anne Sullivan Macy: The Story behind Helen Keller* (Garden City, N.Y.: Doubleday, Doran, 1933); Sheaffer, *O'Neill,* p. 13.

41. Jacob Riis, *The Children of the Poor* (New York: Charles Scribner's Sons, 1892), pp. 68, 84-86; L. E. Caswell, *Report of the North End Industrial Home, from January 1880 to April 1881* (Boston: Frank Wood, 1881), p. 25; Sarah Mytton Murray, *An Englishwoman in America* (London: Thomas Richardson, 1848), p. 8; Elene Foster, "An Irish Mother: A Monologue," *Century* 63 (1903):616-18.

42. *I. W.,* March 1, 1873, p. 4; John Cannon O'Hanlon, *Life and Scenery in Missouri: Reminiscences of a Missionary Priest* (Dublin: James Duffy, 1890), pp. 1, 144; Finley Peter Dunne, "Molly Donahue, Who Lives across the Street from Mister Dooley," *Ladies' Home Journal:* 17, no. 1 (1899):6, 7; no. 2 (1900):6; Fanning, *Mr. Dooley,* pp. 120-23.

43. Robert A. Woods and Albert J. Kennedy, *Young Working Girls: A Summary of Evidence from Two Thousand Social Workers* (Boston: Houghton Mifflin, 1913), p. 55; Louise Boland More, *Wage Earners' Budgets: A Study of Standards and Cost of Living in New York City* (New York: Henry Holt, 1907), pp. 68, 89; Mary Kingsbury Simkhovitch, *The City Worker's World* (Macmillan, 1917), p. 115.

44. Andrew M. Greeley, *That Most Distressful Nation: The Taming of the American Irish* (Chicago: Quadrangle Books, 1972), p. 135; Marvin K. Opler, "The Influence of Ethnic and Class Subcultures on Child Care," *Social Problems* 3 (1955):12-21; Opler and Jerome Singer, "Ethnic Differences in Behavior," *International Journal of Social Psychiatry* 2, no. 1 (1956):11-23; Rita F. Stein, *Disturbed Youth and Ethnic Family Patterns* (Albany: State University of New York Press, 1971); Elise de la Fontaine, "Cultural and Psychological Implications in Case Work with Irish Clients," in *Cultural Problems in Social Case Work* (New York: Family Welfare Association of America, 1940), pp. 21-37.

45. Terrence V. Powderly, *The Path I Trod* (New York: Columbia University Press, 1940), p. 4; William O'Connell, *The Letters of His Eminence Archbishop of Boston,* (Cambridge, Mass.: Riverside Press, 1915), vol. 1 (1876-1901), pp. 48-49; William O'Connell, *Recollections of Seventy Years* (Boston: Houghton Mifflin, 1934), p. 1; James John Corbett, *The Roar of the Crowd: The True Tale of the Rise and Fall of a Champion* (London: Phoenix House, 1925), pp. 122-45; Stuart William Graham, "Finley Peter Dunne: The Archey Road Perspective," senior honor thesis, Harvard University, 1967, p. 3; James T. Farrell, "Chicago South Side: The World I Grew up In," *Commonweal* 83, no. 20 (February 25, 1966):606-11.

CHAPTER 4

1. Arnold Schrier, *Ireland and the American Emigration, 1850-1900* (Minneapolis: University of Minnesota Press, 1958), pp. 107-13.

2. Kerby Alonzo Miller, "Emigrants and Exiles: The Irish Exodus to North America, from Colonial Times to the First World War," Ph.D. diss., University of California, Berkeley, 1976, pp. 232, 387, 432-36, 777; Schrier, *Ireland,* pp. 24-31, 38, 75.

3. T. W. Hancock, "On the Remittances from North America by Irish Emigrants, Considered as an Indication of Character of the Irish Race," *Journal of the Society for Social and Statistical Inquiry of Ireland,* 1873, pp. 280-90.

4. Niles Carpenter, *Nationality, Color, and Economic Opportunity in the City of Buffalo* (Buffalo: University of Buffalo Press, 1927), p. 190.

5. Alice Henry, "Mrs. Winifred O'Reilly: A Veteran Worker," *Life and Labor,* 1911, pp. 132-36.

6. Miriam Allen deFord, *They Were San Franciscans* (Caldwell, Idaho: Caxton Printers, 1941), pp. 114-15.

7. See, for example, Albert Gibbs Mitchell, "Irish Family Patterns in Nineteenth-Century Ireland and Lowell, Massachusetts," Ph.D. diss., Boston University, 1976, p. 316; Mary Catherine Mattis, "The Irish Family in Buffalo, New York, 1855-1875," Ph.D. diss., Washington University, 1975, pp. 136-38; Carole Groneman Pernicone, "The 'Bloody Ould Sixth': A Social Analysis of a Working-Class Community," Ph.D. diss., University of Rochester, 1973, pp. 125-28; Charles J. Bushnell, *The Social Problem at the Chicago Stock Yard* (Chicago: University of Chicago Press, 1902); Robert Coit Chapin, *The Standard of Living among Workingmen's Families in New York City* (New York: Russell Sage Foundation, 1909), p. 58; Walter B. Palmer, "Woman and Child Workers in Cotton Mills," *Quarterly Publications of the American Statistical Association* 7, no. 94 (1911):588-617; Anna S. Daniel, "Tenement House Labor," *Journal of the American Social Science Association* 30 (1892): 73-85.

8. Virginia Penny, *The Employment of Women: A Cyclopaedia of Woman's Work* (Boston: Walker, Wise, 1863); Pauline Goldmark, *Notes on an Industrial Survey of a Selected Area in New York City, with Respect to Sanitary Conditions in the Factories* (Albany: State Printers, 1912), pp. 322, 344; Agnes Hannay, "A Chronicle of Industry on the Mill River," *Smith College Studies in History* 21, no. 1 (1935):7-142; Mary Van Kleeck, *Women in the Bookbinding Trade* (New York: Survey Associates, 1913), pp. 36, 39; "Industrial Opportunities for Women in Cambridge, 1910," box 7, no. 15, WEIU Papers;

9. Massachusetts Bureau of the Statistics of Labor, *Twentieth Annual Report* (Boston: Wright and Potter, 1889), p. 575; Bureau of Labor Statistics of the State of Minnesota, *First Biennial Report for the Two Years Ending December 31, 1887-1888* (St. Paul: Thomas A. Clark, 1888), p. 136.

10. See also Carroll D. Wright, *The Working Girls of Boston* (Boston: Wright and Potter, 1889); U.S. Immigration Commission, *Occupations of the First and Second Generations of Immigrants in the United States* (Washington, D.C., 1911); Edward P. Hutchinson, *Immigrants and Their Children, 1850-1950* (New York: Russel and Russell, 1956); Helen Campbell, *Women Wage-Earners: Their Past, Their Present, and Their Future* (Boston: Roberts, 1893), p. 207.

11. John Lancaster Spalding, *The Religious Mission of the Irish People* (New York: Catholic Publication Society, 1882), p. 73; George F. O'Dwyer, *The Irish Catholic Genesis of Lowell* (Lowell, Mass.: Sullivan Brothers, 1920), p. 43; Lucy Larcom, "Among Lowell Mill Girls: A Reminiscence," *Atlantic,* 1881, pp. 593-612; Mitchell, "Irish Family Patterns"; Steven Jan

172 NOTES TO PAGES 75-84

Dubnoff, "The Family and Absence from Work: Irish Workers in a Lowell, Massachusetts, Cotton Mill, 1860," Ph.D. diss., Brandeis University, 1976.

12. Donald Cole, *Immigrant City: Lawrence, Massachusetts, 1845-1921* (Chapel Hill: University of North Carolina Press, 1963); Maurice B. Dorgan, *Lawrence: Yesterday and Today: 1845-1918* (Lawrence: Dick and Trumpold, 1919); *I.W.*, October 3, 1874, p. 8.

13. Constance McLaughlin Green, *Holyoke, Massachusetts: A Case History of the Industrial Revolution in America* (New Haven: Yale University Press, 1939); *1870-1970: The Catholic Observer Reviews 100 Years of the Springfield Diocese* (Springfield, Mass.: 1970), p. 3; *I.W.*, August 10, 1872, p. 8.

14. Carole Groneman, "'She Earns as a Child—She Pays as a Man': Women Workers in a Mid-Nineteenth-Century New York Community," in *Immigrants in Industrial America, 1850-1920*, ed. Richard L. Ehrlich (Charlottesville: University Press of Virginia, 1977), pp. 33-46; Mable Hurd Willett, *The Employment of Women in the Clothing Trades* (New York: Columbia University Press, 1902); Elizabeth Beardsley Butler, *Women and the Trades* (New York: Charities Publication Committee, 1909), p. 23; Jesse Eliphalet Pope, *The Clothing Industry in New York* (New York: Columbia University Press, 1905); Lorinda Perry, *The Millinery Trade in Boston and Philadelphia: A Study of Women in Industry* (Binghamton, N.Y.: Vail-Ballou, 1916); "Working Women in Chicago," in *Seventh Biennial Report of the Bureau of Labor Statistics, 1892* (Springfield, Ill.: H. W. Rokker, 1893), pp. 80-81, 115-31.

15. Helen Sumner, "History of Women in Industry in the United States," *Report on Conditions of Women and Child Wage Earners in the United States*, 61st Cong., 2nd sess., 1910-13. S. Doc. 645, vol. 9; Matthew Carey, *Letter to the Editor of the New York Daily Sentinel on the Rate of Wages Paid to Women* (Philadelphia, 1830).

16. NYAICP, *Annual Report, 1875*, p. 73; Colorado Bureau of Labor, *Biennial Report for the Year Ending in 1886*, p. 122.

17. Elsie C. Parsons, "Women's Work and Wages in the United States," *Quarterly Journal of Economics* 29, no. 2 (1915): 201-34.

18. David M. Katzman, *Seven Days a Week: Women and Domestic Service in Industrializing America* (New York: Oxford University Press, 1978), particularly pp. 3-43; Louisa May Alcott, *Work: A Story of Experience* (Boston: Roberts Brothers, 1873); Catherine E. Beecher, *The True Remedy for the Wrongs of Women, with a History of an Enterprise Having That for Its Object* (Boston: Phillips, Sampson, 1851), pp. 39-40; Helen Campbell, *Prisoners of Poverty: Women Wage-Workers, Their Trades, and Their Lives* (New York: Roberts Brothers, 1887) pp. 228-29, quoted in David Emerson Fite, *Social and Industrial Conditions in the North during the Civil War* (New York: Macmillan, 1910), pp. 186-87.

19. Helen Campbell, "Why Is There Objection to Domestic Service?," *Good Housekeeping* 11 (September 27, 1890):255-56.

20. "Employment Office, Boston YWCA," n.d., box 7, no. 48, WEIU Papers.

21. Frances A. Kellor, "The Immigrant Woman," *Atlantic* 100, no. 3 (1907):401-7; Virginia Yans-McLaughlin, "Like the Fingers of the Hand: The Family and Community of First-Generation Italian-Americans in Buffalo, New York, 1880-1903," Ph.D. diss., State University of New York, Buffalo, 1970, pp. 346-49; Rose Cohen, *Out of the Shadows* (New York: George H. Doran, 1918), pp. 158-59; Katzman, *Seven Days*, p. 67; Domestic Reform League, *Bulletin* 3, no. 2 (January 1909).

22. WEIU, *Report of the Committee on Domestic Reform No. 1: The Effort to Attract the Workers in Shops and Factories to Domestic Service* (Cambridge, Mass.: Cooperative Press, 1898), p. 12; Martha Major, "The Domestic Problem," *Everybody's* 7 (1906):642-47; Lucy M. Salmon, "A Statistical Inquiry Concerning Domestic Service," *Quarterly Publications of the American Statistical Association* 3, no. 18 (1892):89-118.

23. *I.W.*, December 3, 1870, p. 6; John Francis Maguire, *The Irish in the United States* (New York: D. & J. Sadlier, 1868), p. 294; William E. Rowley, "The Irish Aristocracy of

Albany, 1798-1878," *New York History,* 1971, pp. 287-91; *Massachusetts Bureau of the Statistics of Labor, Eighteenth Annual Report* (Boston: Wright and Potter, 1887), p. 266.

24. Goldwin Smith, "Why Send More Irish to America?," *Nineteenth Century* 13, no. 76 (1883): 913-19; NYAICP, *Annual Report* (New York: Office of the Association, 1860, 1866, 1868, 1875).

25. Josephine Clara Goldmark, *Pilgrims of '48* (New Haven: Yale University Press, 1930), p. 232.

26. Caroline Dall, *The College, the Market, and the Court, or Woman's Relationship to Education, Labor, and Law* (Boston: Lee & Shepard, 1867), p. 145.

27. Frances A. Kellor, *Out of Work: A Study of Employment Agencies* (New York: G. P. Putnam, 1904), p. 130.

28. See, for example, Alfred Bunn, *Old England and New England, in a Series of Views Taken on the Spot,* 2 vols. (London: Richard Bentley, 1853), 1:23, 62; Matilda Charlotte Houston, *Hesperos, or Travels in the West,* 2 vols. (London: John W. Parker, 1850), 1:109-10, 165, 2:67.

29. See, for example, Margaret Allston, *Her Boston Experiences: A Picture of Modern Boston Society and People* (Boston: Curtis, 1899), pp. 116-17; Sara Josepha Hale, *"Boarding Out": A Tale of Domestic Life* (New York: Harper and Brothers, 1846); Harry Spofford, *The Mysteries of Worcester, or Charley Temple and His First Glass of Liquor* (Worcester, Mass.: H. J. Clapp, 1846); Thomas Cooley Grattan, *Civilized America,* 2 vols. (London: Bradbury and Evans, 1859), 1:262-65; R. R. Bowker, "In Re: Bridget," *Old and New* 1 (1871):497-501; Francis Walker, "Our Domestic Service," *Scribner's* 11, no. 18 (1857):273.

30. Mary Dean, "The Goings and Doings of Hired Girls, *Lippincott's* 7 (1877): 589-96.

31. Mary Allen West, "Domestic Service," *Our Day* 4, no. 3 (1889): 401-15.

32. Elspeth MacDonald, "Hired Girls I Have Met," *Success,* 1907, pp. 334-35; Edwin Lawrence Godkin, *Reflections and Comments, 1865-1895* (New York: Charles Scribner's Sons, 1895), pp. 29-39, 56-66.

33. Christine Terhune Herrick, "Which Is Mistress?," *Ladies' Home Journal* 3, no. 5 (1886):7; Margaret Polson Murray, "Women's Clubs in America," *Living Age* 7 (1861)558-64; "American Hotels, by a Cosmopolitan," *Putnam's* 5, no. 25 (1870):23-30; "Diaries," Harriet Jane Hanson Robinson Papers; Claudia Bushman, "A Good Poor Man's Wife," Fourth Berkshire Conference on the History of Women, August 23-24, 1978; Annie Adams Fields, quoted in Nathan I. Huggins, "Private Charities in Boston, 1870–1900: A Social History," Ph.D. Diss., Harvard University, 1962, p. 298.

34. Katzman, *Seven Days,* pp. 70-71; Lawrence Admiral Glasco, "Ethnicity and Social Structure: Irish, Germans, and Native-born of Buffalo, N.Y., 1850-1860," Ph.D. diss., State University of New York, Buffalo, 1973, pp. 205-6, 208, 216-17; idem, "The Life Cycles and Household Structure of American Ethnic Groups: Irish, Germans, and Native-Born Whites in Buffalo, New York, 1855," *Journal of Urban History* 1, no. 3 (1975):339-64.

35. Don Harrison Doyle, *The Social Order of a Frontier Community: Jacksonville, Illinois* (Urbana: University of Illinois Press, 1978), p. 114; Grace McDonald, *History of the Irish in Wisconsin in the Nineteenth Century* (Washington, D.C.: Catholic University of America Press, 1954), pp. 66-68, 75.

36. Massachusetts Bureau of Labor, *Trained and Supplementary Workers in Domestic Service, Prepared in Collaboration with the Women's Educational and Industrial Union, Boston, Massachusetts* (Boston: Wright and Potter, 1906), p. 25; Rev. Stephen Byrne, *Irish Emigration to the United States: What It Has Been and What It Is* (New York: Catholic Publications, 1874), pp. 37, 73-74, 137-38, 155-57.

37. State Federation of Womens' Clubs, "Domestic Science Exhibit, 1908," box 7, folder 1, WEIU Papers; Mary Gove Smith, "Immigration as a Source of Supply For Domestic Workers (Based upon a Study of Boston)," 1905, Box 7, no. 48, pp. 14-18, WEIU Papers; idem,

"Immigration as a Source of Supply for Domestic Workers," *Bulletin of the Inter-Municipal Research Committee* 2, no. 8 (1906):4-9; Lucy Maynard Salmon, *Domestic Service* (New York: Macmillan, 1901), pp. 91, 969-1000; J. H. Tuke, "Irish Emigration" *Nineteenth Century* 3 (1881):361-62; Salmon, "A Statistical Inquiry," pp. 89-118.

38. Dennis Alphonsus Quinn, *Heroes and Heroines of Memphis* (Providence, R.I.: E. L. Freeman, 1887), p. 99; Maguire, *The Irish*, p. 334; Michael Flood Davin, *The Irishman in Canada* (Toronto: Maclear, 1877), p. 65; *I.W.*, November 16, 1872, p. 8.

39. *I.W.:* December 21, 1872, p. 8; January 11, 1873, p. 7; Spalding, *The Religious Mission*, pp. 112-13; *Catholic Mirror*, April 7, 1877, p. 1; "The Irish in America," *Brownson's Quarterly Review* 3, no. 4 (1885):538-47; quoted in Arthur W. Calhoun, *A Social History of the American Family: From Independence through the Civil War*, 2 vols. (Cleveland: Arthur H. Clark, 1918), 2:163; *Irish Harp* 1, no. 4 (1864):177-81; John Joseph Hogan, *On the Mission in Missouri, 1857-1868* (Kansas City: John A. Heilmann, 1892), pp. 37-38; *Irish American*, November 29, 1856, p. 2; George Deshon, *Guide for Catholic Young Women: Especially for Those Who Earn Their Own Living*, (New York: Catholic Book Exchange, 1897), p. 53.

40. *Irish Miscellany*, May 1, 1858, p. 190.

41. Rev. William Byrne, "One Hundred Years of the Catholic Church in Boston," 1880, Archives of the Roman Catholic Archdiocese of Boston; *The Cross and the Shamrock, or How to Defend the Faith: an Irish-American Tale of Real Life Descriptive of the Temptations, Sufferings, Trials, and Triumphs of the Children of St. Patrick, in the Great Republic of Washington* (Boston: Patrick Donahoe, 1853); Ella McMahon, *Irish Faith in America: Recollections of a Missionary* (New York: Benziger, 1881).

42. Lucille Eaves, *A History of California Labor Legislation: With an Introductory Sketch of the San Francisco Labor Movement* (Berkeley and Los Angeles: University of California Press, 1910), pp. 136, 311-17.

43. Jane Addams, "A Belated Industry," *American Journal of Sociology* 2 (1896):536-50; idem, "Domestic Service and the Family Claim," *World's Congress of Representative Women: 1893* (Chicago, 1893), 2:626-31; Massachusetts Bureau of Statistics of Labor, *Social Conditions in Domestic Service*, p. 13; "Investigations: Domestic Service, 1914-1917," folder 400, Consumers' League of Massachusetts Papers; "Immigrant Women and Girls in Boston: A Report," box 7, folder 49, WIEU Papers.

44. See also, "The Life Story of an Irish Cook," in Holt, *The Life Stories*, p. 145; James Michael Curley, *I'd Do It Again: A Record of All My Uproarious Years* (Englewood Cliffs, N.J.: Prentice-Hall, 1957), pp. 9-10; Domestic Reform League, *Bulletin: 3*, 1907, Domestic Reform League Papers; "Early Newspaper Notices, 1877-1887," folder 67, Rutland Corner House Papers; Lilian Pettengill, *Toilers of the Home: The Record of a College Woman's Experience as a Domestic Servant* (New York: Doubleday, 1903), pp. 41-42.

45. Robert A. Woods and Albert E. Kennedy, *Young Working Girls: A Summary of Evidence From Two Thousand Social Workers* (Boston: Houghton Mifflin, 1913), p. 58.

46. Edward A. Ross, *The Old World in the New* (New York: Century, 1913), pp. 35-36.

47. Rheta Childe Dorr and William Hard, "The Woman's Invasion," *Everybody's* 20, no. 1 (1909):82.

48. Carpenter, *Nationality, Color, and Economic Opportunity*, pp. 190, 136. See also Don Walsh, *The Stranger in the City: The Working Girl Problem: The Catholic Woman's Club, Life of Father Bouchet* (Louisville, Ken.: Hammer Printing, 1913), p. 71; Sue Ainslie Clark and Edith Wyatt, "Working Girls' Budgets," *McClure's* 35, no. 6 (1910):610.

49. E. P. Hutchinson, *Immigrants and Their Children, 1850-1950* (New York: Russell and Russell, 1956), p. 88; Pauper Institutions Trustees of the City of Boston, *Annual Report, 1898-1899* (Boston: Municipal Printing Office, 1899); Sisters of the Reparation of the Congregation of Mary, *"Blessed Are the Merciful": The Life of Mother Mary Zita, Foundress* (New York: 1953); John Talbot Smith, *The Catholic Church in New York*, 2 vols. (New York: Hall and Locke, 1905), 2:493.

50. See *Dictionary of Notable American Women* (hereafter cited as *NAW*), *s.v.* Arthur, Julia; Cline, Maggie; Coghlan, Rose; Herne, Chrystal; Heron, Matilda; Rehan, Ada; Russell, Annie; Shaw, Mary; and Taylor, Lauretta.

51. Jessie B. Rittenhouse, "The Charm of Louise Imogene Guiney," *Bookman* 52, no. 6 (1921):515-20; "Irish-American Poets," *Irish Monthly* 14, no. 154 (1886):194-200; K.S.G. McGuire, ed., *Catholic Builders of the Nation* (Boston: Continental Press, 1923), pp. 184-203; Donna Merwick, *Boston's Priests, 1848-1910* (Cambridge, Mass.: Harvard University Press, 1973), pp. 166-71; "An Irish Poet's American Critics," *Irish Monthly* 14, no. 155 (1886):274-76; "Donnelly, Miss Eleanor Cecilia," in *A Woman of the Century*, ed. Frances Willard and Mary Livermore (Buffalo: C. W. Moulton, 1893), pp. 251-52; "Conway, Miss Katharine Eleanor," in Willard and Livermore, *A Woman*, pp. 202-3; Myra B. Lord, *History of the New England Woman's Press Association* (Newton, Mass. Graphics, 1932), pp. 98-99; William R. Stanton, "The Irish of Memphis," *West Tennessee Historical Society Papers* 6 (1952):106; Elliott O'Donnell, *The Irish Abroad: A Record of the Achievements of Wanderers from Ireland* (New York: E. P. Dutton, 1915), p. 365.

52. Agnes Geneva Gilman and Gertrude M. Gilman, *Who's Who in Illinois: Women—Makers of History* (Chicago: Electric, 1927), p. 14; Katharine O'Keefe O'Mahoney, *Famous Irishwomen* (Lawrence, Mass.: Lawrence, 1907); Mary C. Donelin, "American Irish Women 'Firsts,'" *Journal of the Irish-American Historical Society, 1925* 24, pp. 215-21; *NAW*, s.v. Ahern, Mary Eileen, and Regan, Agnes Gertrude.

53. Among the women of Irish birth or Irish parentage who appeared in the 1910 *American Catholic Who's Who*, there were two physicians, two librarians, three social workers, one astronomer, four journalists, seventeen writers, ten educators and six listed as "miscellaneous."

54. Ivy Pinchbeck, *Women Workers and the Industrial Revolution, 1750-1850* (London: Routledge, 1930), p. 299; Herbert G. Gutman, *Work, Culture, and Society in Industrializing America* (New York: Vintage Books, 1977), p. 34; Elizabeth C. Lynch, "Margaret Gaffney Haughery," *Journal of the American Irish Historical Society, 1929-1930* 28, pp. 153-54.

55. Jeremiah O'Donovan, *A Brief Account of the Author's Interview with His Countrymen* (Pittsburgh: Author, 1864), pp. 72, 92, 161, 167, 178, 191, 195; Albert Benedict Wolfe, *The Lodging House Problem in Boston* (Cambridge, Mass.: Harvard University Press, 1913), pp. 52-53; John D. Crimmins, *Irish-American Historical Miscellany* (New York: Author 1905), p. 190.

56. Alvin F. Harlow, *Old Bowery Days* (New York: D. Appleton, 1931), pp. 487-88; Herbert N. Casson, "The Irish in America," *Munsey's*, 1906, p. 94; John Paul Bocock, "The Irish Conquest," *Forum*, 1894, pp. 186-95.

57. George A. Kelly, *The Parish as Seen from the Church of St. John the Evangelist, New York City: 1840-1973* (New York: St. John's University, 1973); "The Convent Graduate," *Donahoe's* 10 (1883):178-79; Bernard O'Reilly, *The Mirror of True Womanhood: A Book of Instructions for Women of the World* (New York: Peter F. Collier, 1878), pp. 398-400; Thomas Edward Shields, *The Education of Our Girls* (New York: Benziger, 1907), p. 42; *A Voice from the Roman Catholic Laity: The Parochial School Question—An Open Letter to Bishop Keane, Rector of the New Catholic University at Washington, D.C.* (Boston: Arnold, 1890), p. 15.

58. Diane Ravitch, *The Great School Wars: New York City, 1805-1973—A History of the Public Schools as Battlefield of Social Change* (New York: Basic Books, 1974), p. 102; Howard Ralph Weisz, "Irish-American and Italian-American Educational Views and Activities, 1870-1900: A Comparison," Ph.D. diss., Columbia University, 1976, p. 374; David B. Tyack, *The One Best System: A History of American Urban Education* (Cambridge, Mass.: Harvard University Press 1974), pp. 104-5.

59. James W. Sanders, *The Education of an Urban Minority: Catholics in Chicago, 1833-1965* (New York: Oxford University Press, 1977), p. 163; John Swett, *History of the Public School System of California* (San Francisco: A. L. Bancroft, 1876); Powers, "Invisible Im-

migrants"; O'Dwyer, *The Irish Catholic Genesis*; Rowley, "The Irish Aristocracy of Albany," p. 296; Weisz, "Irish-American and Italian-American Educational Views," p. 83.

60. Ross, *The Old World*, p. 41.

61. *I.W.*, September 4, 1872, p. 4; *Catholic News*, October 13, 1889, p. 4; Thomas Beer, *The Mauve Decades: American Lives at the End of the Nineteenth Century* (New York: Alfred A. Knopf, 1962), p. 145.

62. Doris Smith, "American-Irish Women in Education," *Recorder* 34 (1973): 33-39.

63. Jones, *Autobiography*; Barbara Stuhler and Gretchen Kreuther, eds., *Women of Minnesota: Selected Biographical Essays* (St. Paul: Minnesota Historical Society Press, 1977); Alice Clare Lynch, *The Kennedy Clan and Tierra Redonda* (San Francisco: Marvell, 1935); A. J. McKelway, "Kate: The 'Good Angel' of Oklahoma," *American* 66, no. 6 (1908):587-93.

64. Ruth Delzell, *The Early History of Women Trade Unionists of America* (Chicago: National Women's Trade Union League of America, 1919), p. 15; John B. Andrews and P. D. Bliss, *History of Women in Trade Unions* (Washington, D.C.: Government Printing Office, 1911), pp. 18-19, 45-49, 144-45; Daniel J. Walkowitz, *Worker City, Company Town: Iron and Cotton-Worker Protests in Troy and Cohoes, New York, 1855-1884* (Urbana: University of Illinois Press, 1978), p. 174.

65. M.E.J. Kelley, "Women and the Labor Movement," *North American Review* 166, no. 4 (1898):408-17; Lydia Holt Farmer, *What America Owes to Women* (Buffalo: Charles Wells Moulton, 1893), pp. 440; *Women's Journal* (hereafter cited as *W.J.*): December 11, 1888, p. 380; April 7, 1888, p. 15; "Report of the General Investigator of Women's Work and Wages," *Proceedings of the General Assembly of the Knights of Labor, 1887*, pp. 1582-84; *1888*, pp. 1-4, 9-10; *1889*, pp. 1-2, 6.

66. George E. Barnett, *The Printers: A Study in American Trade Unionism* (Cambridge, Mass.: American Economic Association, 1909), pp. 313-14; George Tracy, *History of the Typographical Union* (Indianapolis: Hollenbeck, 1913), pp. 250-55.

67. Alice T. Toomy, "A Great Forward Movement," *Catholic World* 58, no. 346 (1894): 483-88; *W.J.*, June 8, 1907, p. 4; Mary Van Kleeck, *Women in the Bookbinding Trade* (New York: Survey Associates, 1913); Mary E. Kenney, "Organization of Working Women: Address," *World's Congress of Representative Women*, 2 vols. (Chicago, 1893), 2:871-75.

68. Florence Hovey Howe, "Leonora O'Reilly: Socialist and Reformer, 1870-1927," Honors thesis, Radcliffe College, 1942; Henry, "Mrs. Alice Winifred O'Reilly", pp. 132-36.

69. Lizzie Swank Holmes, "Women Workers of Chicago," *American Federationist* 12, no. 3 (1905):506-10.

70. Dorr and Hand, "The Woman's Invasion," pp. 798-810; S. M. Franklin, "Agnes Nestor of the Glove Workers: A Leader in the Women's Movement," *Life and Labor* 3, no. 12 (1913):370-74; Agnes Nestor, *Woman's Labor Leader* (Rockford, Ill.: Bellevue Books, 1954).

71. Tyack, *The One Best System*, pp. 65, 255-68; deFord, *They Were San Franciscans*, pp. 114-15; William Hand, "Chicago's Five Maiden Aunts," *American* 62, no. 5 (1906):481-87; "The Maid of Chicago," *Journal of Education* 54, (1901):103; "Women in the *NEA*," *Journal of Education* 54, (1901):92-93; Mary J. Herrick, *The Chicago Schools: A Social and Political History* (Beverly Hills: Sage Publications, 1971), pp. 97, 107, 125; Shields, *The Education of Our Girls*, p. 23. The first court case in which a teacher challenged the law that female teachers may not marry was brought in 1903 by Mary Murphy of Brooklyn; Murphy v. Board of Education of City of New York, New York State Reporter, vol. 118, November 9-December 21, 1903.

72. Alice Henry, *Women and the Labor Movement* (New York: George H. Doran, 1923); Andrews and Bliss, *History of Women in Trade Unions*.

73. *Life and Labor* 3, no. 9 (1913):264-65.

74. *I.W.*, February 8, 1873, p. 8.

75. Louise Tilly and Joan Scott, *Women, Work, and Family* (New York: Holt, Rinehart & Winston, 1978), noted that servants in Europe generally "married late and often had substantial savings," p. 122;

76. Homer L. Calkin, "The Irish in Iowa," *Palimpsest* 45, no. 2 (1964); Jo Ellen M. Vinyard, "The Irish on the Urban Frontier: Detroit, 1850-1880," Ph.D. diss., University of Michigan, 1972, p. 124.

77. *Arguments in Favor of the Freedom of Immigration at the Port of Boston: April, 1871: To the Committee on State Charities of the Massachusetts Legislature*, p. 25.

78. Stephan Thernstrom, *Poverty and Progress: Social Mobility in a Nineteenth-Century City* (Cambridge, Mass.: Harvard University Press, 1964); Peter R. Knights, *Plain People of Boston, 1830-1860: A Study in City Growth* (New York: Oxford University Press, 1971); Thernstrom, *Other Bostonians*; Gitelman, *Workingmen of Waltham*; Stewart Blumin, *Urban Threshold: Growth and Change in a Nineteenth-Century American Community* (Chicago: University of Chicago Press, 1976); Dean Esslinger, *Immigrants and the City: Ethnicity and Mobility in a Nineteenth-Century Midwestern Community* (Port Washington, N.Y.: Kennicot Press, 1975); Stephen Gredel, "Immigration of Ethnic Groups to Buffalo, Based upon Census of 1850, 1865, 1875, and 1892," *Niagara Frontier,* 1963, pp. 42-56.

CHAPTER 5

1. Robert Ernst, *Immigrant Life in New York City, 1825-1863* (New York: Columbia University Press, 1949), p. 56; NYAICP, *Seventeenth Annual Report: 1860* (New York: John F. Trow, 1860), pp. 48-49; Byron C. Matthews, "A Study in Nativities," *Forum* 26 (1898):621-32; John J. D. Trenor, "Proposals Affecting Immigration," *Annals of the American Academy of Political and Social Science* 24, no. 1 (1904): 221-36; Edith Abbott, *The Immigrant and the Community* (Chicago: University of Chicago Press, 1926), pp. 190-91.

2. NYAICP, *Third Annual Report: 1843* (New York: John F. Trow, 1844), p. 3; idem, *Thirty-fourth Annual Report: 1877* (New York: John F. Trow, 1878), p. 33; "Report of Aid Given to Destitute Mothers and Infants, 1875," Collection of the Boston Children's Services Association; Mary Roberts Smith, "Almshouse Women," *Quarterly Publications of the American Statistical Association* 4, no. 31 (1895):219-62.

3. Quoted in William A. Sullivan, *The Industrial Worker in Pennsylvania, 1800-1840* (Harrisburg: Pennsylvania Historical and Museum Commission, 1955), pp. 5-6.

4. "Records, January 2-January 18, 1893," folder 4, Denison House Papers; "Letters, No. 46-181," Charles P. Daly Papers, New York Public Library.

5. Joseph Lash, *Helen and Teacher: The Story of Helen Keller and Anne Sullivan Macy* (New York: Delacorte, 1980).

6. Matthews, "A Study in Nativities," p. 622; Rollin H. Burr, "A Statistical Study of Patients Admitted at the Connecticut Hospital for Insane from the Years 1868 to 1901," *Quarterly Publications of the American Statistical Association* 8, no. 62 (1903):313-15, 327-29; David Rothman, *The Discovery of the Asylum: Social Order and Disorder in the New Republic* (Boston: Little, Brown, 1971), pp. 283-87; Brendan Walsh, "A Perspective on Irish Population Patterns," *Eire-Ireland* 4, no. 3 (1969):9.

7. Quoted in Ernst, *Immigrant Life*, p. 55.

8. Austin O'Malley, "Irish Vital Statistics in America," *Studies* 7 (1918):631.

9. Nancy Scheper-Hughes, *Saints, Scholars, and Schizophrenics: Mental Illness in Rural Ireland* (Berkeley and Los Angeles: University of California Press, 1978).

10. William H. Guilfoy, *The Influence of Nationality upon the Mortality of a Community, with Special Reference to the City of New York* (New York: Department of Health of the City of New York, 1917).

11. William H. Davis, "The Relation of the Foreign Population to the Mortality Rates of Boston," in *Medical Problems of Immigration* (Easton, Penn.: American Academy of Medicine, 1913), pp. 50-85.

12. David Ward, *Cities and Immigrants: A Geography of Change in Nineteenth-Century America* (New York: Oxford University Press, 1971), p. 115; Smith, "Almshouse Women"; Pauper Institution Trustees of the City of Boston, *Second Annual Report* (Boston: Municipal Printing Office, 1900), pp. 51-52.

13. Massachusetts Bureau of the Statistics of Labor, *Eighth Annual Report: 1877* (Boston: Rand and Avery, 1877), pp. 200-201; idem, *Twelfth Annual Report: 1881* (Boston: Rand and Avery, 1881), pp. 487-88, 518-19, 524-25.

14. John White, *Sketches from America* (London: Sampson Low, Son and Marston, 1870), p. 356; Marie Thérèse Blanc, *The Condition of Women in the United States: A Traveler's Notes* (Paris: A. Colin, 1895), pp. 233-34.

15. Eliza Mosher, "Health of Criminal Women," *Boston Medical and Surgical Journal* 108 (1882):316-17; Caroline H. Woods, *Women in Prison* (New York: Hurd and Houghton, 1869); Pauper Institution Trustees of the City of Boston, *Annual Report, 1898-1899* (Boston: Municipal Printing Office, 1899), pp. 21-23; idem, *Annual Report, 1899-1900* (Boston: Municipal Printing Office, 1900), pp. 21-23.

16. William Round, "Immigration and Crime," *Forum* 8 (1889):428-40; Rebecca E. Leaming, "A Study of a Small Group of Irish-American Children," *Physiological Clinic* 15, no. 1 (1923):18; Joel Tyler Headly, *The Great Riots of New York: 1712-1873* (New York: E. B. Treat, 1873), pp. 154, 163-64.

17. For example, *I.W.:* May 11, 1872, p. 5; March 1, 1873, p. 1; April 12, 1873, p. 5; Auguest 20, 1874, p. 6.

18. Smith, "Almshouse Women," pp. 219-62; O'Malley, "Irish Vital Statistics," p. 630; Robin Room, "Cultural Contingencies of Alcoholism: Variations between the Nineteenth-Century Urban Ethnic Groups in Alcohol-Related Deaths," *Journal of Health and Human Social Behavior,* 1968, pp. 99-113.

19. Reliable figures on late-nineteenth-century sexual behavior are unavailable. Studies of prostitution in a number of large cities provide only an inconclusive picture. Women arrested for prostitution often gave false names and addresses. Police enforced antiprostitution ordinances selectively and sporadically. Other measures of sexual deviance, like illegitimacy, also are problematic in that particularly among the poor registration of vital statistics was not universal.

20. Matthew Josephson and Hannah Josephson, *Al Smith: Hero of the Cities* (Boston: Houghton Mifflin, 1969), pp. 26-29.

21. George Kibbe Turner, "The Daughters of the Poor," *McClure's* 16 (1909):46, 59; William T. Stead, *If Christ Came to Chicago* (London: Review of Reviews, 1894), pp. 18-34; "Underground Life," *Harper's* 17 (July 12, 1873):603.

22. William W. Sanger, *The History of Prostitution: Its Extent, Causes, and Effects throughout the World* (New York: Harper & Brothers, 1859), pp. 460, 537-38, 559, 562-64.

23. "Undated Newspaper clipping by Arthur D. Howden Smith," folder 46, Ellen Martin Henrotin Collection.

24. Donald B. Cole, *Immigrant City: Lawrence, Massachusetts, 1845-1921* (Chapel Hill: University of North Carolina Press, 1963), p. 35; Earl F. Niehaus, *The Irish in New Orleans: 1800-1860* (Baton Rouge: Louisiana State University Press, 1965), p. 68.

25. Louisa Harris, *Behind the Scenes. or Nine Years at the Four Courts* (St. Louis: A. R. Fleming, 1893, pp. 204-7.

26. James A. Froude, "Romanism and the Irish Race in the United States," *North American Review* 129 (1879-80):522-23; Charles Loring Brace, *The Dangerous Classes of New York,* pp. 148-50; Edward A. Ross, "The Celtic Tide," *Century* 87, no. 6 (1914):952.

27. Jane Addams, *A New Conscience and an Ancient Evil* (New York: Macmillan, 1912); New England Female Moral Reform Society, *Third Annual Report,* October 3, 1838 (Boston: George P. Oaks, 1838), pp. 16-17; see also volumes from 1851 to 1868.

28. "1909 Vice Study," box 8, folder 2, WIEU Papers; Vice Commission of Philadelphia, *A Report on Existing Conditions, with Recommendations to the Honorable Rudolph Blankenburg, Mayor of Philadelphia* (Philadelphia: Vice Commission, 1913), p. 84; Committee of Eighteen, Morals Survey Committee, *The Social Evil in Syracuse* (Syracuse, 1913), p. 103.

29. George Kneeland, *Commercialized Prostitution in New York* (New York: Century, 1917), pp. 174, 176, 208-11; U.S. Immigration Commission, *Immigration and Crime,* vol. 36, pp. 23, 151, 157.

30. Massachusetts Bureau of the Statistics of Labor, *Twelfth Annual Report,* pp. 487, 518-19; U.S. Immigration Commission, *Immigration and Crime,* pp. 100, 142-43, 192-93, 228-29; U.S. Immigration Commission, *Report,* vol. 37 (1911), pp. 62-65, 76; Albert Gibbs Mitchell, "Irish Family Patterns in Nineteenth-Century Ireland and Lowell, Massachusetts," Ph.D. diss., Boston University, 1976, pp. 342-49.

31. John Francis Maguire, *The Irish in America* (New York: D. and J. Sadlier, 1868), pp. 94, 333-34; Ella McMahon, *The Irish Faith in America: Recollections of a Missionary* (New York: Benziger, n.d.), pp. 121-25; "Statistical Studies," n.d., Archives of the Roman Catholic Archdiocese of Boston; John Lancaster Spalding, *The Religious Mission of the Irish People and Catholic Colonization* (New York: Catholic Publications Society, 1880), pp. 113-14; Auguste J. Thebaud, *The Irish Race in the Past and Present* (New York: D. Appleton, 1873), p. 473; *I.W.:* May 27, 1871, p. 3; May 25, 1872, p. 4.

CHAPTER 6

1. Quoted in Richard O'Connor, *The First Hurrah: A Biography of Alfred E. Smith* (New York: G. P. Putnam's, 1970), p. 19. See also Willard L. Hadsell, "A Sociological Study of Certain Irish Organizations and Families of New York," Master's thesis, Columbia University, 1910; Robert A. Woods, *The City Wilderness* (Boston: Houghton Mifflin, 1898), pp. 114-23; Rev. Patrick F. McSweeney, "Old-Time Temperance Societies," *Catholic World* 62, no. 370 (1896):482-86; Board of Charities, Massachusetts, "Responses to Questionnaires, Private Charities, 1873," Massachusetts State Archives, Boston; State of Connecticut Bureau of Labor Statistics, *Seventh Annual Report for the Year Ending, November 20, 1891* (Hartford: Fowler and Miller, 1892), 1:617-719; Edward F. Roberts, *Ireland in America* (New York: G. P. Putnam's, 1931).

2. *I.W.,* July 19, 1873, p. 4.

3. Kerby Alonzo Miller went through the vast immigrant letters collection in archives in the United States and Ireland and concluded that "none of the extant letters, diaries, journals, or memoirs written by Irish immigrants indicate that either the authors or their associates received aid from Irish benevolent societies in North America"; "Emigrants and Exiles: The Irish Exodus to North America, from Colonial Times to the First World War," Ph.D. diss., University of California, Berkeley, 1976, p. 720.

4. Robert Ernest, *Immigrant Life in New York City, 1825-1863* (New York: Columbia University Press, 1949), pp. 7, 243.

5. Earl F. Niehaus, *The Irish in New Orleans, 1800-1860* (Baton Rouge: Louisiana State University Press, 1965), p. 138.

6. T. W. Page, "The Transportation of Immigrants," *Journal of Political Economy* 19 (1911):746.

7. Carl F. Wittke, *The Irish in America* (Baton Rouge: Louisiana State University Press, 1956), p. 19.

8. Harold A. Williams, *History of the Hibernian Society of Baltimore, 1803-1857* (Baltimore: Hibernian Society of Baltimore, 1957), p. 38.

9. *Constitution By-Laws and History of the Charitable Irish Society of Boston* (Boston: James F. Cotter, 1882), pp. 91-92; William H. Talman and Charles Hemstreet, *The Better New York* (New York: Baker and Taylor, 1904), p. 7.

10. Charlotte Smith O'Brien, "The Emigrant in New York," *Nineteenth Century* 16 (1884):530-49; Helen M. Sweeney, "Handling the Immigrant," *Catholic World* 63 (1896):497-508; Richard C. Murphy and Lawrence J. Mannion, *The History of the Society of the Friendly Sons of Saint Patrick in the City of New York: 1784-1955* (New York: J. C. Dillion, 1962), p. 388; John O'Grady, "Irish Colonization in the United States," *Studies* 19 (1930):407.

11. William Geary, "Limerick Men's Benevolent and Social Association, Inc., 1890: Record of Its Accomplishments," in *Remember Limerick: 75th Anniversary Book* (New York: LMBSA, 1965); Sister Joan Marie Donohoe, "The Irish Catholic Benevolent Union," Ph.D. diss., Catholic University of America, 1953; Sister Martha Julie Keehan, "The Irish Catholic Beneficial Societies Founded between 1818 and 1869," Master's thesis, Catholic University of America, 1953.

12. Cornelius J. Kirkfleet, *The Life of Patrick Augustine Feehan* (Chicago: Matre, 1922), pp. 246-47.

13. Maurice Francis Egan and John B. Kennedy, *The Knights of Columbus in Peace and War*, 2 vols. (New Haven: Knights of Columbus, 1920); Christopher Kauffman, *Faith and Fraternalism* (New York: Harper & Row, 1982).

14. A few individual Irish men attempted to assist women in their communities. Judge Charles P. Daly in New York expressed a general sympathy for the appallingly low pay and poor work conditions for females and in 1864 helped found the Working Women's Protective Union. William Corcoran, the successful son of Irish immigrants in Washington, D.C., endowed a home for indigent women. Matthew Carey's concerns for poor women have been treated extensively in the literature.

15. Edward A. Ross, *The Old World in the New* (New York: Century, 1913), p. 28.

16. Carole Groneman Pernicone, "The 'Bloody Ould Sixth': A Social Analysis of a Working-Class Community," Ph.D. diss., University of Rochester, 1973.

17. See Madeline Gray, *Margaret Sanger: A Biography of Birth Control* (New York: Richard Marek, 1979), for one example of an Irish family support network in action.

18. *I.W.*: October 24, 1874, p. 8; December 28, 1872, p. 8; Keehan, "Irish Catholic Beneficial Societies," pp. 70-73.

19. Margaret Haley, "Manuscript of and Material Related to Margaret Haley's Unpublished Autobiography," boxes 32-34, pp. 617-633, Chicago Teachers Federation Papers, Chicago Historical Society.

20. Michael Flood Davin, *The Irish in Canada* (Toronto: Maclear, 1877), p. 378; Alice E. Smith, "The Sweetman Colony," *Minnesota History* 9 (1928):340-41.

21. Helen Campbell, *Prisoners of Poverty: Women Wage Workers, Their Trades, and Their Lives* (New York: Roberts, 1887), pp. 164-72; *Darkness and Daylight, or Lights and Shadows of New York Life: A Woman's Story of Gospel, Temperance, Mission, and Rescue Work* (Hartford, Conn.: A. D. Worthington, 1892), pp. 97-98, 109; Ruth S. True, *Boyhood and Lawlessness* (New York: Survey Associates, 1914), pp. 66-67; Jacob Riis, *The Battle with the Slum* (New York: Macmillan, 1902), pp. 316-21; William Dean Howells to Finley Peter Dunne, March 27, 1903, Finley Peter Dunne Collection, Library of Congress (my italics).

22. Mary Blake, quoted in Donna Mewick, *Boston Priests, 1848-1910: A Study of Social and Intellectual Change* (Cambridge, Mass.: Harvard University Press, 1973), p. 168; D. W. Mitchell, *Ten Years in the United States* (London: Smith, Elder, 1862), p. 145. See also William B. Sullivan, "Celtic Danvers," *Historical Collections of the Danvers Historical Society* 1 (1913):85; James H. Tuke, "News from Some Irish Emigrants," *Nineteenth Century* 20 (1889):434.

23. For example, see Joseph P. Barrett, *The Sesquicentennial History of St. Denis Parish* (Havertown, Pa.: St. Denis Church, 1975), p. 83.

24. *I.W.*, August 30, 1873, p. 7.

25. *O'Neill's Irish Pictorial*, May 7, 1859, p. 200.

26. Sister Joan Bland, "Hibernian Crusade: The Story of the Catholic Total Abstinence Union of America," Ph.D. diss., Catholic University of America, 1951; Sister Francis Joseph McKeon, "The Formation of the Catholic Total Abstinence Union of America," Master's thesis, Catholic University of America, 1946.

27. *W.J.*, February 6, 1886, p. 48; Ira B. Cross, ed., *Frank Roney: Irish Rebel and California Labor Leader* (Berkeley and Los Angeles: University of California Press, 1981), p. 80; John Devoy, *Recollections of an Irish Rebel* (New York: Charles D. Young, 1929), p. 113.

28. John O'Dea, *History of the Ancient Order of Hibernians and Ladies' Auxiliary* (Philadelphia: Keystone, 1923), vol. 2; Ladies' Auxiliary, Ancient Order of Hibernians, *Official Constitution* (Syracuse: Catholic Sun, 1914).

29. Ruth Margaret Piper, "The Irish in Chicago, 1848 to 1871," Master's thesis, University of Chicago, 1936, p. 31; Michael Gordon, "Irish Immigrant Culture and the Labor Boycott in New York City, 1880-1886," in *Immigrants in Industrial America, 1850-1920*, ed. Richard L. Ehrlich (Charlottesville: University Press of Virginia, 1977), pp. 111-12; *W.J.*, September 22, 1888, p. 308.

30. Richard J. Purcell, "The New York Commissioners of Emigration and Irish Immigrants: 1847-1860," *Studies* 29 (1948):30.

31. Mary C. Donelin, "American-Irish Women 'Firsts'," *Journal of the Irish-American Historical Society* 24 (1925), pp. 219-20.

32. NYAICP, *Thirteenth Annual Report: 1856* (New York: John F. Trow, p. 25; *John O'Hanlon's Emigrant's Guide for the United States* (New York: Arno Press, 1976); Oliver MacDonagh, "The Irish Catholic Clergy and Emigration during the Great Famine," *Irish Historical Studies* 20 (1947):287-302.

33. Society of St. Vincent de Paul, *Third Annual Report of the Central Council of Boston: For the Year Ending December 31, 1891* (Boston: J. L. Corr, 1892).

34. Anna Shannon McAllister, *Flame in the Wilderness: Life and Letters of Mother Angela Gillespie, C.S.C., 1842-1887* (South Bend, Ind.: Sisters of the Holy Cross, 1944), pp. 275-82; Henry Joseph Brown, *The Parish of St. Michael, 1857-1957* (New York: Church of St. Michael, 1957). Nuns made up the second largest group of women of Irish origin in the 1910 *American Catholic Who's Who*.

35. A. A. McGinley, "The Catholic Life of Boston," *Catholic World* 68, no. 397 (1898): 20-34.

36. St. Joseph's Home for Sick and Destitute Servant Girls, *Annual Reports, 1870-1880 Inclusive*; Peter A. Baart, *Orphans and Orphan Asylums* (Buffalo: Catholic Publication Co., 1885), pp. 55-56; *A Century of Catholic Culture in Boston: Sisters of Notre Dame de Namur, 1849-1949*; Bernard O'Reilly, *The Mirror of True Womanhood: A Book of Instruction for Women in the World* (New York: Peter F. Collier, 1878), pp. 181-82; Robert Lord, John E. Sexton, and Edward T. Harrington, *History of the Archdiocese of Boston: In the Various Stages of Its Development*, 3 vols. (New York: Sheed & Ward, 1944), 2:371-76, 379-80; 3:315-16, 184, 367, 379, 82; Massachusetts Board of Charities, "Survey of Charitable Institutions, 1879," Massachusetts State Archives; *I.W.*, October 11, 1873, p. 2; Louis S. Walsh, *Origins of the Catholic Church in Salem and Its Growth in St. Mary's Parish and the Parish of the Immaculate Conception* (Boston: Cashman, Keating, 1890), p. 76.

37. Richard H. Clarke, "Catholic Life in New York City," *Catholic World* 62, no. 398 (1898):206-11; Browne, *The Parish of St. Michael*, pp. 15-16; Richard H. Clarke, "Catholic Protectories and Reformatories," *American Catholic Historical Quarterly* 20, no. 79 (1895):607-40; John Talbot Smith, *The Catholic Church in New York*, 2 vols. (New York: Hall and Locke, 1905), 2:342, 493; Sisters of Reparation of the Congregation of Mary, "*Blessed Are*

The Merciful": The Life of Mother Mary Zita, Foundress (Patterson, N.J.: St. Anthony Guild, 1953).

38. Sister Mary Evangela Henthorne, "The Career of the Right Reverend John Lancaster Spalding, Bishop of Peoria, as President of the Irish Colonization Association of the United States, 1879-1892," Ph.D. diss., University of Illinois, 1930, p. 38; Bessie Louise Pierce, *A History of Chicago* (New York: Alfred A. Knopf, 1947), 3:447.

39. Lelia Hardin Bugg, "Catholic Life in St. Louis," *Catholic World* 68, no. 403 (1898):14-30.

40. *I.W.,* November 28, 1847, p. 8; Sister Mary Loretta McHale, "The Catholic Church in the District of Columbia (Later Period: 1866-1938)," Master's thesis, Catholic University of America, 1938, p. 99.

41. See *Sadlier's Catholic Directory, Almanac, and Ordo* (New York: D. & J. Sadlier), for the years 1867-74; *I.W.,* February 1, 1873, p. 8.

42. A Sister of St. Dominic, *History of the Catholic Church in the Diocese of Brooklyn* (New York: Benziger, 1938), p. 16; Mary Loretto O'Connor, *Mercy Marks the Century* (Providence: Sisters of Mercy, 1951); Michael Scanlan, *History of the Parish of St. Rose, Chelsea, Massachusetts* (Chelsea: Author, 1927), p. 13.

43. Henry J. Browne, *St. Ann's on East 12th Street, New York City: 1852-1952* (New York: St. Ann's Church, 1952), p. 21; Horace A. Wadsworth, *A History of Lawrence, Massachusetts* (Lawrence: Hammon Reed, 1880), p. 84.

44. *I.W.:* October 26, 1872, p. 8; February 22, 1873, p. 8; February 1, 1873, p. 8; March 1, 1873, p. 8.

45. James W. Sanders, *The Education of an Urban Minority: Catholics in Chicago, 1833-1865* (New York: Oxford University Press, 1977), p. 163; Sister Mary Ancilla Leary, *The History of Catholic Education in the Diocese of Albany* (Washington, D.C.: Catholic University of America Press, 1957), pp. 16-17, 23, 27, 138, 164; George A. Kelly, *The Parish as Seen from the Church of St. John the Evangelist, New York City: 1840-1973* (New York: St. John's University, 1973), p. 39.

46. Margaret Mary DuFief, "A History of Saint Aloysius' Parish, Washington, D.C.: 1859-1909," Master's thesis, Georgetown University, 1961, pp. 124-25.

47. Katharine A. O'Keefe O'Mahony, *Famous Irishwomen* (Lawrence: Lawrence Publishing, 1907), pp. 123-28; Sister Helen Louise, *Sister Julia* (New York: Benziger, 1928); Katharine Burton, *Mother Butler of Marymount* (New York: Longmans, Green, 1944); *Pioneers and Builders: Centenary Chronicles of the Sisters of the Holy Cross* (South Bend, Ind.: St. Mary's of the Immaculate Conception, 1941); James J. Walsh, "Mother Xavier Mehegan and Her Work," *Catholic World* 121, no. 725 (1925):624-32; R. N. Taylor, "Educated above Their Station," *Catholic World* 53, no. 314 (1891):172-77; Katharine Tynan, "The Higher Education for Catholic Girls," *Catholic World* 51 (1890):616-21.

48. Francis E. Lane, *American Charities and the Child of the Immigrant* (Washington, D.C.: Catholic University of America, 1932), pp. 104, 109, 128-29.

49. *Familiar Instructions of Reverend Mother McAuley, Foundress of the Institute of the Religious Sisters of Mercy, Dublin, Ireland: Edited by the Sisters of Mercy, St. Louis, Missouri* (St. Louis: Ev. E. Carreras, 1888); *Rules and Constitutions of the Religious Sisters of Mercy* (Baltimore: John B. Piet, 1882); Katharine Burton, *So Surely Anchored* (New York: P. J. Kennedy, 1948); Savage Roland Burke, *Catherine McAuley: The First Sister of Mercy* (Dublin: M. H. Gill, 1949).

50. All projects undertaken by the Sisters of Mercy are catalogued by city and date in *Supplemental Manual to the Sisters of Mercy Historical Sketches, 1831-1931* (New York: Macmillan, 1931). See also Elinor Tong Dehey, *Religious Orders of Women in the United States: Catholic Accounts of the Origin, Works, and Most Important Institutions* (Hammond, Ind.: W. B. Conkey, 1930), pp. 285-373; Kathleen Healy, *Frances Warde: American Founder*

of the Sisters of Mercy (New York: Seabury Press, 1973). The standard history of the order in the United States is Sister Mary Eulilia Herron, *The Sisters of Mercy in the United States: 1843-1928* (New York: Macmillan, 1929).

51. Maguire, *The Irish*, p. 341.

52. Ibid., p. 503. See also Helen M. Sweeney, *The Golden Milestone, 1846-1896: Fifty Years of Loving Labor among the Poor and Suffering by the Sisters of Mercy of New York City* (New York: Benziger, 1896); James Roosevelt Bayley, *A Brief Sketch of the Catholic Church of the Island of New York* (New York: Edward Dunigan, 1853), pp. 122-23; Smith, *The Catholic Church in New York*, 1:197-98; *Leaves from the Annals of the Sisters of Mercy*, 3 vols. (New York: Catholic Publications Society, 1889), 3:151, 172-82; Katherine Burton, *His Mercy Endureth Forever* (Terrytown, N.J.: 1946), pp. 77, 98; Henry J. Comman and Hugh N. Camp, *The Charities of New York, Brooklyn, and Staten Island* (New York: Hurd and Houghton, 1868), pp. 497-501; Kelly, *The Parish as Seen from the Church of St. John*, p. 39.

53. *Mercy, by a Sister of Mercy* (Rochester: George P. Burns, 1932); Sister Mary Innocenta Fitzgerald, *A Historical Sketch of the Sisters of Mercy in the Diocese of Buffalo, 1857-1942* (Buffalo: Mt. Mercy Academy, 1942).

54. *I.W.*, November 7, 1874, p. 8; Michael J. Shea, *A Century of Catholicism in Western Massachusetts* (Springfield: Catholic Mirror, 1931).

55. Mary Veronica McEntree, *The Sisters of Mercy of Harrisburg: 1869-1939* (Philadelphia: Dolphin Press, 1939), pp. 90-91.

56. Katherine E. Conway, *In the Footprints of the Good Shepherd: New York, 1857-1907* (New York: Convent of the Good Shepherd, 1907).

57. Dehey, *Religious Orders*, pp. 282-84; O'Grady, *Catholic Charities*, pp. 166-81; Lily Alice Toomy, "The Organized Work of Catholic Women," *World's Congress of Representative Women* (Chicago: Rand McNally, 1894), vol. 1; Patrick Joseph Dooley, *Fifty Years in Yorkville, or Annals of the Parish of St. Ignatius Loyola and St. Lawrence O'Toole* (New York: Parish House, 1917), p. 294; Comman and Camp, *Charities of New York*, pp. 469-73. On the work of the Sisters of the Good Shepherd outside of New York, see Pierce, *A History of Chicago*, 2: 442-43; "Episcopal Register, 1856-1888," Archives of the Roman Catholic Archdiocese of Boston; "Immigrant Women and Girls in Boston: A Report Based on Five Hundred Schedules for the Intermunicipal Research Committee during Their Recent Investigation of Immigrant Women in the Cities," Box 7, no. 49, WEIU Papers; Hugh Nolan, *The Most Reverend Francis Patrick Kenrick, Third Bishop of Philadelphia, 1830-1851* (Philadelphia: American Catholic Historical Society, 1948), pp. 387-88; *Historical Sketches of the Catholic Churches and Institutions of Philadelphia* (Philadelphia: Daniel T. Mahoney, 1895), pp. 68, 194-99; Sister Constance Marie De Foe, "A History of the Catholic Social Welfare Agencies in the Archdiocese of St. Paul," Master's thesis, Catholic University of America, 1946, pp. 25-26, 38-39, 45-48; Andrew Arnold Lambing, *A History of the Catholic Church in the Dioceses of Pittsburgh and Allegheny* (New York: Benziger, 1880), p. 517; Joseph M. Flynn, *The Catholic Church in New Jersey* (Morristown: Publishers' Printing, 1904), pp. 628-29.

58. Mary Frances Cusack, *Advice to Irish Girls in America* (New York: F. Pustet, 1886); Irene ffrench Eager, *The Nun of Kenmare* (Cork: Mercier Press, 1970); *I.W.:* April 10, 1872, p. 6; June 6, 1874, p. 8.

59. Baart, *Orphans*, pp. 100-105; Browne, *The Parish of St. Michael*, pp. 18-19; *I.W.*, February 10, 1872, p. 7; Sherwood Healy, "The Cathedral Fair, Report, 1872," Archives of the Roman Catholic Archdiocese of Boston; *History of St. Joseph's Boston* (1902), pp. 11, 15.

60. *O'Neill's Irish Pictorial*, July 2, 1859, p. 334; Katharine O'Keefe, *A Sketch of Catholicity in Lawrence and Vicinity* (Lawrence, Mass.: Sentinel, 1882), pp. 12-13, 87-96, 147; Record Group no. 5, "Parish Reports," Archives of the Roman Catholic Archdiocese of Boston; Charles W. Evans, *History of Paul's Church* (Buffalo: Matthews-Northrup, 1903), p. 149; Thomas S. Duggan, *The Catholic Church in Connecticut* (New York: States History, 1930),

p. 110; *St. Mary's Parish Centennial Commemoration: 1853-1893* (Providence, 1953). See also *History of St. Joseph's Boston,* p. 35, 48; *Old St. Mary's Church of the Society of Jesus in Boston, One Hundred Years: 1874-1974,* p. 17; Laurence J. Kelly, *History of Hòly Trinity Parish: Washington, D.C. 1795-1945* (Baltimore: John D. Lucas, 1946), p. 96; Dooley, *Fifty Years in Yorkville,* pp. 305, 308-10, 326-28; Katharine F. Mullaney, *Catholic Pittsfield and Berkshire* (Pittsfield, Mass.: Sun, 1897), pp. 89, 91; *Historical and Souvenier Program to Commemorate the One Hundredth Anniversary of St. Patrick's Parish, Watertown, Massachusetts, 1847-1947,* pp. 24, 36, 40; "Journals of the Archdiocese of Boston," scattered entries from 1836-1863, Archives of the Roman Catholic Archdiocese of Boston; "Holy Cross Cathedral Scrapbook, 1872" Archives of the Roman Catholic Archdiocese of Boston; *I.W.:* April 12, 1873, p. 8; May 10, 1873, p. 8; April 11, 1874, p. 8; Evans, "The Spirit Is Mercy," 72-73; Wammes, "The Sisters of Mercy in the Archdiocese of Cincinnati," p. 22.

CHAPTER 7

1. Finley Peter Dunne, "Mr. Dooley's Christmas Scene," *Ladies' Home Journal* 19 (1902):14.

2. Howard M. Gitelman, *Workingmen of Waltham: Mobility in American Urban Industrial Development, 1850-1890* (Baltimore: Johns Hopkins University Press, 1974), p. 60; Merle Curti, *The Making of an American Community* (Stanford: Stanford University Press, 1959), p. 401; Marie M. Gearson, *The Early Irish Settlers in the Town of Gardner, Massachusetts* (Gardner: Author, 1932), pp. 42-44.

3. A few Irish men supported women's suffrage. Bishop McQuaid of Rochester was one while John Lancaster Spalding began his ecclesiastical career as an opponent, but by the 1890s reversed his position. Terence Powderly of the Knights of Labor supported women's suffrage as did Mayor Hugh O'Brien of Boston. They contrasted sharply to most Irish-Americans. See James Edmund Roohan, "American Catholics and the Social Question: 1865-1900," Ph.D. diss., Yale University, 1952, pp. 419, 421; Powderly, *The Path I Trod* (New York: Columbia University Press, 1940), pp. 11-12.

4. Mary K. Simkhovitch, *The City Workers' World in America* (New York: Macmillan, 1917), p. 131; Charles Dickens, "The Irish in America," *All the Year Round* 22 (May 1, 1869): 513; Louis Boland Moore, *Wage-Earners' Budgets; A Study of Standards and Cost of Living in New York City* (New York: Henry Holt, 1907), p. 38.

5. Thomas L. Nichols, *Forty Years of American Life* (London: J. Maxwell, 1864), 2:73.

6. Albert Gibbs Mitchell, "Irish Family Patterns in Nineteenth-Century Ireland and Lowell, Massachusetts," Ph.D. diss., Boston University, 1976, p. 231.

7. Robert H. Lord, et al., *History of the Archdiocese of Boston,* 3 vols. (New York: Sheed & Ward, 1944), 2:80-83, 119-39; Lois B. Merk, "Massachusetts and the Women's Suffrage Movement," Ph.D. diss., Harvard University, 1956; James J. Kenneally, "Catholicism and Women's Suffrage in Massachusetts," *Catholic Historical Review* 53 (1967):34-57.

8. *I.W.,* December 31, 1870, p. 8.

9. *I.W.:* June 10, 1871, p. 3; February 24, 1872, p. 8; December 3, 1870, p. 8; May 16, 1874, p. 7; February 10, 1872, p. 3; *O'Neill's Irish Pictorial,* May 7, 1859, p. 200.

10. Finley Peter Dunne, "Molly Donahue, Who Lives across the Street from Mr. Dooley," *Ladies' Home Journal* 17, no. 1 (1899):6.

11. Ibid., 17, no. 2 (1900):8; 17, no. 3 (1900):8; 17, no. 4 (1900):6; Finley Peter Dunne, "Mr. Dooley on Woman's Suffrage," 1909, Scrapbook, article no. 15, Houghton Library, Harvard University.

12. Katherine A. Conway, ed., *Watchwords from John Boyle O'Reilly* (Boston: Joseph George Coupples, 1891), pp. 13, 15, 16, 20, 24; "The Woman Question," *Catholic World* 9, no. 50 (1869): 145-59; Francis G. McMananin, "The American Years of John Boyle O'Reilly,

1870-1890," Ph.D. diss., Catholic University of America, 1959, pp. 217-19; Francis Robert Walsh, "The *Boston Pilot:* A Newspaper for the Irish Immigrant, 1829-1908," Ph.D. diss., Boston University, 1968, pp. 109-209.

13. *I.W.,* October 5, 1872, p. 4.

14. *O'Neill's Irish Pictorial,* June 11, 1859, p. 283.

15. John Boyle O'Reilly, *Boston Pilot,* January 4, 1871, p. 3.

16. Ibid.

17. *I.W.:* August 10, 1872, p. 5; August 18, 1873, p. 7; *O'Neill's Irish Pictorial,* September 17, 1859, p. 516.

18. *I.W.,* January 21, 1871, p. 4.

19. *I.W.,* August 17, 1872, p. 6.

20. *I.W.,* January 27, 1871, p. 4.

21. James Michael Curley, *I'd Do It Again: A Record of All My Uproarious Years* (Englewood Cliffs, N.J.: Prentice-Hall, 1956), p. 2.

22. *W.J.,* December 12, 1885, p. 398.

23. *W.J.:* December 7, 1895, p. 389; April 10, 1886, p. 199.

24. *W.J.:* December 25, 1886, p. 412; November 14, 1886, p. 359; August 4, 1888, p. 245.

25. *W.J.:* August 4, 1888, p. 246; June 30, 1888, p. 207; September 19, 1885, p. 297; Arthur Mann, *Yankee Reformers in the Urban Age: Social Reform in Boston, 1880-1900* (New York: Harper & Row, 1954), p. 44.

26. Thomas Steven Duggan, *The Catholic Church in Connecticut* (New York: State History, 1930), p. 326; John J. Kane, "The Irish Immigrant in Philadelphia, 1840-1880: A Study in Conflict and Acculturation," Ph.D. diss., University of Pennsylvania, 1950, p. 185.

27. Quoted in Mann, *Yankee Reformers,* pp. 212-13.

28. *W.J.,* February 25, 1889, p. 4.

29. *W.J.:* March 29, 1884, p. 1; September 1885, p. 380.

30. *W.J.:* October 21, 1871, p. 6; January 31, 1885, p. 1; September 12 1885, p. 4; November 14, 1885, p. 359; September 12, 1885, p. 292; November 7, 1885, p. 358.

31. *W.J.:* January 16, 1886, p. 18. See also *W.J.:* January 23, 1886, p. 32; February 6, 1886, p. 48.

32. Merk, "Massachusetts," 1:122; Aileen S. Kraditor, *The Ideas of the Woman Suffrage Movement, 1890-1920* (New York: Columbia University Press, 1965), pp. 232-33; Lucille Rogers, *Lights from Many Candles: A History of Pioneer Women in Education in Tennessee* (Nashville: McQuiddy, 1960), p. 140.

33. "An Irish Woman on Woman's Rights," *I.W.,* July 9, 1871, p. 3.

34. Katherine E. Conway and Mable Ward Cameron, *Charles Francis Donnelly: A Memoir* (New York: James T. Wright, 1909), pp. 29-31.

Index